Fifty Ways of Letting Go

Shadow Work for Spiritual Practitioners

BY ROBERT KANDO CORNELL

BALBOA
PRESS

A DIVISION OF HAY HOUSE

Bible quotations are all from the New International Version®, NIV® Copyright © 1973,
1978, 1984, 2011 by Biblica, Inc.® Used by permission. All rights reserved worldwide.

Balboa Press books may be ordered through booksellers or by contacting:

Balboa Press
A Division of Hay House
1663 Liberty Drive
Bloomington, IN 47403
www.balboapress.com
1 (877) 407-4847

Because of the dynamic nature of the Internet, any web addresses or links contained
in this book may have changed since publication and may no longer be valid. The views
expressed in this work are solely those of the author and do not necessarily reflect the
views of the publisher, and the publisher hereby disclaims any responsibility for them.

The author of this book does not dispense medical advice or prescribe the use of any technique
as a form of treatment for physical, emotional, or medical problems without the advice of a
physician, either directly or indirectly. The intent of the author is only to offer information
of a general nature to help you in your quest for emotional and spiritual well-being. In the
event you use any of the information in this book for yourself, which is your constitutional
right, the author and the publisher assume no responsibility for your actions.

Any people depicted in stock imagery provided by Thinkstock are models,
and such images are being used for illustrative purposes only.
Certain stock imagery © Thinkstock.

Print information available on the last page.

ISBN: 978-1-5043-7357-9 (sc)
ISBN: 978-1-5043-7359-3 (e)

Library of Congress Control Number: 2017901143

Balboa Press rev. date: 03/20/2017

Dedicated to two wonderful Teachers of the Heart, Drs. Ron and Mary Hulnick, founders of the University of Santa Monica.

Pages 1, 254: Poems of Rilke translated by myself with assistance from Jochen Strak.

Pages 294-295: Poem "Father II" about her father Don Thomas by kind permission of Gillian Kessler.

CONTENTS

Letting in Love

Growing Up

Loosening The Grip on Who We Think We Are

Letting Go of Worldly Things

Challenging Practices

Being of Service: the Ultimate Practice

APPENDICES

ACKNOWLEDGMENTS

No book is written in a vacuum. I want to first thank my wife Marna for supporting me on this project that has taken many nights over the last three and a half years to finish. She read and proofed it and gave me great encouragement. She also gives me the support of a loving home environment that lets me spend my evenings after work writing! I want to thank men in the Brothers on the Journey group at my church that read it and gave me some good feedback: Kevin Wilson, Phil Spradling, and Jochen Strak.

Jochen also helped me with the Rilke poems to understand some of the idiomatic usages of German I might otherwise not get; but any errors of translation are mine. My good Dharma friend Dana Dunlap gave me one of the few quotes from a Zen master that mentions the heart. My friend Phil Spradling donated some of his beautiful photos for backdrops for several of my original poems. I couldn't use them in this book for practical reasons but I hope in a future version of this book to be able to use them! My long time therapist Constance Wells not only encouraged me but also read the entire manuscript and gave me many helpful corrections. How many people have therapists that will do that for them!

I would like to thank Zelda Kennedy, Associate Pastor at All Saints, for her many years of support for my work as group leader of Sacred Journeys, Brothers on the Journey, Practicing the Habit of Stillness, and other workshops and small groups that I have led at the church. She has put much trust in me over the years and let me experiment with many different type of groups and workshops. Some materials from these groups find their way into this book. Thanks also to Jon Dephouse our associate minister in charge of spiritual formation at All Saints; I have thoroughly enjoyed his friendship and collegiality.

I want to thank a dear deceased friend, Kathleen Stroup, who wrote the beautiful poem in chapter 44 and who helped me so selflessly in some of my workshops. I sorely miss her! And last but not least, I want to thank Gillian Kessler for letting me use her beautiful tone poem about her father, Don Thomas who is a fellow congregant at All Saints Episcopal Church in Pasadena.

INTRODUCTION

Why Did I Write This Book?

The closer you get to the Light, the more of your shadow you see. Thus truly holy people are always humble people. As one master teacher cleverly put it, "Avoid spirituality at all costs; it is one humiliation after another!"

Richard Rohr

Back in 1982, I had been practicing Zen in Los Angeles for 13 years, nine as an ordained Zen Buddhist monk, and I was studying to become a teacher. My Zen teacher was always something of an enigma to me; he could be warm and engaging at times (especially when you were drinking with him) but then he could pull back and feel very distant. As someone with a father wound, I was hungry for his attention and approval and this alternating warmth and distance really hooked me. I drove myself to practice harder in my meditation at least in part to gain his acceptance, if truth be told. As they say in program, I "white knuckled it", trying to gain enlightenment through sheer effort.

Then the truth finally came out when he went into rehab for alcoholism: he had been involved sexually with many of his women students even though he was married and had children. I went from a rather naive idealization of Roshi to feeling outraged and betrayed by him. Soon after the secrets came out, I went to an Alanon meeting, full of anger and pain. I shared my story and outrage in the group and one person came up to me later and asked me, "What was your part in this drama?" I really resented their question; I was so angry and hurt and I was not ready to see that the answer to that question eventually might bring me some clarity and freedom.

A year later, I left the Zen Center, remarried and became a layman with a landscape design and construction company that I had started as a monk a few years earlier. But serious questions stayed with me as I tried to make sense of what had happened at the Zen Center and with Roshi – and most importantly with myself. These questions became deep ongoing subjects of inquiry for me. These were my personal Koans; deep questions that I had to live with and keep inquiring into. As I explored these issues and studied psychology and participated in therapy, it became clear that one could have deep experiences of realization and still have issues that can cause problems for yourself and your relationships.

In the early to mid 80's there were many serious examples of abuse of power and sexual acting out by senior Buddhist teachers at many other Buddhist practice centers. We Buddhists thought we were superior to those crazy Bible thumping Christians but it turned out that we had serious issues to address as well. In terms of the institutional issues involved, it is clear that the concentration of unchecked, unaccountable power in the hands of the teachers at these training centers was a big part of the problem.

And their presenting themselves as gurus who had all of the answers was another part of the problem. This set them up to be potentially isolated and to have neither peer support nor accountability. However, there was still the troubling question of how such well-trained so-called enlightened teachers could behave so badly and be so far off track from the teachings they purported to teach and uphold. The truth that came to me over time is that we all have unexamined parts that we cannot see by ourselves. This is the shadow that depth psychology speaks of. Even talented well-trained spiritual teachers can have serious unexamined shadows that can wreak havoc on their communities.

Thus it is important for people who are spiritual teachers to have others they can check in with on a regular basis to be sure they are not acting out their unresolved issues on their loved ones and their students. Not only that but they need to be in spiritual community themselves so that other peer teachers can both support them and hold them accountable. And most of us who are serious about our spiritual practice need to do regular shadow work in the form of psychotherapy, spiritual direction, ongoing counseling or group work of one form or another. That is what this book is for: assisting you in exploring where your shadow might be interfering with your spiritual journey, perhaps even distorting how you see spiritual practice and what it is really about.

I see a lot of spirituality even today that concentrates on having spiritual highs and looks askance at psychology and any exploration of the dark unexplored side of human consciousness. Many of these spiritual seekers focus on charismatic gurus and healers, crystals, power vortexes, pyramids and magical nonsense of all kinds, hoping that someone or some thing can take away their troubles and take them to higher states of consciousness. This is such a sad thing and my sincere hope for them is that they will grow up and see that no one can do the real work for them. We each must engage with our life and our wounds. We can have teachers and therapists who can assist us but ultimately we have to do the inner work ourselves. And a critical part of this work is shadow work: the surfacing, exploration and healing of our unconscious wounds and defensive strategies.

What is Letting Go?

You have not to do anything in the positive sense of the word, in order to realize God. Simply undo what you have done in making your prison house and there you are, God already, truth personified already.

Sawan Singh

The Guru

There is a funny spiritual story about a man who goes on a pilgrimage up in the mountains to find a guru who can give him spiritual guidance. He starts out along the winding path in the morning in the bright sunlight, but as he continues through the day, the clouds come over the sun and it starts to rain and become very dark. As he slogs along the narrowing trail, he loses his footing and slips over the side of the sheer cliff. Luckily, he is able to grab onto a small bush on the cliff but he can't get enough purchase with his feet to be able to haul himself back up onto the trail. In his desperation, he calls out, "Help, help! Is anyone there?" To his surprise and relief, God answers him back in a deep clarion voice, "Yes my son. I am here." The man shouts back to God, "Help me!" And God replies to him gently, "Let go my son." The man is quiet for a moment and then he shouts, "Is there anyone else up there?"

On this funny note is where the story usually ends; but let's take it a bit further. There is no answer, so the man hangs on until morning and then notices in the increasing light of daybreak that there was a ledge just a little under his feet. Had he listened and let go, he could have rested on that ledge and then easily pulled himself up in the morning. Instead, he had to struggle to haul himself with great difficulty back up on the trail. And as he lay there exhausted, he realized he didn't need to go up to the guru for advice. He had gained the wisdom he had been looking for from his own struggle the night before: trusting when to let go.

In the story above, a man goes on a journey, seeking wisdom in the words of a guru far removed from the noise of everyday life. But instead he finds himself facing his own survival, hanging onto the edge of a cliff. He is looking for wisdom outside of himself and instead life circumstances bring him to hanging desperately onto a small bush over the edge of a cliff. (Has life ever done this to you?) And then God tells him, kindly, to let go! The poor guy doesn't trust God and hangs on for dear life. But his struggle is what in fact leads him to the very wisdom he has been seeking.

Isn't this how we spiritual seekers often are: looking for a guru or a book or a philosophy that will tell us what to believe or what to do to gain wisdom, when the very thing that will lead us to real wisdom is our life itself that we struggle with, distrust, resent and resist? So this book is not a compendium of easy advice to solve your problems but rather some suggestions on how you might relate more wisely and willingly to the difficulties and challenges (cliffs) and the opportunities to let go more gracefully. In this book, I invite you to engage with your life, as it is, not the idealized, elevated spiritual life that you wish you could attain, but to engage with the very nitty-gritty life that you have now, with all of its ups and downs and challenges. Yes, that life!

We will explore many ways of Letting Go (in fact 50) of all the things that we want to hold onto that neither serve the greater good nor give us personal satisfaction or peace. Letting go of fear and judgment and moving into loving connection with ourselves, with God/Spirit/True Self and with the world around us. Letting go of our personal agenda in favor of a desire to be of service. Letting go of the desire for fame and fortune and being led by caring and enthusiasm into a wonderful endeavor.

Paradoxically, at least in terms of what our individualistic capitalist culture would have us believe, the more we let go of the ego's agenda and move into love and service, the happier and more meaningful our lives become. And so that is the gist of this book: let go and become larger than you think you are. Let go and have more joy. Let go, forget your limited personal agenda and become the loving future of the human race, now.

You may think that the direction this book is taking looks like giving up – after all isn't that what letting go means? But in actuality, what I am inviting you to do is to take the most courageous step of all: to face your false fears and unhealthy impulses directly and compassionately, without anger or grasping, without numbing out, and without running away. This is the spiritual journey we human beings are called to walk: to let go of what does not serve our greater sense of Self and to keep our hearts and minds open to the people around us, as well as to all living things. This is true spirituality; as the Dalai Lama said, "My religion is kindness."

And let's also be clear about another thing: letting go of something is not the same as getting rid of it. Often we will lament that we can't "let go" of something when in fact what we really are complaining about is that the issue won't go away on our timetable and the way we want it to. We haven't been willing to let the thing be and heal on it's own; rather we are involved with trying subtly -or not so subtly- to get rid of it. Basic to letting go is a willingness to let something be with us instead of fighting against its presence. True letting go paradoxically involves letting something be with us until we are capable of letting it go of its own accord.

The Buddha profoundly said over 2,500 years ago that Samsara IS Nirvana. In plain English that means that this very world of pain and confusion, joy and love (Samsara) is in fact heaven (Nirvana) itself! When we first start out on the spiritual path, we often have the hope that we will have some kind of exalted enlightenment experience that will help us to totally transcend the pain of living in this world. What the path of spiritual liberation actually relieves us from is our resistance to the unavoidable pain and challenges of being human.

It has taken me some forty years to come to some realization of the profound truth of the Buddha's statement. It is not a statement of doctrine but rather a statement of fact that can be experienced and verified by anyone who sincerely practices a path of letting go of the False Self and its fears and pseudo needs. If the Buddha's statement is a puzzle to you now, perhaps you will understand it better after engaging with the material in this book. At least that is my hope.

So I share these short chapters on letting go with you as one who has been on the path for many years. I am seventy two years old now and I love my life and it keeps expanding in new directions even though my body doesn't always have the youthful health and energy it once had. My life keeps opening up in the proportion that I do not let myself shut down or close off because of some temporary disappointment or challenge. Perhaps something I say here will resonate with you that will be helpful to you on your spiritual journey, just as many spiritual teachings, books, and workshops have resonated deeply with me and been a boon to my journey.

In keeping with the growing inter-spirituality movement, this book uses practices, symbols, images, language and stories from many of the world's great wisdom traditions. I invite you to be open to these different expressions of religious and spiritual realization as representing the many facets on the Jewel that we call the Divine, God, True Self, Allah, Spirit or the Beloved – my favorite word. As the Zen people so aptly remind us, all of our mental concepts, spoken and written words, images, rituals, etc. are just fingers pointing at the Moon – the greater reality shining above them. While important and extremely useful to our awakening, they are not the Moon (reality) itself.

So I invite you to be open to these expressions from different religious traditions, for they might surprisingly unlock some place deep inside of you that has been waiting for just such a key to open it. And if some particular words or expressions of religious or spiritual truths are just too loaded with baggage from your past, then discard them and use other ones! You get to choose what resonates with you. You get to discard what leads you astray. This is your journey.

Seeing with Contemplative Eyes

No problem is ever solved at the same level of mind that created it.

Albert Einstein

The work in this book is about learning to look at ourselves and the world with contemplative eyes. What does that mean? It means seeing clearly without judgment, preconception, grasping or aversion. To see our own blindness and shortcomings requires that we be willing to see beyond our limiting beliefs and to accept what we see, as it is. Without our preconceptions and judgments, we just see what is: not what we want to see or don't want to see, but just what is. This is non-dual, direct awareness.

All too often, when we begin to become aware of our shortcomings and our fears, one of two things happens. One, we begin to feel bad about ourselves and to judge ourselves as shameful, unworthy, etc.. We may then reject ourselves, slide into depression and want to numb out or distract ourselves from looking at the issue. Or we blame others for our feelings and angrily deny that we have any responsibility for the problem. Either way, we are not available for the feedback from life that could help us to see what we need to do to heal our issues and to grow spiritually and psychologically.

Perhaps paradoxically, the more self accepting and self forgiving we are, the more able we are to see and admit our shortcomings. Self Acceptance has no edge to it, it has no desire to pick a fight with others if they criticize us. It also has no desire to lead us into shame and self rejection. It is humble and open to feedback. When we can think about ourselves without heavy emotion laden self judgment or defensiveness, we can more objectively evaluate the feedback life gives us about our beliefs and our behavior. With Self Acceptance, we can be open to other's praises or criticisms of us with equanimity. And we are more able to use this feedback, "good" or "bad," about ourselves to effect positive change in our thoughts and behavior.

The Interweaving of Psychology and Spirituality

In the end, just three things matter: How well we have lived, How well we have loved, How well we have learned to let go.

Jack Kornfield

Many of the world's deep spiritual traditions help their practitioners realize the states of bliss, love, and non-duality, but few help them to fully integrate their newfound realizations with living in the everyday world of human relationships. Spirituality, as it has been viewed traditionally, often seems to be preoccupied with transcendence and not with how to live fully in this less than perfect material world with its less than perfect human beings. Psychology on the other hand gives us great insights into how human egoic consciousness distorts reality through the processes of defense formation, introjection, transference and projection. Psychology brilliantly delineates how egoic consciousness is profoundly conditioned by our families and cultures and gives us many good tools for healing and overcoming our dysfunctional patterns of cognition, emotion, and behavior. But psychology mostly accepts the human ego's limitations and tries to work around its edges to help people live within the accepted constraints of the prevalent culture and norms.

Today we have the wonderful opportunity to practice an integrative spiritual psychology that does not privilege the realization of non-duality over the healing and further maturation of one's personality. Both psychology and spirituality can be vital tools for the full realization of human consciousness. We have an increasing amount of information on how to use both psychological methods and spiritual practices in an integrated manner to transform our consciousness and bring out the best in our nature. A. H. Almaas, Drs. Ron and Mary Hulnick, Fr. Richard Rohr, Bill Plotkin, Jack Kornfield and Ken Wilbur are just some of the leaders in the ongoing development of integral psycho-spiritual practices that address how to heal and transform our body, heart, and mind, our connection to nature, our past traumas and also the effects of culture, and systems of human organization on our consciousness.

These integral practices can help us move our consciousness out of the House of Fear, where we human beings often live, into the House of Love. They can assist us in healing our old wounds, increasing our awareness, unleashing our creative capacities and nurturing our ability to love. With the love, courage and clarity of heart and mind that we develop within ourselves with these practices, we can begin to address the root causes for the systems and structures in our cultures that debase and oppress our humanity. This is our best hope as individuals and for the human race at this critical point in time.

This book is about a type of integrated psycho-spiritual practice sometimes called "shadow work" where the unintegrated and disowned parts of our consciousness are worked with. This can be a challenging practice at times, requiring the willingness to face in ourselves what we have long been afraid of and avoided. This book is not about some New Age methods for lifting yourself up into eternal bliss away from all pain, confusion and suffering in ten easy steps. And it is also not a book to be engaged with only on the mental level as some kind of interesting theological or spiritual writing. I hope that you will be both challenged and encouraged by what I write here. The work I invite you to do in this book is not easy but, in the long run, it is this kind of courageous work (heart work) that builds our character and deepens our spiritual maturity.

On Being Human

I do not understand what I do. For what I want to do I do not do, but what I hate I do.

Romans 7:15 NIV Bible

We human beings are a recent phenomenon, geologically speaking, having evolved only a few hundred millennia ago along the shores of Africa. Recent anthropological theories propose that the desertification of the African savannahs where our ancestors lived made them increasingly inhospitable and they were forced to the margins of the continent to eke out a living in this new environment. The pressures of adaptation caused a surge in our ancestor's evolutionary development and they evolved to become the cerebrally gifted animals we are today.

I'm so often in amazement that the intellectual capacities our Paleolithic hunter-gatherer ancestors bequeathed us have allowed us to develop the complex interconnected technological societies that we live in today. But as we well know from our recent history, our psychological and spiritual growth have lagged far behind our technological development, leaving us in the situation where our ingenious inventions and our fear and greed could well lead to us destroying life as we know it.

As human beings, each of us has potential - and also challenges and shortcomings. We can see by the deeds of great men and women that we have the potential within us to be wise, compassionate, and generous. But we can also see by the daily stories in the newspaper that we are capable of doing incredibly stupid and horrific things to each other and to our earth. Most of us, and this is especially true of those interested in spiritual matters, are trying our best to act decently and to care about others. But even with good intentions, we realize that often we don't achieve what we hoped for. Something gets in the way.

As neuroscientists study the structures of our brains and their functions, it is becoming evident how our evolutionary heritage has given us both great gifts and great challenges. Evolution, being a conservative process, added the neocortex on top of the older structures of the reptilian and mammalian brains, to create a human brain that functions less than optimally for the complex societies we find ourselves living in today. Our brains worked quite adequately in the context of survival in late Paleolithic tribal cultures, but not so well now in our interconnected global technological societies.

Now our very survival as a species is dependent upon our more fully comprehending and appreciating our fundamental connection to and interdependence with each other and with our earth home. We need an ability to react intelligently on a global basis to very long term complex issues such as climate change, not as competing tribes or warring nation states- or battling political ideologies. The common level of human consciousness is not up to what is being required of us. The only way we are going to be adequate for the task ahead of us to preserve and further advance our civilization is to grow our minds and hearts in new ways. This requires us to develop spiritually and psychologically, as well as socially, intellectually and technologically.

If we want to grow psycho-spiritually, it is necessary for us to face, without shame and without self justification, the less than wonderful aspects of our human nature that get in the way of our best aspirations. We can be selfish at times, angry, envious, jealous, fearful, greedy, resentful, hurt, etc. These are feelings and impulses that we have all experienced many times in our lives. They are a part of our basic human nature and we are not going to eliminate them by shaming and beating ourselves up or, on the other hand, by allowing ourselves to wallow in them and act them out. We need to find a Middle Way between severe asceticism and self indulgence, much as the Buddha taught some 2500 years ago.

HOW TO WORK WITH OURSELVES

The Basic Steps to Practice

There are two fundamental practices that help us to grow psycho-spiritually beyond the limitations of our biology and our upbringing. One of them is the further development of our capacity to love. Love is the "mother" emotion that allows us to have empathy, to care for others (and ourselves) and that enables us to heal our neurotic needs and addictive desires. The other practice is the development of the ability to detach, to see beyond our limiting beliefs, emotions and alienating judgments, thus transcending our usual myopic self-centered, dualistic way of seeing things. Without this detachment, Love lacks clarity and can be naïve. But without love, this ability to be detached from our thoughts and feelings can be cold and uncaring. When spiritual groups emphasize detachment over love, something very important is left out of their practice.

One of the most important questions about human psychological and spiritual growth is this: what to do with our difficult negative thoughts, feelings, and impulses, which can come upon us so suddenly, intensely and persistently? This is a book about how to work with, heal and let go of our less than helpful ways of thinking, feeling, and behaving.

The basic formula for this work is:

1) Self Awareness,
2) Self Acceptance and Compassion,
3) Refraining from acting out,
4) Investigation,
5) Loving, Healing, and
6) Letting Go.

Without <u>SELF AWARENESS</u>, we just blindly act out of our thoughts, feelings and impulses with no consideration or self reflection. We are then little better than other animals for we are not using one of the greatest gifts given to us by our evolutionary inheritance: the ability to step back from ourselves and to intelligently observe our thoughts, feelings and impulses from a detached position. The practice of non dual awareness or Mindfulness as it has come to be called is an incredible boon to us in helping us to fully develop and use this gift of self detachment for our own spiritual and psychological growth.

One thing important to note is that the word for "mind" that is used in Eastern religions actually means something like heart/mind, which more fully encompasses our whole being. It is that meaning we will use here, for this is a holistic mind/heart/body awareness. We are not a mind residing in a body where the mind is a little homunculus up in the control tower, directing the whole show. That is a very simplistic and dangerously inaccurate model of how consciousness actually works.

SELF ACCEPTANCE and SELF COMPASSION, are equally important, because without them, when we become aware of our negative impulses and feelings, we are likely to turn away from our awareness to avoid shame and self rejection. This turning away can be either to judge ourselves or to project the issue onto others when we can't tolerate seeing it in ourselves. The more self accepting we are, the more we are able to see and acknowledge our emotional reactions and impulses. With the abilities to be self accepting and self aware, we can then begin to work more skillfully with our human shortcomings. Part of letting go of our harsh self judgment is the simple realization that all of mankind has these issues and struggles with them. Each of us is no better and no worse than others.

To avoid doing harm to ourselves and to others, we need to REFRAIN from acting on negative thoughts, emotions and impulses. The more we can catch and let go of negative trains of thoughts, not identify with negative emotions and resist the impulses to act out, the less we have to clean up and repair the damage from our acting out of our old dysfunctional patterns of thought and behavior. But of course, this is easier said than done! Awareness is key in this, but even being aware of our temptation, as Saint Paul notes in his letter to the Romans quoted above, we may still end up doing what we hate.

Interestingly enough, recent studies of the issue of self control or discipline (concepts that have only recently been studied by the psychological field) show that it is not rational thought and conscious efforts to resist temptation that are the most effective means of self control. In fact, the use of will power actually takes considerable psychic energy that can reduce our ability to resist further temptations. What works far better is using the positive emotions of love and gratitude to support our refraining from negative actions. I suspect that further studies will bear out what many spiritual traditions have known for a long time. Meditations on love, generosity, kindness, compassion and other positive attributes create a general state of mind that can resist temptation far better than the old fear based moralistic haranguing that much conservative and fundamentalist religion still holds onto and perpetuates.

As we learn to become more aware of our inclinations and impulses and refrain more and more skillfully, we find many opportunities to <u>INVESTIGATE</u> below the initial impulses to the deeper issues hiding below them. This means first focusing on the sensations and feelings in our body below any story that our minds might make up. So often what we find under these feelings and impulses are wounds from our childhood. As we inquire, we begin to become aware of the compulsive dysfunctional patterns of thinking, feeling and acting that we took on to protect ourselves (or so we thought) from being hurt further as children. This is the way our brains so often work: from a survival standpoint. These dysfunctional protective mechanisms that are part of our consciousness I will be calling egoic consciousness or the False Self in this book.

As we become aware of these specific childhood wounds without reactivity and judgment, we begin to develop a more compassionate attitude towards ourselves and we open ourselves to the <u>HEALING</u> power of Love: love of self, love of God, love of our fellow human beings. Love and other positive states of mind not only help us to resist temptation but help us to heal our emotional reactivity that comes from trauma and wounds from our past experience. This work of loving ourselves is often not easy. We have had years of abusing, neglecting and abandoning ourselves; so it takes time to develop a loving, nurturing relationships with ourselves. Finally, as we refrain from our compulsions and are able to stay lovingly present with our wounded self, we are able to <u>LET GO</u> more and more easily. And this letting go is not something we do just once but is an ongoing noticing and sloughing off of negative thoughts and impulses.

The Critical Importance of Personal Practice

Do not say," when I have leisure I will study." You may never have leisure.

Rabbi Hillel the Elder

I have a colleague at my counseling center who is very bright and insightful, understands much about spirituality, but he balks at the notion that he should need to *practice* spirituality. "Why should I have to practice in some Dharma Center, meditating long hours, while normal people just go on about their daily lives? They seem to get along just fine without all of this rather dreary spiritual labor, so why shouldn't I?" he asks. And there is another more subtle argument that he makes against practice. Basically it boils down to this: spiritual practice can be hijacked by egoic consciousness and its agenda into unhealthy and non-productive directions. This is true; the False Self inevitably will try to insert itself into whatever approach we take to spirituality. However, for me that is not a reason to doubt the value of spiritual practice, but rather a good reason to be on the lookout for wherever the False Self may show itself, including in our spiritual practice.

At this point, there is no way I can convince him of the need for practice. The motivation to practice will have to come from him. From what I have seen, there are two basic reasons we are motivated to engage in spiritual practice. The first is that we have had a taste of Divine Love, we can't forget it and we keep searching for our way back to it. The other is that we experience suffering in our lives and find that we need some kind of practice/inquiry into the causes of our suffering to free ourselves from our self imposed bondage. We human beings are forgetful creatures. We can have an amazing experience of God's abundant Love and then lose sight of it the very next day- or minute for that matter. For that reason we need to practice consistently, just as we eat our meals and brush our teeth every day. This does not mean we have to retreat into a monastery or convent. But it means we have to be very intentional as to where we find the times and places in our daily life to practice.

In dealing with our suffering, we could say that those of us who are motivated by it are the lucky ones, for it pushes us to dig deeper and more consistently into our lives than most people want to. Many AA members come to thank their addictions for forcing them to deal with their issues and consequently make their lives better. Whatever motivates us to engage in spiritual practice, it is important that we find the right practices for our particular needs and personal issues and that we make time for them in our all too busy and distracted lives.

Bottom line is, if you want your life to improve, you will find the time to practice. It won't happen any other way. Just reading about spirituality and knowing a lot about it will not get you there, trust me! As you find the time and you practice consistently (not slavishly) your life becomes more peaceful and enjoyable and you spend less and less time involved in upset, distraction and living on the surface of your life. Spiritual practice is not something that magically makes your life perfect; rather, it helps you to gradually see the perfection that was there to begin with, even in the difficult things that will show up in your life.

If you already have an established practice regimen in your life and you belong to a spiritual practice community, then this book could be a useful tool for considering additional practices to undertake. It could help you especially with healing and integrating your shadow: that part of your consciousness that remains hidden from you and causes you much unnecessary suffering. In any case, work with the inquiry questions and practices in each chapter of this book that call to you, not all of them. One of them might be a key to clarifying and healing some issue that has been nagging you for some time. And for those of you who are spiritual workaholics, take it easy! You don't need to do everything I propose in this book. Dear ones, that would just set you up for more guilt and feelings of inadequacy which you probably have enough of already!

For those of you who identify yourselves as spiritual but not religious, consider these words from someone who has been on the spiritual journey for some forty-five years: for all the faults and failings of religious communities, they are still useful and even essential supports for remembering who we really are. We all need community to practice within. Alone and without support we are very likely to fall away from the conscious life. We need community for its resources, its support - and for holding us gently accountable when we fall back on old unhealthy ways. This community of practice might be a Twelve Step Program. It might be a church, temple or mosque. It might be a Buddhist practice center or a Hindu ashram. But make no mistake, for most of us this is essential to our spiritual growth.

The Lone Ranger, Do-it-yourself, buffet style spirituality of many spiritual seekers today leaves them susceptible to many mistakes and self deceptions. This is the disease of our Western obsession with personal freedom and unlimited choices. When we run solo we have few checks and balances on our own unconscious and unskillful behaviors and attitudes. Left to our devices, we are likely to run towards what is pleasant and fun and avoid the difficult work of engaging with our shadow.

All of these institutions are imperfect because they are filled with imperfect human beings who can really screw up. So choose wisely, but choose to work in community. You will at times be upset with people in the community that you think are stupid or worse. And you will of course make your own blunders! But if it is a healthy religious / practice community it will be of great assistance to you on your spiritual journey. And, make no mistake about it, your experience of friction with the less than perfect people (you included) in this community will actually be a critical part of your learning!

The Trap of Self Criticism and Shame

It is important for me to talk about something that many of us in our western culture are prone to that can get in the way of the work done throughout this book. Because of our culture's overemphasis on individualism and our personal achievements and attributes, we are prone to harsh self criticism, self rejection and a deep sense of shame about our personal inadequacy. When we start becoming more aware of our less than desirable traits in the shadow work we will engage with in this book, it is extremely important for us to be able to manage our Inner Critic. For some of us, this Inner Critic will just not let us off the hook when it perceives that we are not living up to its exacting standards.

If you are anything like most people you will find this to be true: as you approach your shadow (the parts of yourself that you have disowned, repressed and/or are unaware of) your egoic consciousness will get more and more upset, defensive, and resistant. You will be tempted to turn away from this challenging work. And one of the things that can easily cause us to turn away is harsh self criticism and shame. When these arise, all desire for clarity, healing, and transformation disappear. Another way that we can turn away is to project our shadow material onto other people and get angry and judgmental towards them.

So be aware of and prepared for this to happen! Otherwise your Inner Critic might come upon you unexpectedly when you encounter something in one of the chapters that really points to your issue and this might discourage or distract you from getting spiritual and psychological healing. That is why the initial chapters on Self Forgiveness, Self Acceptance and Trust are so important for the work that we will be doing together in this book. I want to be sure that you are ready to use these tools when the demons of shame and blame attempt to take you down into their lairs of self rejection and self condemnation or paranoia and blame of others.

HOW TO BEST USE THIS BOOK

To read spiritual books but not to engage in regular spiritual practice is like reading books about physical fitness and never doing physical exercise.

This book is an example of Integral Psycho-Spiritual Practice – the weaving together of spiritual and psychological wisdom and practice to address our full nature as human beings, both our everyday psychological issues and our desire for transcendence. My standpoint is that, without an integrated healed healthy ego, transcendence by itself will not serve you very well. This book invites you to explore a variety of spiritual and psychological practices that address body, mind and spirit. Most of our problems are not held at the mental level; they are carried on the emotional and unconscious levels and are often deeply felt in our bodies. So I will be inviting you to especially address these deeper levels in the exercises in this book.

While this book is broken down into easy to read chapters, I encourage you not to rush to one that sounds just like your "issue of the day." There are beginning chapters, including this introductory material, that are basic to using the rest of the book productively and they give you the appropriate psychological and spiritual tools to facilitate your work. This book deals with challenging issues that may trigger reactions of self judgment, shame, fear, etc. One thing we know about our psychology as human beings is that if we get bogged down in self judgment, shame or fear, or anger and judgment of others, we can lose any desire for the healing, self knowledge, and the emancipation that would otherwise be available.

Here are a few important ways to both increase your engagement with the material and increase what you will derive from it:

1) Read Chapters 1-10 first to prepare yourself to engage with the rest of the book skillfully. These chapters contain foundational practices and processes that will allow you to maximize the benefits you will get from engaging with the material in each of the succeeding chapters.

2) Always go back to the exercises on Self Compassion and Self Forgiveness when you find yourself slipping into self judgment, or shame. This will support and protect you when you find yourself being attacked by your Inner Critic.

3) Read *s l o w l y*, one chapter at a time. Chew on and digest the self reflection questions and engage the practices. Don't skip quickly from one subject to another, just reading the main explication. This will keep you on the mental level and very little healing occurs there. The material in these chapters is meant to be read with a contemplative mind and body. The poems and stories at the beginning and the Invitation sections at the end of each chapter are designed to lead you into a deeper contemplative level; reflect on them and perhaps do a Lectio Divina (slow meditative reading) exercise with them. It would be helpful to devote a whole evening (or perhaps even a whole week) to one chapter and to meditate or do some kind of centering process for 10-15 minutes before and after engaging with a chapter in order to deepen and integrate the work.

4) Each chapter will have exercises and reflection questions for you to engage with the subject matter on an experiential basis. Chose the ones that most speak to you. Not all of them will. There will be prompts in these sections to access your deeper perceptions and feelings about an issue. You are encouraged to process the material through self-compassion and somatic (body) exercises such as Focusing and Heart Centered Listening. (See appendices 3 & 4 for further information on these practices.) Write your responses to the questions; this encourages a deeper engagement with the inquiry process. Keep an ongoing journal for this.

5) To support yourself in coming to this work with the right frame of mind, you might want to read and engage the material in this book in your own sacred space. This would be a clean, attractive area away from the hubbub of your regular life where you ideally have an altar and pictures and symbols of your connection with Divinity. Another thing conducive to working on a deeper level is the use of quiet sacred music, particularly when you engage in the Inquiry section in each chapter.

6) Another good support for working more deeply with this material would be doing it in a study/practice group. These days lots of people are getting together to read spiritual works and to reflect upon them. With such apps as Meet Up.com available as well as plain, old fashioned networking, it is easy enough to find an existing group or to form a new group yourself. Look at Appendix #9 for some suggestions on how to make such a group work well.

Letting in Love

There are two ways of letting love into our lives. One way is to eliminate the barriers that we have to letting love in. Usually we are not conscious of these barriers, because they are based in our unconscious egoic programming and they cannot be undone with rational thinking. They are held on a deep emotional level in our bodies, hearts and minds. The other way to heal the resistance to letting love in is to actively invite love into our hearts and minds. This needs to be done as a regular spiritual practice and is best done with rich imagery, meaningful ritual, and often with others in spiritual and religious community.

CHAPTER 1

Falling into the Arms of God

The great Chan master of the Song dynasty, Da-hui Zong-gao said, "Just let go and make your heart empty and open.

translation by Dana Dunlap

Autumn

The leaves fall, fall from afar
   as if faded from heaven's gardens
   they fall with negating gesture.
And in the night falls the earth
   away from all the stars in its loneliness.
We are all falling. This hand here falls
   And look at the other one. It's in all of them.
And yet there is one who holds this falling
   in His unendingly gentle hands.

Rainer Maria Rilke, translation by Robert Cornell

Introduction

This book is basically many variations on one central theme: how to let go and fall into the arms of God. Or, to put it in Buddhist terms, letting go of the small self and realizing our Buddha Nature. The greatest challenge in life for us all as the imperfect human beings that we are, is to be able to let go of our fears and self centered desires, our limiting stories about ourselves and the world around us and to open up to a bigger picture of what Life is about besides me, mine, and myself. The individuals that we, as a healthy culture, most revere are the ones who were able to transcend their personal situations, identify themselves with humanity and to give themselves to a purpose that framed their lives of service and undergirded their inspirational leadership.

In order to expand our sense of who we are and what our calling is beyond our limited sense of ourselves, we need to let go of many things that do not serve us or our world. A deep faith in God or some other transcendent entity such as what Buddhists call the True Self or Buddha Nature or the Twelve Step traditions speak of as our Higher Power can support us in moving beyond our character defects, our psychological complexes and our all too human limitations. These religious and spiritual concepts and the sacred texts, writings, rituals, traditions and cultures that they are embedded in become, for those of us who commit to a particular faith journey, the wind in our sails, the safe ship that conveys us to our ultimate destination; the other shore, the Kingdom within.

The image of letting go and falling into the arms of God can elicit some fear in us as to whether or not there is Someone or Something there to catch us when we do let go. After all, fear of falling is one of the basic instinctual fears we humans have! And falling is a great metaphor for the challenges that are part of spiritual practice: to let go into the unknown, let go of our need for too much control, too much self protection and to move way beyond our comfort zone. For our ego, this letting go can feel as if we are going to fall into a bottomless abyss of darkness.

This is why the spiritual journey requires us to develop an ever growing and deepening faith in order to make possible this inner movement of letting go of our fears and allowing ourselves to be held by Something Greater than our little egoic consciousness. This faith journey that we are on is one where we regularly remind ourselves through meditation, prayer and ritual of our being held by/within the Beloved, the Tao, Divine Spirit, Buddha Nature. As the imperfect, conditioned human beings that we are, we need these ways of worshipping and practicing to grow and strengthen our connection with and trust in the Beloved.

Many years ago, my Zen teacher talked to us his students about throwing ourselves into the House of the Buddha. Several times a year we would renew our vows at the Zen Center as both lay members and monks. We would recite as we bowed, "Namo Buddha, Namo Dharma, Namo Sangha." I take refuge in the Buddha, I take refuge in the teachings, and I take refuge in the practice community. Every religious tradition reminds us that we have to give over our self centered ways, because our self centeredness is exactly the cause of our own suffering- and the suffering of mankind in general.

Personally, I like the image of falling back into my Big Self – my deep and true Self that has let go of fear, of self judgment and is playful and relaxed. Sometimes I picture

2

myself being on a rolling log (my ego) such as lumberjacks compete on and then suddenly and joyfully letting myself fall back into the water. Other times, I like to hold my hands upwards towards God in a gesture of surrender and receiving His Love. These ways of picturing letting go and letting God encourage me, when I am tempted to get uptight and defensive about something, to just relax and let go.

We inevitably will get triggered at times and our old automatic emotional reactions and defensive patterns of behavior will manifest themselves. If we practice letting go on a regular basis, then when the ego defenses are triggered, we have something to literally fall back on! When we are reactive, it is so helpful to have a way of relaxing, letting go and abiding in Divine Love. This is a love that we all rest in, and when we forget, we use our spiritual practices to re-member that we are an essential part of this Love. This is why the practice of "letting go and letting God" (or however you name the great mystery) is so foundational to our spiritual life.

Because the templates of how we see the world and ourselves are so deeply set in our consciousness and can take over in our minds and hearts so quickly, we need to regularly practice letting go of our thoughts, beliefs and impulses. Recently, I had a spiritual directee share with me a funny example of this. She was in a parking lot and happened to look over at a woman that she had never seen before in her life, and BAM her mind immediately stereotyped this woman as 'poor white trash" and came up with a whole back story just from this brief encounter.

This is a perfect example of the workings of the part of our brain that Daniel Kahneman in his book, *Thinking Fast and Slow*, called "a machine for jumping to conclusions." And we all have it as part of our brain that is designed to respond quickly -and emotionally- to external stimuli. Because of our evolutionary heritage and our brain's bias for remembering negative experiences over positive ones, our first impressions can take us deep into negative emotional territory very quickly. That is, if we don't have ways of catching ourselves and overcoming our tendency to go to fear and anger with practices that increase our self awareness and deepen the channels in our brains that engender love and compassion.

We now can say, based upon neuroscience, that what was once regarded in Western Christianity as original sin is in fact the product of our less than perfect human brains that are programmed for survival. Our brains have been molded by evolution to be easily triggered into greed, lust, anger, fear and other negative emotions as survival mechanisms. As we practice the many ways of letting go and letting God that are described here in fifty chapters, we will learn more and more how to overcome these less than angelic parts of ourselves.

Self Inquiry & Practice:

Love is letting go of Fear.

- Gerald Jampolsky

If you belong to one, your spiritual community probably has many rituals, images, prayers, and ways of worshipping that can help deepen your faith in the Beloved and engender love and compassion in your heart. Besides these, are there other images, symbols, music, words of scripture or writings from the world's wisdom traditions, poetry or rituals that you find most helpful to let go into God / the Universe? Without being too concerned if they meet the criteria of correctness for your spiritual community, explore which might be best for your own spiritual development. This is so important! There are no universal images, texts, rituals, etc. that work for everybody.

We know from psychological studies such as Neuro-Linguistic Programming that different people learn through different modalities of the senses. Some are visual learners, others auditory, still others kinesthetic, etc., etc. I encourage you to find your own touchstones and talismans that help you to remember how to let go. It is your privilege as a conscious human being – and your responsibility - to care for your spiritual well being and find what is most encouraging, consoling and empowering to you, given your unique history, gifts, and inclinations.

In meditation, practice using guided imagery with a picture, symbol, or words about letting go that you have chosen to represent this falling / relaxing into God's / the Universe's care. Perhaps with music of your choice, meditate on these images, symbols, word pictures that invite you into this surrender, this falling into God's arms. If you are visually oriented you might make a collage of God / the Goddess holding you in their arms that you could place on your altar at home. Perhaps poetry or scriptural passages call you deeply into Source. Have verses memorized that you can bring to mind when you need to remember your connection to the Beloved.

Sometimes, people like to have a loving dialogue with God/Source to find their way to this peace in His/Her arms. Try this out. Talk to Him/Her as you would a loving Father/Mother and tell Him/Her about your fears, your hurts and concerns and see if you can let Him/Her heal and comfort you. Or just talk to Him/ Her as you would your Beloved as He/She most certainly is! Do this from your Heart Center so that it isn't just coming from your head. You might put your hand over your heart as you have this dialogue to keep centered in your heart space.

Important Practice

Relax in a safe space that feels inspiring and quieting to you. This could be your sacred space at home or in nature somewhere. Lie down on your back and deeply let go. Breathe out deeply, and let your breath breathe you. And allow yourself to feel supported by the earth (or floor). With every outbreath, allow yourself to relax more and more deeply, falling gently into the arms of the Beloved / the Universe / Buddha Nature.

Assuming that the place where you are is peaceful and safe, if you find your peace being disturbed in any way as you try to enter more deeply into these practices, pay attention to what is going on inside of you. Is it the call of duty, feeling guilty for giving yourself this "unproductive" or "irresponsible" time? Is it a feeling that something bad will happen to you if you let yourself be this relaxed and undefended? Is it a feeling gnawing away at you that something is wrong with you that must be fixed? If none of these scenarios fit (or schemas as psychologists say), feel into your body and see if you can find images and/or words to match the feelings that you are having.

Remember that, while it may seem strange to you now, it can be very valuable to feel and compassionately explore your dis-ease, to make friends with it and to inquire into its source. This will be a topic that we will pursue in many other chapters of this book. The key to working with our dis-ease is to be as loving and accepting with it as we would with a child, for indeed that is what it is: our own wounded Inner Infant, Inner Toddler, Inner Child, Inner Adolescent. Depending upon at what stage in our development we have been hurt by parents, peers or others, we have psychic wounds and egoic structures that protect these soft spots.

Our work to heal the ego is not to attack it but rather to heal and nurture the parts of ourselves that were wounded in our growing up so that we no longer need the ego's rigid protection. As we become familiar with our wounded selves, we may intuitively begin to sense what these young parts of ourselves suffer from and what they need from us. If it is a very young infant part, it needs our tangible, physical holding and nurturing. If it is a toddler or older child part of us, it may need permission to play and to make its own choices. If it is a preadolescent, it may need our encouragement and recognition for its accomplishments.

Much of our work in this book is body oriented, because the thinking mind, while very useful to us, is often not able to bring about the healing that we are looking for. Insight onto our issues often in and of itself does not heal the issue. We need to touch into our hurts in the body. To that end, Yoga is a wonderful way for us to learn how to relax, stretch, and let go with our body. This goes far beyond mental effort and becomes a way to embody letting go. If you tend to be mentally oriented, as so many of us are, Yoga offers us a gateway to Spirit through the body. We can practice using breath and asanas (postures) to let...go. Consider adding Yoga to your spiritual practices if you continue to find sitting still in meditation difficult. It could very much help you to find the doorway into inner silence.

Invitation

Let nothing disturb you, nothing trouble you. He who has God has everything.

Saint Theresa of Avalon

Know that no effort is needed in this Letting Go, this Falling. You just...let go. Let go of worrying about the future. Let go of trying to make something happen. This Falling happens on its own as you let it. Let go of judging yourself as not worthy, let go of feeling afraid, let go of needing to know what is happening... Let go of being in control. Wheeee! Let go like a child playing. Let go like a lover making love to their beloved. Let go like a bone tired person falling asleep at night after a busy day at work, thankful for the comfort of their bed...

Inside yourself, fall back into your deepest Self, deep below the thinking mind with all its concerns of right and wrong, gain and loss, beyond all its worries and concerns. Dive deep into the dark oceanic abyss that resides within you and swim there, buoyed by the Beloved. Making no effort, abide there, floating in the current, gently being guided deeper and deeper into this unknown dark realm of rest and bliss. This is your true home as a spiritual being. Rest and let no concern disturb your contemplation of the unknown Knower of you - which is you yourself, the Beloved in whom you are always immersed.

When you know this place, you then know the way Home. You will know how, even in difficult circumstances, to find your way through the thicket of fears, concerns and desires to this place of abiding. Remember to practice this falling and abiding regularly, for then you can remember well the Way home. This is the work of the mystic: to let go into the Dark Abyss within and to sink into Love and Unknowing and to abide there over and over again until this becomes an indelible memory that infallibly leads you back to your true Home.

CHAPTER 2

Opening to Love

Love is simple. Love is the Way, the only way for us humans. Love is Life itself. Without Love there would be no human life as we know it.

The Beloved

We look for the Beloved, but
we look for Her in all the wrong places.
Until, at last, trusting in ourselves,
far beyond the wiles of the World,
our Heart rests in its heart of hearts,
Where true love is found.

Robert Cornell

Introduction

For some time I have marveled over the amazing length of time it takes for a human being to be reared, to be nurtured and taught enough by its parents and other adults to be able to fend for itself. Evolutionary biologists have talked about how the human mother's pelvis has had to evolve so as to allow for the size of the baby's head to come through the birth passage. They also discuss that one of the reasons for the child's need for a long period of nurturance is that the infant's brain, while large for an animal, is not nearly fully grown at birth and, because the mother's pelvis can't expand any further, this further brain development must occur after birth over a long period of time.

But they seldom speak about the absolute need for parental love that would allow this nurturance to continue for such a long duration- and that this nurturance is actually essential for the further development of the human brain. This part of Darwin's theory of evolution regarding the importance of love and nurturance in the development of human beings and expounded in his book *The Descent of Man*, has been ignored and instead evolutionary biology and evolutionary psychology have taken up the theory of the Selfish Gene. It seems that our individualistic culture even affects our scientists so that they cannot conceive of anything beyond self-interest, even if this selfishness has to be placed in our genes in order to ignore the critical importance of generosity and selfless love in the very survival and continued evolution of the human race.

So for them, this generosity can only be explained as an evolutionary advantage that gives our "selfish" genes a higher chance of survival. What pray tell is a "selfish gene"? How can a gene be considered selfish or unselfish? Isn't that rather an anthropomorphically based concept? How does the concept of selfishness even make sense on the biological level? And what about the holistic view of how living beings fit into the great scheme of things?

While evolutionary psychology, which is based upon the selfish gene theory of evolution might be a meta theory that leads to interesting theories about human consciousness in terms of what behaviors and predispositions have in the past lead to human survival, it provides no inspiration for what we aspire to become as an evolving human race. And it offers no inkling of how we are to grow beyond the limitations of our biological inheritance. That role must be taken up by philosophy, religion and spirituality. For what will enable the human race to survive and the world to survive our folly will not be human selfishness (or genetic selfishness) but rather human compassion and wisdom.

I suspect there is a strong correlation between the ability of an animal to love and nurture its offspring and the level of intelligence that animal species can have, purely on the basis of biological considerations. We now know how much critical human brain development occurs after birth and it is instigated by the interaction of the parents with the child. Without parental love, this level of nurturing interaction could not be sustained. We also know from studies of infants given adequate physical nurturance but raised without prolonged warm human interaction, that development in such children is severely stunted, mentally, emotionally – and spiritually.

So much of human intelligence is the result of parent-child interaction and without that interplay the brain of the infant would not develop to its potential. In other words, intelligence is not just decided on the basis of the biological structure of the infant brain but also is very much dependent upon the quality of interactions it has with its caregivers. Our big brains require a long period of positive and active interaction with our caregivers and their creating a safe environment for us to explore. Incidentally, this is why it is extremely unlikely that there ever will be intelligent monsters; they could never care enough for their offspring for them to develop intelligence! Intelligence is not a given at birth. The brain and consciousness do not develop in a vacuum. Without love and the continued nurturance it motivates, it is simply impossible for intelligence to be fostered. They go hand in hand.

And it is fatherly love in particular that has probably made the difference for human beings. Maternal love is much more common in the animal kingdom. Without our male forebear's love and commitment to the support of his family, his children would have been unlikely to survive this long developmental period in times past. It seems that the further evolution of the ability to love in our male forebears would have been absolutely necessary to enable our ancestors to evolve into what we are today. And given the trouble that young males can cause in all societies today, it would be reasonable to say that one of the greatest needs of our human race is for young men to be mentored in the art of love and nurturance earlier in their lives.

What our western culture often does not fully appreciate is that our brains aren't the only part of what informs and supports our consciousness. The love we feel is not restricted to the brain itself. The heart and the field of consciousness it forms with the brain and the rest of the body are very much part of what allows us to love and what makes us human. The brain doesn't function as a homunculus separated from its passive robot body; it would be better to talk about the brain/heart/body/mind system. The development of a more loving "mind/heart" is the most needed capacity that will allow our human race to evolve to the next level of consciousness. Without this increased ability to love, which we can learn through spiritual practice, we probably will not survive as an advanced civilization.

As human beings, one of our greatest needs is for love in all of its manifestations: parental, brotherly/sisterly, spiritual and sexual. It is as basic as the need for food, shelter, and physical safety. One might think that love is much higher on the hierarchy of needs than these physical concerns, but we have these studies of infants raised with their physical needs met- but not being tangibly loved – to indicate how basic love is for our very survival. This is true of adults as much as infants: without the support and love of those close to us we cannot thrive and grow either intellectually, physically, or spiritually. So often our growth has been stunted by the lack of love in our lives or the conditions placed on love by our caregivers and loved ones in our childhood.

To engage in spiritual practice without a container of love to support us and encourage us is undesirable and sometimes downright dangerous. We may come to an intellectual understanding by our own practice and self-study, but without a container of love, we will tend to hold back in our defensive postures and remain in our heads, not our hearts.

We will want to keep ourselves safe from a world that, to our wounded selves, seems undependable and even hostile.

Without the support of others who love us just as we are, we are vulnerable to being used by unscrupulous or zealous people for their own agendas. Many cults and fanatical groups are founded on the adherent's need for love and acceptance and the leader's ability to manipulate and control the group by giving and withholding love from them, And even in more mainstream religious traditions, as many of us so painfully know, love has not always been offered without soul destroying conditions.

In our current secular culture there is a pervasive valuing of the intellect, technology and information and a devaluing of the wisdom derived from being in our bodies, with our feelings, and being connected to the natural world. Even in the field of psychology we find more and more emphasis on technology, evidence-based practices with their protocols, and a kind of fix-it mentality. While this is useful in many cases, it can also lead us away from the spiritual work of the heart, which in reality is more of an art than a science. We may imagine that we are so much more technologically advanced than our forebears but in doing so we neglect the teachings of the many wise spiritual elders who over the centuries have called us to the work of the heart.

In order to let go, spiritually speaking, we need the assurance that "someone up there loves us." The hapless climber in the story from the introduction who hangs all night from the cliff clearly wasn't sure that he could trust God, that God loved him and wished the best for him. I don't want to propose here a simplistic theology of a loving super hero up in the sky who will save us at every crisis. But let's face it: most of us are to some degree or another like this guy hanging from the cliff. We are not so sure we can trust the universe or God or whatever we call that bigger picture of life to provide for us and over a lifetime we develop many strategies for protecting ourselves and for looking out for number one. We won't be willing to let go of our limited sense of self unless we know that we are loved and that someone or something cares about us.

Every religious tradition has some form of loving figure that serves to reassure its proponents and that supports them in the difficult and sometimes frightening process of shedding the ego's protective layers. In the Abrahamic religions, the focus is on a loving, merciful God. In nontheistic religions such as Buddhism, the locus of care and compassion may be a guru/teacher or a mythic figure such as the Buddha himself or the myriad Bodhisattvas described in the Mahayana sutras.

In Buddhism, the Bodhisattva known as Avalokitesvara in India, Kwan Yin the Goddess of Mercy in China and Kannon in Japan is the symbol of compassion. Literally the name means "the master who looks down" (on this world of suffering) or the one who hears the cries (of the world.) This Bodhisattva is dedicated to assisting all human beings in overcoming their suffering and ignorance and is often represented with manifold hands and arms that offer myriad kinds of compassionate aid to the human realm.

In your engagement with the material in this book, it is vital to bring Unconditional Love into your work. The very essence of this spiritual work is to bring Unconditional Love to whatever you are experiencing. Love is what ultimately heals our consciousness of its fears and limitations. If you have a symbol such as God, Christ, Buddha, Kwan Yin or perhaps a guru figure that represents this love in your tradition, let it/him/her hold you in its/his/her arms as you engage this work-- for it can sometimes be very challenging. As a vulnerable human being you need the reassurance that Love is there with you, not judging, always encouraging. Let yourself be the beloved that is loved by the Divine Presence as much as you can. Anytime you feel fear, abandonment, self-judgment, self rejection, or shame arising as you do the work in this book, come back to Love.

To aid in engendering this loving energy it would be an excellent thing to have a sacred space where you read this book and do the exercises. In that space, you could have images of your divinity, incense, sacred music- anything that helps you to link your mind with the divine loving energy that would be supportive of doing this challenging and important work. Try your very best to accept and love yourself, knowing that at times this may be difficult, especially for those of you who have been abused and rejected.

Your egoic consciousness may act out in anger, fear, self loathing, self rejection and self abandonment. Know that this is not your True Self, but rather an inheritance from your family and dysfunctional culture. Know that Love will bring you back to who you really are: you are the beloved who can surmount any challenge with acceptance and letting go. For some of us this is extremely hard to believe, but try to allow at least the possibility that you are loved. It is no wonder that Jesus, at the very beginning of his ministry, after he was baptized and before he was led into the desert for his trials and testing, felt God's love fall upon Him. And God said, " This is my son in whom I am well pleased." This was the source of Jesus's assurance and obedience to his call from God. It is this Divine Unconditional Love that heals and empowers us and turns us towards our own callings and ministries.

Self Reflection & Practice

Darkness cannot drive out darkness: only light can do that. Hate cannot drive out hate: only love can do that. - Martin Luther King

How much do you feel lovable and loved? Bring to mind the people who love you and what they say about you-- what you perhaps have a hard time letting in. Putting your hand on your heart, allow to come to mind what your best friends say about you that you know is, well, true but that feels awkward to admit to yourself. Let yourself remember in detail what good things they have said about you, for they know you well.

Perhaps you have a pet that adores you, follows you around wanting your attention, wanting to hang out with you, just to be near you. Try to see yourself from their perspective. See if you can feel the love that wells up in you towards them and let it come back towards you. Why do they like to snuggle up to you, lick you or purr when you pet them?

How much can you love yourself? Think about how you judge and reject yourself. Does this really serve you? How much can you let yourself be loved by others? For many of us, this is sadly a most difficult task, harder by far than loving our spouse and children, or even loving our neighbor.

Why should it be so difficult to love yourself? You have spent your whole life in your own company and, if anyone could understand you and be sympathetic to your pain, wouldn't that be you? But so often, you close your heart and stand in hurtful judgment of yourself, unable to forgive yourself for the shortcomings that you could easily forgive others for. If you can let go of your judgments of others, why can't you do so for yourself? With your hand on your heart, reflect carefully on this.

Can you recognize your basic goodness? If so, bring to mind some of your best traits and qualities. Write them out artistically and keep them on your altar with a picture of yourself. Also add to the list things that you would like to aspire to, with God's help.

Acknowledge to your self how you want to love and care for others and extend that loving to yourself each and every day. Can you imagine yourself to be the Beloved of God or the Beloved of the natural world? Try doing this as part of your meditation practice for each day, visualizing being embraced by Divine Love. Through the eyes of your heart, look upon yourself and see your preciousness.

Did you ever experience as a child the simple joy of being connected to the world and dancing and playing in the natural delight of living? Did you have a doll or imaginary playmate that you loved and that loved you? Think of some ways to connect with your younger innocent self by putting things from your childhood on your altar: an old toy or doll, a picture of a natural space that you experienced as a child. What might you place there?

One of the most important things that we can do to help ourselves to heal and grow is to develop within us a loving witness for ourselves that functions from the heart space. This is a part of us that can step back from the drama of our emotions and be lovingly present with us as we go through our challenges and ups and downs. This may seem like developing a split personality but is an essential psycho-spiritual skill. It is like having a loving wise parent present with us 24/7. This is our loving wisdom self that is connected to Spirit. This part of ourselves, as we develop it, will be there to comfort us, advise us, even to correct us lovingly when we need it. To start developing this wise loving part in you, here are some things to practice:

IMPORTANT PRACTICE: (Also, see appendix 3)

Spend time practicing loving kindness, sending loving thoughts and wishes, and loving energy towards yourself. You can support this kind of consciousness by putting your hand over your heart space and letting your awareness sink into this space. Your mind goes into a very different, loving state when you place your hand over your heart. Rather than all of the criticisms that your mind will make of you when you are on the mental level, you connect with yourself with compassion and appreciation through the heart space. Or put one of your hands on your heart and the other hand on your abdomen as you do this to emphasize the heart/body centered nature of this work. Make this a regular part of your meditation practice, especially if you find it difficult to care and accept yourself. This will pay big dividends if you do it consistently!

When you are upset about something, journal about it. First, meditate to center yourself as much as you can. Next, with your hand on your heart, let the part of you that is upset write about it. Then see if you can step back and be your own wise counselor, the one whose presence you feel when you are meditating calmly. Let this calm loving voice dialogue through writing with the upset part of you. First let it give you empathy and support and then perhaps this wise part can give you some advice on how to proceed with the upsetting incident more skillfully.

If you find it hard to connect with yourself emotionally when you are hurting, try caressing yourself where the hurt is. Put your hands there and softly pat and stroke and soothe the hurt. Try rocking yourself back and forth like a mother would soothe a hurting child. For that is often what is present below the level of your awareness: a very young, hurt, abandoned, neglected part of you.

Try to overcome any reluctance, embarrassment, or even revulsion for doing this. These critical, rejecting feelings are what have kept this part of you stuck in pain for so long. And don't judge the resistance to doing this self nurturing either. This is what you learned from how you were treated when you were growing up! Be gentle even with your resistance.

Invitation

As soon as Jesus was baptized, he went up out of the water. At that moment heaven was opened, and he saw the Spirit of God descending like a dove and alighting on him. And a voice from heaven said, "This is my Son, whom I love; with him I am well pleased."

- Matthew 3: 16-17 NIV Bible

You were once a child and you were lovable, innocent, vulnerable, needing kindness and protection. You needed somebody to love and care for you. If you were not loved as a child how much more you deserve to be loved now and taken care of now, to be held, caressed and nurtured now. In your mind's eye picture yourself when you were a child, how you played, how your parents took care of you- or didn't. Imagine yourself now as your adult self, caring for the child that you once were. That child is still present in you, needing your love and nurturance. In your heart's eye, go to that child you were and embrace them. You are now the parent of that child within you, so take good care of them!

When your heart feels tight and closed, be kind and gentle to it. This is the only way for it to open up again. As long as you are beating yourself up, it will remain afraid and closed. Your heart space can feel so vulnerable at times, just as you as a young child would feel when you were frightened. Place your hands over your heart and allow yourself to gently feel into your heart space; feel its warmth and openness or even (especially) its pain and tightness with gentleness and care. And breathe, breathe into your heart. Breathe out fear, hurt and self criticism. Breathe in love and peace.

In contemplation, allow your heart to be open like a chalice and offer it up to a loving God or the Universe and gently hold yourself open to receive His/Her/Its love. Imagine God's / the Universe's love like a golden sun beam, streaming down into the chalice of your heart, filling it to the brim with Love. Breathe in this love and breathe it back out to God / the Universe as an offering of your love. Love speaks to Love. Love touches Love. Love listens to Love. You are both the Lover and the Beloved.

CHAPTER 3

Developing Basic Trust

Welcome, You belong Here

I have been waiting for you
a thousand million years and more.
You were in my mind when I made
the universe so long, long ago.
Now you sit on your little spinning world
amidst so vast a number of stars and galaxies
and wonder if you mean anything.
You mean so much to me and
hopefully you know you are made of
the same star stuff divinity as I!

-Robert Cornell

Introduction

In Erick Erickson's stages of psychosocial human development, the formation in the infant of Basic Trust in its mother to meet its needs consistently is Stage One. This is the foundation for all succeeding stages of development. If this basic trust is not met, the infant will have a difficult time developing normally, gaining a sense of autonomy, developing social skills, etc. And no matter how well we are nurtured, human nature seems to conspire with our past negative experiences so that we are never as trusting as we would ideally be about the basic nature of our world. We have to work at developing further this foundation of trust in our spiritual work.

Our species developed in a different world when the dangers surrounding our forebears in their environment were much graver and more prevalent than today (at least for those of us lucky enough to live in peaceful, developed nations.) So from an evolutionary standpoint, the bias of our brains and nervous systems towards sensing danger is what allowed our species to survive in past times. Now we need a different kind of consciousness: one that can see the inter-connectedness of things more clearly than the threats to our survival. And we humans don't have the luxury of waiting for our bodies and minds to evolve biologically towards this more loving and caring attitude. In order to ensure the survival of our species as well as life on the planet in general, we must develop and deepen this attitude of basic trust through psychological healing and spiritual development.

For some of us, a deep distrust of the world, of others and even distrust of ourselves comes from our past suffering of neglect, abuse, abandonment and lack of nurturance in our families. In childhood, we are profoundly dependent physically and emotionally on our caregivers and, if they treat us badly, it leaves deep wounds in our psyches. Because of this dependence, we are exquisitely attuned to our parent's attitudes towards us and we bend our very natures to fit what our parents want from us.

To put it bluntly, this is what our very survival depended upon: to keep our parents happy enough with us that they wouldn't abandon or abuse us (and even then some did). This is the basic way many of us are set up by our biological inheritance and family dysfunction: to distrust the world, others, and even ourselves. And unfortunately this distrust of our parents and the world can transfer to ourselves and to God or whatever image we have of the Ultimate Truth.

The development of trust starts with ourselves because we are the only ones who are with us 24/7 – except for God. In order to develop a sense of basic trust in ourselves, we need to foster a consistent attitude of caring, kindness and reliability towards ourselves. If we cannot depend upon our own selves to care for us then whom can we in fact depend upon? For those of us conditioned to be judgmental or uncaring towards ourselves this will mean gentle, patient work to gradually replace our habitual self-rejection and self-abandonment. These were often learned in response to parental abuse and neglect. Now they can gradually be unlearned through the consistent practice of self acceptance, self love and self care. This is not antithetical to being more caring of others; it is the very basis for caring for others by learning to care for oneself.

Some of us reacted to dangerous and abusive family environments with anger and aggression. We have no trust in other people, so hostility and conflict have become the default mode for how we relate to the world: ready at a moment's notice to defend ourselves and those dear to us. This mode of being in the world can be hard to heal, for in some ways it can feel safe to be angry and to blame others for our problems. We can feel self righteous and empowered, and this feels far better than the vulnerability that we otherwise might feel. Those of us with this aggressive posture need to allow ourselves to sink down below the anger and blame in order to feel the hurt and vulnerability hiding out below the anger.

This is very challenging work as it requires us to be able to stay with our vulnerability, our hurt, and the fear that we have defended ourselves from for so long. Much patience is necessary and an act of faith that, if we remain open and vulnerable, we can then be healed with love and forgiveness. It can be very useful to have a caring counselor to accompany us on this journey of healing, to be there for us when we melt down and are tempted to act out. A "good enough" counselor can love us even when we find it hard to love anyone, ourselves included.

Still others of us earned our parent's love by taking care of them and doing what they wanted from us. We learned to give up our needs and focus on theirs so that we would be given a pittance of care in return. We distrust that we will have our needs met if we do not sacrifice ourselves for others. And we perpetuate this sad deal with those that we come into relationship with. "If I love and care for you the best that I can, then maybe you will deign to love me. For I am not worthy of love just for myself." This is what we have come to unconsciously believe about ourselves: that we are unworthy of receiving what we need from our relationships with others - perhaps even from God.

Some of us retreat inside ourselves to find a safe place where we can't be hurt anymore. This might be in reading books or wandering alone out in nature where we could find some safety and comfort. While this gives us a rich inner life, we are cut off from others and the larger world by this introverted lifestyle. For others of us, this might be found in compulsive use of internet video games, pornography and living in virtual worlds that seem a whole lot safer then the real world which hasn't been too kind to us.

But these are bloodless things devoid of the real human connections that nurture and sustain us. Others of us retreat into drug use and acting out in in self harming behaviors. In all of these ways, we retreat further and further from our painful wounds, and further from ourselves and from our connection to the divine. In my therapy practice with clients, those who are most damaged by their families are the ones who have the most difficulty developing trust in me. Of course, this isn't their fault; they have a lot of good reasons for not trusting anyone. And so my job is to be as consistent as I can in meeting with them and caring for them – and not forcing them to open the door into their secret world of pain.

I can just invite and love them and wait for them to open the door from the inside. Then I do my best to honor and praise them for being courageous enough to trust me and to let me into their lives. Gradually a bond of trust is formed between us and the work can go on from there. But without that trust no work can begin, for the client's walls will be up and they will not let me see anything vulnerable.

Fortunately, trust can be developed; it is not fixed in place forever. One thing we can do for ourselves is to become aware of our reactions to externals and to see without judgment our habitual reactions of fear and distrust. Then we remind ourselves that how we perceive things is not necessarily reality. If we have a history of abuse, we are very likely to suffer from feeling unsafe and have fearful or angry reactions to situations that, to others, might seem nonthreatening.

Our awareness at least begins to help us to not react unconsciously and unskillfully to these perceived threats. The next level of work is to allow ourselves to contact the hurt and frightened parts of ourselves that are hiding out in the basement of our consciousness. These are felt in our bodies, which connect us to the memories of the wounds. We need to own and care for these parts and it can be difficult work requiring considerable courage.

I remember part of my own healing work from thirty some years ago: I was terribly upset about what happened in my Zen Center community when the secrets came out about my teacher's sexual misbehavior. I was doing some Voice Dialogue work, engaging parts of my consciousness with a facilitator around issues with my teacher and a scared part of me came out that hid behind a chair in his office. This wasn't a part of myself that I was comfortable engaging with at that point in my life and after that session, I ended the work. I was not ready to acknowledge that scared little boy that was hiding down in the cellar of my consciousness, rejected and abandoned even by myself. That would come later!

When you are ready to begin this challenging work of reconnecting to the vulnerable, wounded parts of yourself that are hiding within you, recognize that this is a step of great courage. Care for yourself enough to know that this path, however scary and difficult it may seem at first, may be the most important journey you will ever take. Learn to nurture, cherish and honor the parts of yourself that have been abused, blamed, shamed, and cast out. Some day you will realize that these wounded parts are a great gift that led you to seeking wholeness – and to being of service to others on their journey of healing and wholeness.

Self Reflection & Practice

Basic trust is a nonconceptual confidence in the goodness of the universe, an unquestioned implicit trust that there is something about the universe and human nature and life that is inherently and fundamentally good, loving, and wishing us the best.

- A. H. Almaas, Facets of Unity

We can let go of our distrust and self protectiveness when we come to believe in our very hearts -not just intellectually consent to it- that there is Something Greater than our fearful ego identities to which we can entrust ourselves. In order to let go of our fears, we first need to become aware of what they are and what they stem from. This exercise is intended to assist you in identifying what your fears are and what they might be based upon. In engaging with these questions it might be a good idea to play some quiet spiritual music in the background as support for this rather challenging work.

What fears might you have of relying on, falling back into the arms of God / the Universe / your Higher Power? He/She/It won't be there for you? He/She/It isn't dependable? He/She/It is capricious and cruel and not about Love and Grace? You don't deserve this kind of care and support? What other fears might you have of opening up in trust to the Universe/ Life? Journal on this. Explore what deep core beliefs you have about God/the Universe that cause you to be reluctant to trust in His/Her/Its comforting presence in your life. Putting your hand on your heart, let your heart speak of its fears and distrust. Journal on this subject.

Sometimes our mistrust of God comes from the mistrust we had as children of our parents because they emotionally, physically, or sexually abused us or neglected and abandoned us. Or perhaps a member of the clergy abused us as a child or teenager. Does this make sense to you for your particular inability to trust? The causes of our distrust may be fairly obvious or they may not be. In any case, explore this issue of distrust in some detail. This is a fundamental issue deserving your close attention.

If you have not already done so, it would be an excellent step on your spiritual journey to get some supportive counseling about these matters. Often with spiritually based counseling, either psychotherapy or spiritual direction, you can then start to reclaim trust in God – and His /Her representatives here on earth.

Do you even mistrust yourself? Some of us have been taught to distrust our emotions, our intuition, even our bodies themselves. Reflect upon how much trust you have of yourself in these areas. Can you trust your feelings, your thoughts and intuitions, your body? If not, reflect upon where your distrust might have come from. Try having a written dialogue with the parts of you that you do not trust. For example, say you have an uneasiness about a part of your body. Have a dialogue with this part as if it were its own entity and see what the conversation reveals to you. This can be very enlightening work! Touching into a part of the body can surface old painful memories and even traumas, so be gentle with yourself as you do this work.

Let yourself feel into your heart space – the area around but not identical to your physical heart. You can facilitate this by putting both hands gently over your heart and imagine you are breathing into your heart and breathing out of it. When you allow your awareness to descend into your heart in this manner, what do you feel? Do you feel safe resting there? Is there some sensation of numbness or constriction? Can you spend time resting in your heart space or do you feel a panicky need to come back up to the surface of your mind? If so, do you have a sense of what lies behind these fears? Touch in to these feelings in your heart and explore these matters in your journal.

Let your heart speak freely of its fears and concerns without editing or judging. Free form writing might be useful at this point where you just let yourself write freely without any concern about grammar, punctuation, spelling, etc. Be compassionate and understanding to yourself as you write, for you may have childhood wounds that need the salve of your caring attention. Write about what happened to you as a child, staying with the feelings in your heart. Treat any distrust and fear that surfaces as if it were an Inner Child that lives inside of you and that still carries the wounds of your childhood. This may help you to accept yourself with more compassion if you can relate to your feelings of distrust and fear as if they come from your childhood self, for in all likelihood they do.

If you had a difficult childhood, spend some time each day practicing caring for yourself. This could be by learning to eat healthy foods and refraining from junk food. It could be by making sure that you get enough sleep at night or listening to your body for what it needs. Learn to take consistent good care of yourself in all things. Can you be trustworthy to yourself or do you find it hard to stay with yourself when you encounter difficult feelings? This ultimately is the basis for your having deep trust in the world: being able to count on you to not abandon yourself. Don't be hard on yourself if you can't stay with difficult feelings; get help from a loving counselor, friends, and fellow participants in recovery programs to assist you until you can do it for yourself.

Spend time listening to and processing your feelings and comforting yourself with your wise self as in the exercises in the previous chapter. Learn to be present with yourself by putting your hand on your heart often when you feel afraid, hurt or angry. This is what a "good enough" dependable parent would have done for you. But now you can learn to be that dependable parent for yourself. This is how you will grow and deepen your basic trust. Start by being trustworthy for yourself. Deepen your ability to trust yourself by learning to stay present and compassionate with difficult feelings as they arise.

Even for those of us who had "good enough" parenting, there is often the need to learn to be with ourselves more intimately and consistently. This practice is not to be begun when we are in crisis but rather when our world is calm and steady. Spiritual practice only in the 11th hour of crisis or death is not very useful. We so called normal people have the luxury of choosing to practice. We should not be too complacent about our lot in life; it could change for the worse any moment. Now is the time to practice!

Invitation

I think the most important question facing humanity is, "Is the universe a friendly place?" This is the first and most basic question all people must answer for themselves.

-Albert Einstein

Learning to trust is essential to the spiritual journey: learning to trust oneself, learning to be discerning and to trust those who are worthy of our trust. And finally, trusting God and the World to be a safe place for us to live and love in. Our lives are filled with much joy and pain, many challenges and much to rejoice over. This is the human journey. And it is our hearts that contain all of this human experience of joy, sadness, compassion, hurt, fear, and courage. Trust your heart and be trustworthy to it, for your heart is the abode of your truest self. While our minds are marvelously creative, it is our heart, even with all of its wounds and passions that leads us into our authentic lives.

Care for your heart and it will be true to you. Ignore it at your peril, for an untended wounded heart will never let you see clearly, let alone act with compassion or integrity. When your mind is vexed with troubling thoughts, let yourself sink into the depths of your heart where the source of your sorrows lies. Be with your heart and assuage its troubles, for then your heart will be faithful and reliable to you. Open your heart to God's loving presence and let Him/Her heal you.

No matter what your heart feels, endeavor to stay lovingly present with it. Don't abandon it. Your heart needs a consistent and loving parent and you are the Chosen One. No one, not even God, can do this for you. No one can be around you 24/7 other than you yourself. To develop basic trust in the world, be trustworthy to yourself. And ask sincerely for God's help in this challenging work. For God is Love and Love is the thing that ultimately heals us.

Be compassionate with yourself when you cannot stay with your pain. Find help that will support you in feeling the pain and not numbing out or acting out in compulsive or addictive behavior. You are human and have your wounds and sometimes it takes awhile to heal them. Be patient with yourself and find the help that you need: friends who are compassionate and don't judge, a Twelve Step program, a religious or spiritual community, a counselor. Trust means to open yourself even when your mind is saying you should be afraid and close yourself off. You practice trust with a gentle opening of your heart. You practice trust by loving – even when it seems inconvenient. You practice trust by letting Love show you the way. Remember: you are the one you have been waiting for!

CHAPTER 4

Being with Our Vulnerability

Vulnerability is the gateway to spirituality.
> - Dr. Ron Hulnick, President, The University of Santa Monica

The Gateway

Who would know-
the last thing we would want-
would be the gateway?
That raw edge, the heartache,
the anger, the aching hurt
would be the Way that God
could reach into us and heal us.

There is a catch, though.

We have to let the feelings be
and melt into their depths.
And when we surrender,
The dark clouds will open
and the beams of God's love
will enter our hearts.

> -Robert Cornell

Introduction

What we resist, persists.

-Anonymous Program saying

The last thing most of us human beings want is to be in touch with our vulnerability: the fear, discomfort, sadness, the hurt and anger that lie down inside our bodies. No, we don't want to feel any of that, and that is why we spend so much of our time and energy chasing pleasure and distraction and running away from what we fear - even if we know the pleasures and distractions are shallow and lead us away from our truth. We distract ourselves with the banal, the sleazy, with down right stupid acting out. We numb ourselves with TV, the Internet, pornography and sexual promiscuity, overeating, oversleeping, overwork, underperforming ... you name it, all for the purpose of running away from the scary uncomfortable feelings that lie below the surface – in our bodies, in the present moment.

And much of the time we are not even aware of what we are running from (or even that we are running) and it runs us. To avoid the possibility of being hurt (being vulnerable) we have adopted unconsciously a way of being in the world. We become the people pleaser, the good little boy or girl, the overachiever, the bully, the womanizer, the rager, the liar, the one who retreats into their little private world of addiction or fantasy. All these false roles and personas developed to avoid being hurt....again.

We avoid our vulnerability – and our true power and authenticity. For those of us who can be half truthful to ourselves, we may harbor a secret guilt that we are not living our real life, only some pale reflection of what it really could be. And we are often correct in sensing this. For so many of us, our real "sin" (sin as in missing the mark) isn't the sin of commission, it is the sin of omission. Our real sin is that we are not being true to ourselves. In running away from the truth of our direct experience, which is often challenging, we betray the very best that we have to offer the world.

This is what Jean-Paul Sartre called " bad faith." For someone who was a secular existentialist and not a person of faith, this was a profound insight. "But the first act of bad faith is to flee what it cannot flee, to flee what it is." Sartre wrote in *Being and Nothingness*. In our unconscious emotional mind's distorted perspective, being true to ourselves usually carries the risk of being hurt again – most likely in the ways we were hurt as children. To our adult rational minds this makes no sense but on the unconscious emotional level, our minds deeply hold this to be true. If I am my authentic self, I will be ridiculed, hurt, abandoned, rejected, betrayed- even destroyed.

The greatest courage we can have is the courage to meet our life as it is, in the moment, in our bodies; not as we want it to be or as we think it should be. And I emphasize that life is to be lived in the body because so many of us have abandoned our bodies to live up in our heads where we can feel safe. When we stop fighting our direct experience, which feels vulnerable and uncomfortable - even terrifying at times - we are opening ourselves up to reality, to God, to the "I am that I am." And in opening to our feelings of vulnerability in our body, we are living in the present moment where God/Buddha Nature abides and where we can be healed.

It may seem counterintuitive, but one of the best ways we can learn to accept and love ourselves is to open up to whatever we are experiencing in the present moment, whether joy or sorrow, whether love or fear. Why would this be so? It's because we are then bringing our awareness to the vulnerable parts of ourselves that need healing and love. If we push away or avoid the feelings we judge as bad or even threatening, we are rejecting and abandoning the wounded aspects of ourselves.

In her talks on spiritual practice, Pema Chodron talks profoundly about learning "To Stay" - to stay with our experience as it is, whether it is "good" or "bad." We learn to let go of our grasping onto what is pleasant and to allow ourselves to just experience what we dislike, as these arise and pass away. This is the core teaching of Buddhism: overcoming the bondage of aversion and grasping, letting be what is and not trying to escape from or hang on to it.

When you are aware of your inner experience, from time to time, you will feel your body tense up or contract as you encounter unpleasant emotions, physical sensations, memories or threatening thoughts and judgments and your fight or flight responses are triggered. This is part of our common human nature and is the product of an evolutionary process that is by no means perfect or complete. These psychobiological aspects of our human nature are not evil – in fact we need them for our very survival. But they are also very hard to retrain when they have been conditioned by childhood trauma. We could say from a scientific basis that we are biased by our neurobiology to focus on our fears, prejudices, desires, and to tend to be emotionally reactive.

It takes a lot of spiritual and psychological work, engaging proactively with Life and our inner experience, to become a good human being. It doesn't come easily or naturally because our biology has only partially prepared us to live with wisdom and compassion. The potential is there in each of us to be an exemplary human being but it takes a great deal of effort and practice to keep our hearts open. We can clearly see if more of us don't follow this path of wisdom and compassion we are not going to make it as a civilization. Our greed, ignorance and reactivity combined with our technology and our sheer numbers will do us in by destroying the natural world around us and ourselves in the process.

Our human tendency to be overly vigilant as to what might threaten us and to be overly protective of ourselves is what causes humans at the personal, institutional and the national levels to create unnecessary walls between "us" and "them." This is the source of both personal animosity between individuals and conflict between nations. So how do we spiritual learners work skillfully with these human tendencies to be protective, reactive, and resistant to that which we perceive to be threatening? The counter intuitive answer is to drop our protective walls and to feel what we feel. This means allowing ourselves to feel very vulnerable at times, which is just what our defensive structures are there to avoid and resist. This is spiritual unilateral disarmament and it is a radical step, personally, institutionally and politically.

Our egoic defense structures are very much influenced by our childhoods when we had no rational capacity to understand what was happening to us and around us. These defense mechanisms were designed to protect us as children and are based on very partial and distorted ways of seeing the world and these no longer serve us as individuals or as members of institutions or nations. A large part of psychology's gift to spiritual practice is its insights into how these adverse childhood experiences distort our ways of seeing and being in the world. In addition to these insights, we have healing tools such as EMDR, (Eye Movement Desensitization and Reprogramming), EFT, (Emotional Freedom Technique), somatically based therapies and Mindfulness based therapies for reducing the emotional impact of traumatic memory on our consciousness.

Not-so-aware people, who have no insight into the unconscious influences of their childhoods become fearful, angry, hurt, and reactive in situations where they are triggered by situations reminiscent of their childhood trauma. Truth is we "spiritual" people, are often triggered too. We may not be so reactive, but we are often embarrassed and ashamed of our "weakness" or our "emotionality." We may want to avoid such experiences by trying to "bliss out" or avoid them with some other spiritual practices. This can lead to the trap of Spiritual Bypassing. Deeply engaged psycho-spiritual practice invites us to stay present with our experience, neither to identify with it and act out, nor to try to escape from it. But gently and compassionately we stay mindful of the feelings and thoughts and work with them in loving and constructive ways.

If we allow ourselves to rest gently and compassionately in our awareness of our bodily sensations and use the breath to allow us to go further into the experience without resistance, it often will flow through us and be gone. On the other hand, if we resist, the feelings tend to persist. Paradoxically and completely against our common sense, allowing the walls of defensiveness and resistance to melt inside of us is the gateway to a deep change in our way of being in the world. We become less defensive, less reactive, and more open and able to be present with whatever we are facing, "good" or "bad."

The fundamental problem with avoiding and resisting our vulnerability is that it doesn't let us engage with, clarify and heal our issues. "If we don't feel it we can't heal it" could be the motto of this deep work of psychological and spiritual healing. As we allow ourselves to contact these difficult feelings, we begin to solve many of the puzzles we have about our behavior. We can see why something caused us to react angrily, why we resist another's help, why we need to be right in an argument, etc. Our secret and unconscious agendas begin to come to light so that we can heal ourselves and change our limiting beliefs and dysfunctional and reactive behaviors.

Our fear about contacting these buried feelings is typically that we will be dragged back into painful memories and this will get us nowhere but into more pain, and possibly threaten our very survival. So most people just want to "put them behind" and what they end up doing is avoiding and burying them. But that doesn't make these old issues go away; they will remain down in the basement of our unconscious and still erupt from time to time in painful reminders of their unhealed presence. The wonderful thing today is that we have many psychological and spiritual tools for healing our old wounds and growing into our open, spontaneous true selves. This is the potential that we have now and it is what I invite you to work towards with the exercises in this book.

This work of letting go of our resistance to our experience is so foundational to all of the rest of the work in this book that I have spent much more time on it than we will do with many subjects in other chapters. For if you get how to do the work in this chapter, the other chapters will be much easier for having learned the basic processes in this chapter. In addition to the somatic sensing described below, I invite you to learn about Energy Psychology and the tapping work done in the Emotional Freedom technique, which is a relatively new therapy tool that can be so helpful in doing this work. You can see this technique in action and how to do it with yourself on the website www.emofree. com. (Also see appendix #5.)

Self Reflection & Practice

If there is one over riding reason why our world and relationships are in such a mess, is that we try to get rid of our anxiety, fear and shame as fast as possible, regardless of the long term consequences. In doing so, we blame and shame others and in countless ways, we unwittingly act against ourselves. We confuse our fear driven thoughts with what is right, best, necessary or true.

Harriet Lerner

Spend several weeks or more with these exercises if you haven't done much of this kind of body awareness practice before. This is crucial to the work laid out in the rest of this book. Without this kind of ongoing direct experiential contact with yourself you will miss the growing edge, the vitality, and healing potential of much of what is offered in this book. Mostly then you would learn information about spirituality – not the direct experience of being here now in your body, which is what actually heals. Our work in this book is going to be about learning to be with our direct experience - as it is, in the body- "good", "bad" and "indifferent". We learn to stay with our experience in our bodies and not to spin out mentally, creating more stories that filter and distort our reality and create more pain and limitation.

This is why awareness practice is so important to practice on a regular basis. Otherwise, you will not have sufficiently developed the safe container of awareness built up over time that allows you to stay present with challenging experiences that come up for you. Insight Meditation or Mindfulness practice is about learning to be present with and accepting of our experience. Practicing daily is the best way to consistently develop this capacity. If you are not meditating presently, begin. Today. If there are no meditation centers near to you, I suggest that you get a course such as *Insight Meditation* by Joseph Goldstein and Sharon Salzberg or *Mindfulness Meditation for Everyday Life* by John Kabat Zinn to help you with the basics. This kind of meditation practice will be extremely useful to you in your spiritual work as well as in your everyday life.

IMPORTANT PRACTICE

Spend the next several weeks watching how you relate to your direct experience. Keep a notebook and jot down your observations during the day. REMEMBER TO BE KIND TO YOURSELF AND NOT USE THESE OBSERVATIONS AS MORE AMMUNITION AGAINST YOURSELF! Remember that every human being does unconscious things much of the time! You and everyone else have been set up by our common biological and psychological inheritance with these shortcomings. Give yourself a break and be grateful that you at least have become conscious of how conditioned your life is. That is such an important stage to get to even though it can be sobering and upsetting to see how reactive and on automatic we are so much of the time.

Notice when you are lost in thought. If you are, what are you thinking about and how might this relate to keeping yourself safe from potential harm or trying to be in control of your experience of life? Our thoughts so much of the time revolve around fixing, avoiding or figuring out how to deal with situations that we find difficult or threatening. Some of us spend a huge amount of time regretting things we have done or not done. Or we lose ourselves in pleasant fantasies and thereby insulate ourselves from reality. Or we spend time being angry and resenting someone for what they did to us. All a waste of our precious time!

Or we engage in self-pity or being angry with ourselves and beating ourselves up. All of these are ways of solidifying our stories about ourselves and strengthening our conditioned ego consciousness. When you notice yourself lost in these self pity, shame and blame parties, come back to your body. Feel into what you feel there. Gradually this practice will take away the energy of obsessive thinking, because there is less energy left over for thinking when you are feeling.

Notice how you relate to other people. Do you have a particular (happy, placating, apologetic, angry, pleasant, neutral, stand offish, overly friendly) face that you present to others that you know is not your real face? What purpose does that serve for you? Be as explicit as you can about this. Journal about your persona in some detail. Be sure to apply self-acceptance if you sink into self-criticism or depression. Breathe and release anger if it shows up.

Try to notice when you space out. Of course, this is a little difficult when you have, after all, spaced out! So you notice this when you come out of the "space out." Then try to find out what was the trigger for spacing out: were you scared, wanting to retreat inside? Bored? Were you resistant to being present? If so, what in particular were you resistant to? What were you feeling prior to spacing out?

Remember that some people who were traumatized when young will dissociate (a more acute kind of spacing out) when a triggering situation reminds them of the old traumatic event. And this triggering event does not need to be a violent, overwhelming situation. Healing from such trauma often involves learning to stay present to our feelings rather than dissociating.

Notice in your body when you tense up, get fearful or angry. What preceded these reactions? What thoughts or memories came up before, during, or after the event? What judgments of the events stayed with you after it was over? How long did these stay with you and did you struggle with them or hold onto them?

Our emotional upsets are the very stuff of our learning about and healing old emotional patterns. Spirituality is often mistaken to be a kind of exalted unearthly state of leaving your worldly cares (and body) behind. This creates a very unhealthy kind of spirituality that is not grounded and is lived out somewhere in a fantasy world untethered to the body. Engaging the body and our experience in the body is critical to a holistic psycho-spirituality.

IMPORTANT PRACTICE

In a safe place, lie comfortably on your back and allow yourself to feel down into your body. Lying down lets you relax; just try not to fall asleep. Keep attention gently on the breath while you scan with your awareness through your body, say from the feet up through the legs, thighs, pelvis, gut / belly, chest, arms and hands, neck and shoulders, and finally, the head. As you do this, you may find areas that are stiff, numb, painful, or otherwise feel uncomfortable as you gently touch on them with your awareness.

More than likely, these are areas where your body holds resistance to feelings and sensations and perhaps traumatic memories. Be gentle in feeling into and exploring these areas. The more trauma that is related to an area of the body, the more resistance you will experience to doing this. As they say in Yoga, play the edge. Gently breathe into this area as you feel your way into it. When the resistance becomes too much back off. You can always revisit this body area again.

As we engage with the experience we do so with Mindfulness. This means that we are developing a witness awareness that is not identified with the experience that we are having. In practice this means to be aware of our reactions to our experience, how we judge it as "good" or "bad", how we tend to hold onto a "good" experience and resist a "bad" one. We gradually learn to develop equanimity to whatever we are experiencing. This is not an intellectual exercise. It is body focused and in the moment, feeling what we feel and learning to be with what it is. This is the vital fundamental practice that heals us and lets God do His work with us.

This is what we do, over and over again, until there is no resistance to being present to this area and this experience in the body. This sounds so easy in theory but in practice, we will discover over time our many layers of resistance and defensiveness playing out as we attempt to stay present with our bodily experience. We may fall asleep, become distracted by a chain of thought and fall into a fantasy or "planning". Or we may find ourselves overcome by shame and self judgment. These egoic protectors are very strong when we are uncovering some painful issues in our bodily experience.

We may feel so overwhelmed by the experience that we start to panic. This means we are moving into areas of body memory that relate to serious trauma. In this case, it would be highly desirable for you to get professional support for this work. If you have indeed experienced serious trauma, working with a somatic (body focused) therapist could provide you with much healing and opening. Some of the therapies that encompass this area are Touch for Health, acupuncture, somatic psychotherapy, Emotional Freedom Technique, EMDR, Focusing, etc.

One of the best opportunities to work with bodily sensations is when you are triggered and upset about some situation. Instead of going mental and rushing to tell others how upset you are and why, it is better to learn to stay with the sensations in the present moment in the body. Gently breathe into the places in the body that hold these emotions/ feelings/sensations and befriend them. Work without judgment, with curiosity and the practice of being completely present with them.

When you do this, memories and thoughts may come up; these are also to be looked at with detachment and compassion. As we do this kind of exploration, we begin to see what unconscious memories and beliefs may underlie our emotional reactions and thought patterns. And, as we refrain from feeding the bonfire of our stories and our reactivity, we create more spaciousness around our wounds. They begin to heal and less and less box our lives in.

As an antidote to your overly mental level life, Yoga, Tai Chi and other body-focused practices are excellent ways to acquaint yourself with your physical being. I highly recommend these types of practices if you are overly cerebral and not very well connected to your body. If you are a "nerd" or an "intellectual" and are physically awkward, this may seem like a very unfamiliar and uncomfortable world to explore but it could be an excellent way to balance out your overly developed mental approach to life.

Invitation

Be tender with yourself, my dear. For only kindness can heal your wounds. Our wounds are kept from being healed by our fear of being hurt and Love is the way beyond this fear. Do all things with love for yourself. Not the false love of self promotion or entitlement, but rather the humble love that would care for your hurt little self, that would carefully wash off the dust of the world from your feet. Kindness and compassion are the Way. This is the Way of the Heart. This is the Way of Forgiveness of Self and Others. This is the Way of Jesus the Rabbi and Healer.

Your wounds lie in your body so that is where the healing must eventually go. It's where you can feel your vulnerability most poignantly and indeed, sometimes painfully. Give yourself enough trust that you are willing to descend into this body that God gave you. He did not make a mistake by enfleshing you. Remember that Jesus lived in a very human and vulnerable body. So don't avoid your body. Listen to its murmurs, its pleasures and its fears. Your exquisite vulnerability lies within this body – as does your authenticity.

Remember that your body is your earthly temple; do not demean it or reject it. It is your home until you leave this life, so treat it well. If you are living in your mind (as so many of us do), come down out of the attic and learn to live on the ground floor. Your mind may be a great dreamer and visionary, but it can never dwell in the present moment where your body abides. So take a tour through this body of yours. You might be surprised at what you find! Done with awareness, this will lead you back to this present moment that is the Bodhi Mind and the Kingdom that Dwells Within you.

Feel into your breath, now. Know when you are breathing in, and when you are breathing out, now. This is a profound gateway into the present moment, for awareness of sensation only occurs in the present moment. Let your breath be a gentle anchor on your mind, which can be such an unruly horse. And you thought your mind was the master! Silly you. Come back to this breath over and over again. It will never fail to ground you in the present moment as long as you are alive.

And in this body, breathe into whatever you are feeling there, whether pleasant or unpleasant. In this way you will gradually break down the distinction between pleasant and unpleasant, good and bad. Yes, you will sometimes feel a raw unmediated sense of vulnerability but in this, you will know that you are alive! And you will indeed BE more alive to the present moment, which is all that actually exists. Everything else is an idea, a memory, a weak reflection of reality itself. Cherish this present moment in the body - even when it feels uncomfortable. Feel into any bodily sensation with your breath being like a gentle featherlike touch of your awareness.

This is what's real. Whatever the feeling or sensation, it will not overpower you; it is workable. Even the toothache, even a bout of flu, even the embarrassment and anxiety of giving a talk: it's workable. Don't forget this. All you have to do is allow yourself to gently feel into the vulnerability, acknowledge it and go on doing what you are doing. Gradually, as you gently lean into this kind of direct experiencing you will notice a subtle freedom growing within yourself and your life will open up. I promise you, this will happen. And it takes time and your gentle perseverance.

Live your life more directly and authentically. Your body is calling you to abide within it, in this moment. Perhaps you have been absent from it for a long time, living in your mind. It's time to come home to your abode of NOW. Your mind can never know this place like your body can, so let yourself BE your body. Breathe.

31

CHAPTER 5

Letting go of Self Judgment

Self judgment is toxic to the soul; it is the ego's way of trying to protect itself from other's criticisms or to force itself to be better through self punishment.

Why?

Why are you so mean to yourself?
        Do you hope against hope that you can
        flog a dead horse and get it to trot?
        Do you hope to make up for all of your
        imagined shortcomings and transgressions?
        Or perhaps, you want to beat others to the punch?
Put the daggers away, all the instruments of self-torture
        you have collected over the years.
        Bring out the pillows and the sweet tea.
        Rest. Allow yourself to be: as God made you.

Robert Cornell

Introduction

Some of us are habitually used to judging ourselves even though this creates great pain. Why do we do this to ourselves? One important reason for this is that some of us as children were emotionally, physically and / or sexually abused by those we trusted. When children are abused in this way they carry a deep sense of unworthiness and believe that something is wrong with them. In their magical way of thinking, they feel responsible for what happened to them and hence, they believe they are bad. It will take much supportive therapy for adult survivors of child abuse to learn to love and care for themselves.

This tendency to self-criticism often comes from being chronically scolded or attacked as children in our abusive families. When we are young we tend to swallow as the truth, the falsehoods that our parents tell us about ourselves. If you think about how dependent we are upon our parents for our very survival as young children this kind of introjection (as therapists say), this taking into ourselves of our parents' ways of relating to us, makes perfect sense. We literally soak up their behaviors and judgments and their critical voice becomes our Inner Critics.

As counterintuitive as it may seem, we often will use self-criticism as a means of protection. I had a therapy client that used self-criticism as a way to try to protect herself from the unpredictable outbursts of rage that her father would direct towards her. Her unconscious strategy as a child was to be hard on herself and not do anything wrong so that her father wouldn't hurt her. This gave her the illusion that at least she had something she could do that might protect her from her father. She had some sense of control, even if it was to beat herself up.

Today as a middle-aged adult, she still struggles with stopping this deeply entrenched habit of being so harsh in judging herself - though it is intellectually clear to her by now that it no longer serves her as any kind of protection. And when she does let go of her self criticism, she feels a sense of vulnerability, as if she is leaving herself open to being attacked and punished again. Oddly enough, the Inner Critic or Abuser once made her feel protected and now she must tolerate this sense of exposure and vulnerability in order to stay open and present.

In other cases, self-judgment might be used as a means of pushing ourselves to work harder so as to avoid failure and disgrace. Our individualistic culture venerates individual accomplishment and shames failure so this can be a very potent motivation for us to be severe critics of ourselves. If the only winners in society are those judged as the best and most famous, some of us will do anything to avoid the shame of being judged as mediocre, second best. Another downside of this winner–takes-all attitude is that it flattens out our appreciation of the varied expressions of individual talents and gifts to a few categories that can be judged in contests and other superficial and artificial ways of evaluating talent or capabilities.

Our culture creates a toxic environment for women in its standards for a woman's physical beauty. The movies, fan magazines and the internet all present idols of physical beauty. How many women can live up to our culture's unrealistic standards of feminine beauty? Even attractive women often feel ugly and insecure about their looks. This self doubt and self criticism sets up so many women to hate their bodies and to torture themselves with diets and cosmetic surgery and the more life threatening compulsive behaviors of Anorexia nervosa or Bulimia.

The harsh self judgments that many of us are mired in do us no good whatsoever. They may be familiar, habitual, and even believable in our own distorted frame of reference, but they keep us stuck. The energy of self-criticism is very negative and cannot equal the positive energy of enthusiasm, which is the real and proper source of inspiration and motivation to achieve good things. Some of us are so identified with our self-criticism that it would seem impossible to escape it. To suggest letting go of self- criticism is like telling us to cut off an arm or leg, so fused are we with this negative way of relating to ourselves.

When I invite some of my therapy clients who are habituated to criticizing and loathing themselves to practice self caring and self loving, it seems initially like such a foreign, even off putting idea. From a spiritual point of view the kind of harsh criticism I have been describing here does nothing but shut down our awareness and the chance to learn and change from that awareness. When we flagellate ourselves with self-criticism, self reproach, self loathing, regret, etc. we feel guilty, worthless, inherently unlovable, and we painfully fall into shame and depression. In doing this we have closed ourselves off to real learning and healing. And we are closed off to the ultimate healing power of Love.

One way to overcome this habitual harsh self-judgment is to relate back to our vulnerable selves as children. Most people can find some empathy and caring for their child self and this can be a way forward out of the abuse of self-criticism. It is far better to be able to evaluate our sometimes less than perfect behavior from the vantage point of part of us still being a vulnerable needy child. When we can feel love for ourselves it is not so threatening to acknowledge our wrongdoings and shortcomings. And for some of us, it is even difficult to love and care for the child that we were, so engrained is the rejection we experienced from our parents. In this case perhaps there is a nephew or niece or a grandchild that you can love and if you would imagine them going through what you did as a child – then perhaps you could begin to have some compassion for yourself.

It is helpful for us to remember again and again the imperfection inherent in being human. We have a brain and body that are subject to the many imperfections of our biology, chance misfortune, family circumstances, etc. It is clear from looking at the general state of humanity that it takes a great deal of work to overcome our lot as human beings. We are easily triggered into anger, fear, greed, lust, etc. This is the normal if less than desirable human condition. We should not beat ourselves up that we have these kinds of challenging feelings and impulses. Rather, we should give thanks that we can be aware of them and not act them out. Gradually as we develop psychologically and spiritually, we find that our mind and body will settle down and become more manageable.

Self Reflection & Practice

It is easier to try to be better than you are than to be who you are. Perfection does not allow for feeling.

- Marion Woodman

When you can begin to step back and neutrally evaluate your behavior, you have opened up a huge opportunity to learn and to grow spiritually. If you have a habit of being harshly self critical, it is important that you learn to see yourself as you are, good parts as well faults and imperfections. This section is designed to help you work more skillfully with self judgment so that it doesn't impede your spiritual journey.

Where in your life (what capabilities, aspects of your body, your personality, your intelligence, etc.) do you judge yourself harshly? In your safe, sacred, loving environment and centered in your loving self, take an inventory of all the ways that you criticize yourself. In doing this you must be careful not to believe what you are taking stock of. See if you can consistently come from the part of you that is a loving presence that is watching another part of you writing out this list. Make as thorough a list as you can, write without hesitation and don't let yourself get bogged down in depression and feeling bad about yourself. Get it all out of you and then ritually burn it saying "this list of judgments of myself I release and in burning it, I let it go back to the emptiness from which it came."

Important Practice

As a further more focused step, you might want to work with specific judgments that you have against yourself. (At this point you may want to review the Appendix # 3 on the practice of Self Forgiveness.) Take one judgment at a time and release it with this practice: Put your hand over your heart and state: I forgive myself for judging myself as being <u>(fill in the judgment here).</u> As an example: I forgive myself for judging my self as being stupid and a slow learner. You can keep doing the same forgiveness process until you sense a shift, a softening within yourself. With this energetic shift you find you can be more accepting and compassionate towards yourself and you less and less sink into self judgment and self pity. Do this process over and over again with succeeding judgments. Another thing you can do to add to the forgiveness process is, with hand over heart, to state the truth of what is really so instead of the self judgment. For the example above, the statement might be: (hand on heart) The truth is that I have a learning disability and it does not limit my intelligence and I can choose to learn at my own pace.

What is the history of self-criticism in your life? Can you remember when it started and perhaps why it started? Think about your childhood and where you might have learned this habit. Spend time with your Inner Child comforting them about experiences when they were hurt by their parents, siblings or others criticizing them. Be the loving parent for this Inner Child that you did not have at the time. Let them talk about their hurt as you embrace them inside yourself. This could be done while rocking back and forth in a rocking chair or putting your hands over the places inside you that hold the hurt, such as the heart space or the gut.

Try letting go of your self-judging commentary for a moment. Feel into your body and sense the energy patterns present there. Do you feel afraid, vulnerable, unsafe? Or do you feel calm, open, safe, happy? What might this tell you about the purpose of your self-judgment? What might it be trying to protect you from? Journal about this. If you sense your vulnerability, see if you can just stay compassionately present with your vulnerable self in your body instead of going to the mental level where the critic dwells. You may find that this takes the energy out of your Inner Critic, which often is trying to keep you from feeling this vulnerability.

How might you be kinder to yourself? And how do you react inwardly to being asked how you can be kinder towards yourself? What part of your self is making these judgments? Can you separate yourself from the one who judges you or do you become identified with this judgmental part of you? Can you start to separate yourself from their attacks or do they seem implacable and the Voice of Truth? The more fused you are with the voice of self-judgment, the more important it is for you to seek the help of a loving counselor to help you on your healing journey.

How do you see God? Do you see Him/Her as a harsh judge? If so, why would you want to worship and commune with such a God? What experiences in your youth led you to believe that God was vindictive and a harsh judge? What efforts have you made to undo this toxic theology? Where might you find further assistance and resources in undoing this harmful theology?

The Buddhist sutras show the Buddha and his core disciples as perfect enlightened teachers. The students in the sutras usually get the true dharma very quickly after the Enlightened One instructs them. If you are a Buddhist practitioner, do you have some ideal of what the enlightened person is like that you always compare yourself with – and that you always fall short of? Is there an Inner Critic that is always comparing you to a standard of perfection that you confuse with your true Buddha Nature? Is it perhaps the super ego with its own agenda?

It is not uncommon for spiritual practitioners to confuse their Inner Critic (or Super

Egos) with their essential spiritual nature. If this Inner Critic isn't coming from your True Nature, then why do you pay such heed to it? What is the payoff? What is the cost to you?

If you have a spiritual teacher, what is your relationship with them like? Do you feel accepted by them or are you afraid of their judgment? If you do fear them, is it their judgment of you or is it really your own self judgment projected onto them? Does this repeat any old childhood relational patterns with parents or other authority figures? Journal on this!

Especially if you are a woman, try this exercise: Look with kindness at yourself in a mirror and notice any judgments you make about how you look. Afterwards, see if you can move into acceptance of whatever in your physical appearance you have been judging. If you can't, this is a place to work on Self Acceptance first and Self Forgiveness later.

If you have some sense in yourself of "the one who judges you" as a separate presence in your psyche, try having a neutral dialogue with him/her. Don't argue with or kowtow to the judge – and don't believe its criticisms of you. You might write this as a dialogue, starting by asking the Inner Critic questions such as "Why are you in my life? What is your purpose? Why do you come out in me in certain situations like _____?" In this way you may gain some insight into why the Inner Critic is such a prominent part of your psyche.

Examine what circumstances precede your Inner Critic coming out to attack you. It might be when you are feeling vulnerable. It might be when you are feeling bad about something you have done. It might be when you think someone is upset with you. Oddly enough Inner Critics often come out to attack us in such circumstances to protect us. See if that rings true for you. Journal on the purpose of your Inner Critic.

When the Inner Critic comes up, ignore its criticisms and feel into your body where your Inner Child lives. Allow yourself to move towards this Child and embrace, accept, and even love this Child as it feels its fears, its sense of shame, its unworthiness. When you do this, the energy of the Inner Critic will weaken as you have moved towards what it in its misguidedness is trying to protect you from. This is the ultimate gate of liberation: to love the parts inside you that are fearful and hurting.

When you feel yourself in the throes of a self-judgment attack try to soften and feel into your heart space. Put both hands over your heart and become aware of the feelings there. Often there is such hurt in your heart that needs your compassion and your understanding. Listen lovingly to your heart for it does not judge you. It is your mind that judges you. Get out of your head and put your hands on your heart and abide there. You will probably find the energy of your Self Critic diminishing with this exercise.

As you heal, you might feel it useful to personify self-judgment in some humorous way. Give self-judgment a funny image in your mind's eye and a funny name. Then whenever judgment shows up in your awareness you can bring to mind the funny image or name and chuckle at it. Be vigilant and on the lookout for your Inner Critic. Notice it as soon as you can when it flits into your consciousness. The sooner you can catch it with its negative whispers in your ear and not believe it, the better you can keep yourself from falling down the slippery slope of self rejection into the abyss of depression and anxiety.

If you chronically judge and reject yourself, spend some time each day learning to love and care for yourself. Forget anything in the spiritual writings you have read that talks about killing the ego or denying the self. This is not your path! You need to learn to love and care for yourself before you can let go of your self concerns. Find little ways to care for yourself each day, to say something good about yourself that you can admit to being true. This will be a stretch for you initially but it is well worth the effort!

Later still, as you have healed further, you may practice seeing Judgment pass through your awareness like a cloud through the clear blue sky. It comes and it goes away all by itself. For it no longer hooks you. You have released the self-blame game! Sometimes anger may show up when the Inner Critic starts to bash on you. It may be saying in effect, "stop this! This is not my fault!" This is good; you may be starting to defend yourself better against the Inner Critic and your outer critics as well. Then the issue becomes how to lovingly work with the anger so that you don't become stuck in angry victimhood. Welcome the anger because it may lead you in a healthier direction!

Invitation

How would it feel to accept yourself just as you are? What would it be like not to have absolutes of perfection held over your head? To release the relentless judge and heartless jury and to rest in the suchness of yourself as you are day by day? To let your bare face hang out all over and not to worry about how others judge your looks? To enjoy your unique self and let yourself be how God made you, perfect just as you are?

God does not judge you. In fact, She would be overjoyed if you would drop the club in your hand with which you beat yourself up. God is waiting outside the swarm of your self-judgments to embrace you. The minute you let the judgments go is the minute that you will feel your connection to the Divine. Feeling unworthy? You are the one that God is waiting for, so go cry out your feelings of unworthiness in Her arms and let Her embrace you.

If you are chronically forgetful of your basic goodness, each time you fall into self-judgment remind yourself of your essential goodness. Recount this basic goodness with conviction, with your hand on your heart, for your heart is your true sacred text. When you can let the Truth of your Goodness enter deep into your heart, then you will be set free. For the Truth shall be written on your heart. So put your hand over your heart and proclaim: "I am God's Beloved. This is indeed the ultimate truth of who I am."

As you progress in your self healing and release of self criticism, you may be able to watch the self judgments with detachment - as only thoughts floating across your consciousness like clouds across the sky. They are not the truth of who you are, they do not serve you or help you to realize your purpose in life. You are so much more than these negative thoughts can ever encompass. So, let them go, dearest. Day by day, moment by moment, let them all go.

CHAPTER 6

Letting Go of Self Doubt

Self doubt is like a heavy chain around your ankle, holding you back. Notice it and let it go. Self doubt never did anyone any good – unless they were arrogant!

The Way Back to Ourselves

We have lost our Way and
know not the way forward.
For we are lost to ourselves,
having abandoned our bodies and feelings
to fears and dictates long forgotten,
and to the seductions of superficial things.

The way back: to touch the earth body
as One did so long ago when confronted and tempted
by Mara the seducer and deceiver.
And to know what we think and feel,
to know our own body
as the temple of ourselves.
And each breath we breathe
takes us back to ourselves, to Now,
to this very body mind that is
the Bodhi Mind itself.

-Robert Cornell

Introduction

For some of us, we learned not to trust our feelings and thoughts in our families. Our feelings were denied, shamed, condemned to go underground. Some of us did not get the encouragement and guidance to know how to properly engage with ourselves or with the world. And our mentally oriented culture is also conducive to our losing our connection to our bodies and their natural signals that we would otherwise heed and use as good, dependable information. Today's young people are now immersed in a virtual electronic world that increasingly allows them less time for face to face intimacy with others, let alone intimacy with themselves. All of these factors along with self-criticism plant the seed of uncertainty and self doubt within us.

I was four and five years younger than my brothers and I often felt inept, ridiculed and rejected by them when I was young. That and my father's emotional distance set me up early in life for a lot of self doubt about my capabilities. As I grew into my teens I would desperately try to overcome my low self esteem with frantic efforts to prove myself capable. Later as a Zen student I would try to get rid of this self doubt by rejecting it, pushing it away and feeling ashamed of it when it surfaced. Needless to say this never cured me of self doubt! If anything, it made it worse, because on top of the self doubt there would be feelings of shame, self criticism, and self rejection.

The choice we face in trying to free ourselves is either to become aware of this self doubt and engage with it lovingly or to reject it and force it underground into our subconscious where it can surreptitiously lead us away from ourselves. To engage lovingly with self doubt is an act of courage and the way out of its morass of confusion, fear and uncertainty. We can become curious and mindful of how self doubt works in our consciousness.

We can do this with warmth and no judgment. We then can see the workings of self doubt and observe carefully its patterns of thought / feeling / behavior. With this compassionate awareness, we no longer identify ourselves so completely with our self doubt. Finally, we can lovingly hold our doubting selves in our awareness and gently be compassionate with our sense of inadequacy and unworthiness. As we create space around our self doubt with loving awareness, it holds less sway over us.

Another thing that will become clear to us as we become more aware of our self doubt is that we have patterns of thought and behavior that help us to cover it up and protect us from the pain of experiencing it directly. It is quite common for those of us that suffer with self doubt to over perform, over study, over think, over…. everything. We will anxiously over prepare for anything that we might remotely stand a chance of falling short on. We usually succeed with this strategy - but at the price of much anxiety driven compulsive work that has little joy, creativity and spontaneity in it.

Another stance that works (badly) for some of us is being arrogant and boastful. This is rather like whistling past the graveyard at night, thinking that it will protect us from harm. And sadly, some of us, doubting our ability to succeed, just withdraw from any real challenges and stay with what we are familiar with and good at in order to avoid the possible pain of failure.

Clearly, as we work with our self doubt internally we also need to face our fears of failure and to "Just Do It." It isn't any good to wait by the sidelines until we have completely worked up our self confidence. We will gain confidence as we meet our external challenges AND do our inner work. Without the inner work, we may succeed any number of times yet the self doubt will still gnaw at our minds. Without the outer effort, there will never be a chance to disprove our self doubting and to move beyond it.

Self Inquiry & Practice

To heal any aspect of ourselves, first we become aware of how it operates in our lives, moment by moment, as each thought, feeling and impulse arises. We do this with compassion for its presence in our lives. For, if we can't accept its presence, we won't be able to understand its role in our lives and to love it into healing. We will continue to reject it and send it underground where it will continue to sabotage us.

Being compassionate does not mean you have to buy into the story of your self doubt! If you find you are judgmental and rejecting of your doubt, practice self-forgiveness and acceptance of your self doubting. For example: (hand on heart) "I forgive myself for judging myself as weak and stupid for feeling this doubt. I accept that I feel this doubt and I intend to be gentle with myself while I experience this doubting in myself."

Where did doubt first show up in your life? Picture the first time you remember feeling uncertain about your feelings, your perceptions or your abilities. How old were you? Who was there with you and what was said to you? How did you feel? Journal about this in your sacred space. Practice Self Acceptance and Self Forgiveness as needed for we often feel ashamed of or judgmental about our lack of self confidence.

When self doubt arises, sense it in your body. Feel into this internal sense of self doubt and into what qualities it has. What weight, color, texture, movement, etc. does it have? By being curious and open to how you experience your self doubt in your body like this, you create a healing space around it. Oddly enough, getting in touch with the sensations of self doubt in your body you will feel more grounded. You get out of your head where your mind can spin endlessly around in circles trying to resolve the self questioning but never coming to any resolution. Your body can do a better job of resolving self doubt than your mind ever can!

Draw a picture of your self doubt and see what it would look like. Notice how you relate to it in the picture. Is it inside of you or is it outside? Is it above you, beside you or below you? Is it bigger or smaller than you? What might these things imply about how you see your self doubt in relation to yourself?

Form a loving relationship with the Inner Child or Inner Teenager that carries this self doubt. Dialogue with them about their doubts and fears regarding their competency and abilities. Help them to see what a capable adult they have become. Especially when you sense their self doubt within you, check in with them and talk it through. You are on the way to being your own wise and loving parent; the one you needed in the past but didn't have!

Just as with any other long-lived pattern of consciousness, you will probably need to practice Self Acceptance and Self Forgiveness for some time with this pattern of self doubt. Remember that it is perfectly normal for self doubt to show up when you take on something new and challenging. Be willing to practice again and again and gradually the old pattern will heal and fade. And even if it shows up again and again, the important thing is how you will be with yourself when doubt shows up in your inner experience.

Start to forgive yourself for the beliefs you carry with this self doubt. For example: (hand on heart) "I forgive myself for buying into the belief that I am a klutz and completely incompetent when it comes to personal relationships. For the truth is, I wasn't taught these things when I was young and I am now learning how. I am willing to learn and I intend to be patient with myself."

Another practice to utilize with the feelings of inadequacy and self doubt is the Energy Psychology tool called "tapping." Refer to the Appendix #4 Tapping into Healing for a description of these very useful techniques. You might tap on memories of when you were made fun of, ridiculed for failing in something or other times when you were made to feel inadequate or incompetent.

At some point as you work with Self Doubt and the sense of not being good enough, you may feel anger arise. This is a healthy progression from the shrinking in of Self Doubt. Allow it to be and let it play out as you follow the energy patterns mindfully in your body. What movements or stances does the body want to take? Notice if words of protest or challenge want to come to your mind, defending your competence.

Invitation

The small child that was you many years ago was judged, rejected, shamed, made to feel weak, stupid, not good enough. You have carried these feelings and beliefs with you for many years. Perhaps you have been angry towards this scared child when they show up inside you because you believe that they have held you back for so many years in moving ahead with your life. But know this: if you persevere in accepting and loving them, they will bloom and become more and more self confident. And this Inner Child will bring the gifts of play and creativity to your work.

All they need is your care and encouragement. You can be the parent for them that they did not have: the one they can go to and be consoled and reassured. Then, with your encouragement and support you will go out into the world and begin the long delayed work you were called to do. So don't judge this doubt. Let go of shame, self condemnation, and self rejection. These will never serve you and will only keep you imprisoned in self doubt. Love is the Way, the only way. Remember this dear one!

Remember when Self Doubt shows up again and again in your consciousness that this does not mean that you're stupid or incapable as your self judgment may tell you. It just means this is an old deep wound that needs care and love to heal. Some of us have more wounds than others; that is just a fact of life. The best thing we can do is to accept this and wrap our arms around our wounded selves and ask God to be lovingly present with us as we learn gradually to release our self judgment, self doubt, and self rejection.

Gradually, you will heal this pattern of self doubt and feel self confidant. You will not be arrogant, but rather rest quietly in an inner conviction of your own capabilities. And you will seek further challenges to grow yourself into who you truly are…. Just remember, with each new challenge that you take on, you may experience some feelings of self doubt. This is normal and no reason to beat yourself up for experiencing it again! Let yourself stretch and soar for that is how God made you. You were not meant to be small in heart and mind!

CHAPTER 7

Letting Go of Guilt

Guilt is a gift that can keep on giving for our whole lives, if we let it. If we want to free ourselves from guilt, we apply the balm of Self Forgiveness and the sharp insight of the Truth to see how so much of our guilt is not based on reality.

Found Innocent by Love

What did you do wrong?
Guilt always assumes you were
the wretched culprit,
deserve no mercy,
and wants an immediate trial
by firing squad.
What DID you do wrong?
Maybe nothing but standing there
breathing while it happened.
Guilt of course would say
that's quite enough to convict.
Call for the Beloved:
This one sets them all free.
There's no shame in Him;
He just loves too much to see
they deserve to be punished.

- Robert Cornell

Introduction

Some of us are guilt addicts. We can't say no to anyone without feeling guilty and afraid of what their reaction will be. Or the moment anyone is unhappy with us about something, we want to run to them and scream, "It's my fault!", make a full confession of our wrongs, fall down on our knees, groveling for forgiveness. Think this is crazy? Then you are not a guilt addict! Those of you who shake your head in understanding and maybe even relief, that finally someone understands your hidden guilty secret, read on!

Yes, there is healthy guilt. Without our conscience pricking us from time to time, we would likely remain spoiled self centered brats. The people who don't feel guilt we call sociopaths because they can harm others with no compunction. When we do something wrong that hurts another human being or one of God's creatures, it is appropriate for us to feel bad about it and to want to make amends. That is the useful and natural function that guilt should play in our lives as social animals. Healthy guilt gives us a signal that we need to look at something we have done so that we can correct our behavior. But healthy guilt does not lead us down the slippery slope of depression and anxiety.

Unhealthy guilt on the other hand can take us deep into the hellish darkness of fear, self condemnation, self rejection, and shame. None of these feelings are triggered by healthy guilt, so if you experience any of them it means that you are moving into the desolate lands of unhealthy guilt. Most of this toxic guilt we learned as children when our parents in one way or another led us to believe that we were in some way responsible for their needs – and we fell short of their expectations. And as children with no way to differentiate ourselves from our parent's view of the world, we took this guilt on as part of the cost of keeping connected to our parents. As children, we would rather swallow the guilt and take it inside ourselves than risk abandonment, because we truly could not have survived without our parent's support.

Unhealthy guilt causes us to feel separate from God and His/Her forgiveness and love. It can also cause us to hide away from others who could give us a more realistic perspective that could free us from our guilt. Now when we find ourselves unexpectedly triggered by unhealthy guilt, it behooves us to find ways to let go of the morass of depression, anxiety and shame that this kind of guilt can otherwise pull us into. Self Forgiveness is an absolutely vital part of this process of freeing ourselves from the toxic and oppressive feelings of unhealthy guilt.

Recently I found myself caught off guard when my wife became upset with me over a home improvement project that became more complicated, more expensive and took longer than I expected. Usually I can keep calm when my wife is triggered by a situation where something in our house is out of order. And I don't take it on as my fault that she is upset. But this time when she was angry and harshly criticized me, I felt like a deer in the headlights: frozen and unable to say anything in my defense.

Finally, I got in touch with my anger and then to the hurt below the anger; but something in me was still stuck and I could not get out from under the feelings of hurt, fear and sadness. I felt like I could get nowhere with my feelings and that if I shared them with my wife she would just stay in her angry critical mode. When I saw my therapist (whom I see twice a month to keep digging out the old garbage) I finally saw what I was doing. I had taken it on that it was my fault that she was upset because the project had not been finished when I said it would be.

Actually she was responsible for her own upset! When I clearly saw that I had taken on how she felt as MY fault I started to laugh and the whole situation lightened up into the domestic comedy that it surely was. I am sharing this with you to encourage you to have a wise friend or a counselor whom you can check in with and that will help you move out of your blind spots when you fall into them. And this does NOT mean having someone to share with who will support you in feeling like a helpless victim and enable you to perpetuate your story of victimhood. Notice that the road to my deliverance was seeing how I was guilt tripping myself; it was NOT how my wife was guilt tripping me.

This is the important truth about real liberation; it is not about what the other person is doing to you. IT IS ABOUT WHAT YOU ARE DOING TO YOURSELF INSIDE YOURSELF. When I saw that I had been making myself responsible for her upset, I set myself free. Then I didn't even need an apology from her (although I eventually got one) because I was free of MY guilt and hurt. This is very hard for us to understand because so often our bad feelings seem so obviously (to us at any rate) to have been caused by the other person attacking us, putting us down, etc. But what the other person says or does will not hurt us unless there is some part of us that agrees with and even conspires with them. If I had not taken on the responsibility for my wife's upset, her attacks would have bounced off my back as they usually did and she would have deescalated on her own.

Have you gotten this? If not, you will have many situations where you will move into victimhood with no realization that you hold the key to your prison cell in your own hand. This is a hard truth and inviolable law of consciousness: unless we can see how we are the author of our own story of suffering, we will have more of it. The key to our liberation is taking responsibility for our own issues, seeking to understand the inner source of our upset, and then being with what in us causes it. And as we let it be, it will go away on its own.

Robert Kando Cornell

Self Reflection & Practice

Ultimately all self blame comes down to blaming oneself for not being enlightened. Universally, there is a core place within all ego structures where one feels guilty for not being a realized being....The deeper you go into understanding the sense of guilt, the more you realize that you feel guilty for not being real.

- A. H. Almaas, Facets of Unity

Look for those areas in your life where guilt shows up. Keep a journal and record the circumstances that triggered the guilt and look for the commonality of these situations. If you find that you are frequently feeling guilty, I guarantee you that there will indeed be a pattern to them and that this pattern will most likely relate back to episodes in your childhood.

Look carefully at the exact situations that trigger you into guilt: when you turn someone down? When you think you haven't done enough? When someone gets upset with you? When you are accused of something? When you disappoint someone's expectations? When someone criticizes your actions?

When guilt arises, feel into your body and be present with it. Be curious and compassionate towards this feeling, which is a combination of beliefs and feelings. Notice where the feelings reside in your body. Your shoulders? Your gut? Where else? What is the texture, weight, color, shape or other patterns of how guilt shows up in your body? Is there some sense of contraction in the body and if so where? Be willing to be with the guilt and sense into it, to befriend it. Does this sensing of guilt in your body tell you anything about your guilt-ridden memories, your patterns of holding it in your body, etc.?

What role does guilt serve in your life? Is it there to protect you from other's wrath? Is it there to keep you from being rejected or abandoned? Is it there to deflect others unhappiness with you? Does it serve to keep you honest or does it make you overly moralistic and rigid?

Does it make you feel like you are responsible for something that you in fact have no control over? This is a critical point: if you do not have control over a situation, then why do you feel guilty about it? Follow this line of reasoning carefully and you may free yourself from a lot of guilt! Does it bury the resentment you feel for being obliged to meet every one else's needs besides your own? Is it safer to feel guilt than anger?

Has guilt ever showed up in your life when someone close to you has become very ill or died or was killed? What did guilt try to make you believe about that?

If your Guilt were standing over you right now what would it say to you about your level of responsibility (fault) for situations currently in your life? Look around in detail

48

at your life as it now stands and take notes on what Guilt has to say about it. But be careful: don't believe a word that Guilt says to you! Be a neutral reporter, recording what Guilt says. Then thank Guilt for sharing with you. If you do not find Guilt's judgments threatening then by all means keep them in your journal to remind you of how your Guilt tries to guilt trip you! If they still feel threatening, then there is still work to do to let go of your belief in what guilt is saying to you.

<u>IMPORTANT PRACTICE</u>

Letting go of guilt and any other deeply habitual negative patterns of consciousness requires an accepting and caring attitude towards your self. Why is this? It's because the one who feels guilty inside of you was hurt by the judgments and demands of others and doesn't need more rejection and judgment from you! The guiltier we feel, the harder it is to feel compassion and acceptance for ourselves. That is why it is so important to practice Self Forgiveness on a regular basis if you are a person who suffers from chronic guilt.

So when guilt shows up, remember to be especially compassionate towards yourself. This will very likely keep you from sliding into darker states of mind such as depression and self loathing. In this loving state of mind talk to the part of you that feels guilty. This is usually a wounded Inner Child. Talk to it and comfort it and remind it that it isn't responsible for what it feels guilty for.

As you heal this pattern of guilt, you might find it useful to give Guilt a slightly ridiculous name such as "Party Pooper" or "Wet Blanket" and/or find a funny image in your mind for Guilt. As an example, the image of a dried up, judgmental old man/woman who keeps following you, wagging their finger at you and saying "shame on you, shame on you!" If the image creates anything but mirth in you, then try another image!

On a regular basis, practice Self Forgiveness for buying into the belief that you are guilty for something that you know intellectually you are not guilty for, but still feel guilty about. Example: "I forgive myself for buying into the belief that I am responsible for my spouse feeling depressed. For the truth is that they are responsible for how they feel, just as I am responsible for how I feel."

Invitation

Forgive yourself for believing that you owe others every minute of your life. You don't.

Forgive yourself for believing that you are responsible for making everyone around you happy. You're not.

Forgive yourself for believing that someone's anger is all your fault. It's not. Their anger is their responsibility, not yours!

Forgive yourself for believing that you're unlovable because you let others down. You are only a human being. It's not your job- or anyone's - to provide for everyone all of the time.

Forgive yourself for believing that you have to live up to your parents' expectations of you. You have your own life to live. And their expectations may very well not honor who you really are.

Forgive yourself for believing that God only loves you when you are accomplishing something great. He/She is Love. God's only job is to love you regardless of your success or failure.

Forgive yourself for believing that you are only worthy of your own self acceptance when you do everything perfectly. Who do you think you are any way, God?

Let go of guilt; it does not serve you. Once it tried to keep you safe and connected to others through feeling their feelings and owning them as yours to fix. Once it tried to protect you from harm by appeasing the ones who threatened you. Once it thought it had the power to be responsible for the whole world and in this way had some sense of control in a chaotic situation. But all it did was make you feel burdened and...guilty. So let go and give it over to God. Let it go and feel joyful. Let it go and be free to be yourself. Let it go and realize that your love is indeed the love with which God loves you – and so back and forth Love goes!

CHAPTER 8

Letting Go of Shame

Shame is paralyzing and debilitating. ....Being courageous when shame enters the picture requires extraordinary courage because people will do anything to escape from shame or from the possibility that shame will be evoked. It is just too difficult to go there. Even for people who will walk in to the fires of transformation to face fear.

Harriet Lerner – The Dance of Fear

Resurrection

Shame hides in places
    away from prying eyes.
It burns to bury itself
    and never again
    to feel despised.
Come, Love
    and unseal the tomb.
Let Lazarus rise
    from this deadly
    judgment of doom.

- Robert Cornell

Introduction

When shame hits us, any openness and loving in our hearts disappears. We want to hide ourselves from the judgment that seems to hang over our heads and cling to our bodies, telling us how utterly flawed, unworthy and despicable we are. Often we start out on our descent into shame feeling guilty about something we have done or not done and it escalates as our Inner Critic unrelentingly attacks us and we slide down into the abyss of shame and self loathing.

When we are engulfed in shame we have no desire other than to hide out and to go unconscious, to disappear even from ourselves. When we react with shame to some aspect of ourselves we want to run as fast as we can from our awareness of that part of us. When we feel shame, we cannot tolerate any more bad feelings and so we will want to stop any kind of self awareness from occurring- even when it might give us perspective beyond the painful feelings of unworthiness and utter brokenness that shame evokes in us.

Shame is so far below the frequency of Love and Forgiveness that it will prevent them from coming into our consciousness - unless we work skillfully with it. Consequently, learning how to heal our shame is a critically important skill when we start to engage with our unacknowledged shadow material - as I will be inviting you to do in these succeeding chapters. In order to let go of something we first have to acknowledge its hold on us - or our hold on it. In order to heal it you first have to acknowledge and own it as they say in Twelve Step Programs. That is why this and other preliminary chapters are at the beginning of this book - to ensure that you have the skills and compassion to work with yourself when the going gets rough.

And I know that I am giving you some very hard things to look at as we go through all of the ways that we need to heal our shadow material in order to connect more deeply with who we really are. It is my hope that you will not take subsequent chapters as accusations against yourself but rather as the descriptions of how we humans all tend to hold onto one thing or another in our lives. This is the imperfect human condition. If that were not so, all of our lives would be filled with peace and joy and the desire to serve.

One essential skill is to have steady (but not hyper vigilant) awareness of our mental and emotional states. Often, Shame doesn't do a full frontal attack; it comes stealthily from behind with Guilt in the vanguard and the Inner Critic attacking your flank. The more we can be mindful of guilt and self judgment sneaking up on us, the more likely we are able to heal them before we descend into the dark underworld of shame, self loathing and self condemnation.

The other vital skills to have at our disposal are Self Acceptance and Self Compassion. The very ones of us who most need this spiritual first aide are the ones who have such a hard time accessing these self care skills. But they can be learned! It may take practice and patience to gain these skills and it is vital to your healing and growth to do so. Otherwise shame and guilt will often have their way with you and shut you down.

One way to relate in a healthy way to this shame is to see the younger part of our self that carries it. Often the shame comes from neglect, abuse and abandonment that we suffered in childhood. We were innocent but we were hurt badly by a parent, family member or a trusted care giver and because we were too young to properly understand this and protect ourselves from it, we took it upon ourselves that we must be bad to have deserved such treatment. It is usually easier to have compassion for the child that we were and to be able to forgive them for the shame and guilt that we have carried into our adulthood. We can then begin to forgive ourselves just as we can now forgive the child that became us.

Shame is one of the most virulent emotions that we can have. It is generally not subtle. Guilt can be subtle but not shame. It is more like a demolition ball when it hits us. Consequently, when working with shame we are dealing with a powerful energy that can quickly take us down into very dark places. For many of us, working with a good counselor is essential for dealing with our shame. It is easy for us to fall under its spell and it can sink into us bone deep. Where might you find such a support person? A therapist or spiritual director? A counselor at your church, synagogue, mosque or Dharma Center? Do you have referrals from trusted friends you could check out? What kind of person do you feel most comfortable with in sharing difficult things about yourself?

Self Reflection & Practice

For some of you, the key to trauma recovery will be most concerned with reconciling feelings of guilt and shame that have lingered following your trauma.

- Babette Rothschild

Where in your life are you aware that shame shows up? Be specific: something about your sexuality? Something about your childhood? Does it show up in anything about your physical appearance? In regard to your personality, intelligence, social status or skill level? About your race or ethnic identity? Concerning your job situation? Relating to your relationships or lack thereof? What exactly? Journal on this.

What does shame feel like in your body when it does show up? Feel into it; this is a body focusing exercise. Where in your body does it appear? What shape, texture, weight, color, energy pattern, does it have? Does it have any movement associated with it? Remember to feel gently into it all the while breathing into wherever it shows up in your body to gently soften and leaven it. Also, you might imagine a gentle, loving white light illuminating this feeling of shame in your body. This is a healing balm for the sense of heaviness and darkness that shame has.

Connecting to the shame felt in your body, what does it want to say to you? Does it whisper? Does it hiss or scream? Remember that while it feels incredibly real, it is not telling the truth about you. Keep in mind your essential goodness and God's love for you. From this vantage point of acceptance and love see if you can listen to Shame's accusations without getting triggered into depression or anxiety. If not, you can do a series of Self Forgiveness exercises to release the Self Judgment underlying the Shame. (See Appendix #3)

When you connect to the shame in your body, let the feelings take you back to earlier memories in your life. Your body will take you there; you don't have to figure this out. Your body remembers these events only so well. Trust it to take you there; usually your mind will just get in the way. If the memories are very painful, this is material to explore with a good therapist. Be kind to yourself and get help! There is no shame in doing this!

Where has toxic shame got you by the throat? It is critical to give yourself compassion and forgiveness and to let go of toxic shame for, unlike healthy guilt, it will only take you to dark, painful places! Find a good therapist, attend some kind of recovery group and talk to good friends who are proven to be safe and reliable to get perspective on your "terminal uniqueness of awfulness."

It can be helpful to use the Emotional Freedom Tapping Techniques with shame (see Appendix #5.) Example: (set up statement for the tapping) "Even though I feel this burning sense of shame in my face and chest as I think about (the event) I completely accept and love myself." As you work with tapping on a recent episode that triggered shame it may lead to earlier situations that are at the core of this pattern of shame. Then you can tap further on these episodes.

What is your habitual defensive impulse when you feel shame? Be specific. You go unconscious by watching TV, compulsively playing video games, watching pornography, sexual acting out, drinking or drugging or other addictive activities? Do you run away from the feelings through compulsive patterns of behavior such as overwork, people pleasing, enabling others, etc. Do you react to being shamed with anger? Freezing up? Trying to placate? What? Knowing and being aware of your ways of going unconscious and being reactive may at first feel challenging but in the long run they are vital to healing the patterns of shame-based behavior.

Learn to stay compassionately present with the feelings of shame in your body, without spinning out into stories about yourself or acting out through your usual escape routes. Hold/hug yourself and comfort yourself with kind words just as a loving parent would. This is the key to healing shame and any other deeply seated, habitual thought/emotion pattern. Watch the stories that Shame tells you about yourself and don't get hooked by them. They are all lies, lies that were told to you or that you told yourself to explain why you were not loved and cared for as a young defenseless child.

In the story of the Buddha's enlightenment, as he made up his mind to liberate himself, Mara the one who ensnares all beings in delusion tried to stop him. Mara the tempter and evil one demanded to know what right the Buddha had to enlightenment. The Buddha did not reply to Mara but just touched the earth to bear witness to his right to liberation. Find some support group, start an ongoing practice of relating to a loving God, find a place of safety and beauty, let the love of a loved one or a pet remind you of your basic goodness when Shame comes to demand what right you have to walk the earth in peace.

Invitation

No one can make you feel inferior without your consent.

- Eleanor Roosevelt

Shame, the unwanted guest; the one you wish would disappear and never come back. The one you have run away from for so many years. The one you feel overwhelmed by and that you seem to have no control over. The one you so often feel humiliated by, devastated by, crushed down by, wanting to disappear from the very face of the earth. Yes, these are the feelings of shame that seem to corrode the very core of your being.

Yet, Shame is a child who cries in the night, afraid that no one will ever come to comfort them. Shame is the little child that feels bad at its very core because it was abused and shamed. And if you keep pushing Shame away as if it were a demon, it will only get worse. This is the nature of these deep wounds: they need your presence, your compassion, your understanding of what they really are: your Inner Child that has been shamed, abandoned, hurt for so many years – both by an abuser and then eventually by yourself.

Do the one thing you haven't been willing to do before: approach this demon child and hold it with love and caring. When this child feels your consistent embrace, it will eventually melt into the hurt and sadness that it has carried for so many, many years. It will no longer be a demon haunting you but rather the crying lost child that needs your love and acceptance so very, very much. Love it. Love yourself, and let God love both of you. You may dissolve into great sobs and sighs; this is a good sign that you are falling into the original pain and its release. And in your tears God's love can get to you and embrace you at your very core.

CHAPTER 9

Letting Go of Fear

It is not fear that stops you from doing the brave and true thing in your daily life. Rather, the problem is avoidance. You want to feel comfortable so you avoid doing or saying the thing that will evoke fear and other difficult emotions. Avoidance will make you feel less vulnerable in the short run but it will never make you less afraid.

-Harriet Lerner, The Dance of Fear

Introduction

There is a wonderful teaching story about Milarepa, perhaps the most famous lama in Tibetan Buddhist lore. There are many versions of the story and I will recount one of them here, with my own little twist to it. Milarepa was engaged in a long meditation retreat up in a cave in the Himalayan mountains when this story occurs. He left his cave one day to gather firewood and when he returned, he found three hideous demons occupying his cave. At first he tried to use the black magic he had learned in his youth, but this did nothing to dislodge his unwanted guests. They actually liked the negative energy of his spells!

The next day, he tried to educate them that they were empty phenomenon of mind and hence unreal by reciting Buddhist sutras, but they just laughed and did not budge. So he accepted his situation and just sat in the cave with the demons, not trying to get rid of them. With this, one of the demons left. The following day, he was inspired to make tea for the remaining two demons and with this another one of them vanished.

But the ugliest and nastiest of the demons remained in the cave. Milarepa meditated all night for inspiration and in the morning, he walked up to the demon and, with a smile on his face, put his head in the demon's mouth, upon which this last demon vanished to leave Milarepa in peace to continue his meditation retreat.

The story of Milarepa colorfully illustrates how we can learn to work more skillfully with our own inner demons - those things that we dread and fear to face. Initially, he tries to drive them away using black magic. But the Demons feed on the negative energies of the aggression inherent in his black magic spells, so they don't leave. The next day he is slightly more skillful; he tries to use his reasoning and his Buddhist studies to convince them that they are unreal. Still, even though he teaches them that they are only made of mind stuff and hence not fundamentally real, Milarepa in fact wants the demons to leave. Finally, he is willing to accept their presence and to just sit with the demons in the cave, letting go of any effort to get rid of them. So the Demon of Aggression leaves.

Next, he begins to befriend them, offering them tea and the second demon leaves. We might call this demon the Demon of Resistance. Finally, he lets go of all desire to rid himself of the last demon and surrenders fully by putting his head into the very jaws of this Demon. We might call this final demon the Demon of Aversion. And so each demon reflects the mind states of Milarepa: the mind states of aggression, resistance and aversion. As he lets go of any desire for the demons to leave his cave, they leave of their own accord.

Paradoxically and completely against any common sense, Milarepa learns to engage his fears (demons) without aggression, resistance or aversion. First, he stops trying to actively get rid of them. Then he comes to the place of accepting their presence. And finally he gives up all aversion and totally surrenders to the last demon's presence. And when he does, this last and nastiest demon vanishes. He has totally given up trying to push his demons away and guess what: they vanish on their own. This is not just good Buddhist teaching, it is brilliant psychology!

Our fears are the ultimate barrier to our spiritual evolution into the consciousness of Love. More accurately stated it is our aversion to our fears and our attempts to banish them that keep us stuck. And so it is critical in spiritual practice to engage with our fears, first to make them conscious. Our fears are often hidden deeply in our subconscious and we are pulled around as we mindlessly try to avoid experiencing them. Our fears so often run us and we don't even know that this is happening, because our methods of protection and avoidance are so habitual and below our awareness. So it is critical that we learn to make our fears conscious, that we name our demons, as Jack Kornfield says in his book, *A Path with Heart.*

And as we learn to stop our avoidance and resistance to engaging with our demons, we find that they are just our wounded children hiding in the basement of our mind, pleading for our recognition and love to heal them. When we are in the vicinity of our fears, we usually unconsciously play out old habitual behavioral patterns that we have used in the past to protect ourselves from our fears. For some of us, we placate, for others of us, we avoid and numb out, and for still others we will rush towards the feared object with anger and aggression. The problem with all of these unconscious reactions is that they come from our primitive limbic system, our unconscious memories and our habitual responses and they don't reflect the reality of what is actually before us. Instead, these behaviors usually reflect the impact of things that happened to us a long time ago in our families.

More fundamentally, these habitual patterns of self protection do not let us engage skillfully with our old fears and see the emptiness of their threats. As we become more compassionate and interested in relating to these fears, we bring new attitudes and behaviors to the work of engaging with them. Instead of automatically avoiding or moving against a fearful situation we accept it into our experience and are open to learning from it. Finally, when the feared event happens again, we are able to dive right into it, figuratively speaking, and to act courageously and skillfully as Milarepa did in the wonderful story about his demons.

I still remember an incident in second grade. I was new to the school and ill at ease on my first day of class. We had a letter writing exercise and out of fear of the teacher's disapproval, I tried to smudge out a letter I had written poorly, trying to correct it before the teacher spotted it. But the teacher did spot it and put me up in front of the rest of the class to shame me. The next day when I needed to go to the bathroom, I was so afraid to hold my hand up and ask permission that I shit in my pants. This and other incidents cemented into my mind the belief that if I made a mistake that displeased others I was in grave danger.

I can still get triggered at times by the fear of displeasing another person. But if I stay lovingly connected to myself, I get through the feelings and do not let them continue to distort my reality and my reactions. I do this by moving internally towards the feelings of fear with compassion and awareness. My practice of compassion helps me to overcome my aversion to the fear and my practice of awareness helps me to see the fear as it plays out in my mind and body with non-identification. It no longer is so much my fear with its many old story lines but rather just feelings and thoughts that pass through my consciousness and do not stay. With this practice I am no longer building up further limiting stories and negative reactions to the fear.

One of the mistakes that spiritual people can sometimes make about their fears is to beat themselves up for still having fearful reactions. Sometimes they think they should be able to remain in blissful states and no longer experience fear. But then how would you pay attention to the necessary warning signs of real impending dangers if you were constantly blissed out? Also what they fail to realize is that if they want to avoid feeling fear, they are then likely to avoid situations that bring up their fears and in doing so they are not growing spiritually or psychologically. Sometimes those living in monastic situations have opted out of the world because they dislike dealing with the fears that everyday living brings up for them. If a monastic life is too comfortable, it will be tempting for monastics to become lazy in their spiritual efforts.

Then there are the fears triggered by things outside of our usual experience: disasters, loss of health, loss of loved ones to death or divorce, financial loses, legal challenges, etc. With those situations involving a loss of connection, such as loss of a loved one, we will feel the fear in our hearts as we sense this loss of connection to others, to ourselves, and with Spirit. With fears that challenge our very survival we will feel the fear in our gut. We will feel them in our body that is, if we are in contact with our bodily sensations, which often we are not. But just because we are not aware of these feelings does not mean we are free of them. It just means that they can run us without our awareness of them.

The real issue is: can we stay present and open with our feelings of fear, rather than contracting and withdrawing or numbing out? Can we move towards the difficult feelings with compassion and openness? Can we trust that Spirit, God, True Self, Buddha Nature is in this very experience with us and open to this presence beyond the fears? I like very much what Jack Kornfield said in one of his books about difficult experiences, "Everything is workable." Can we hold this in our mind and heart as we engage with these challenging experiences and trust ourselves to go through them?

Engaging skillfully with our fears is one of the most important spiritual practices that we can have, for fear is the ultimate barrier to our moving beyond our limited sense of who we are. The practice is to keep our minds and hearts open as we move into the realm of our fears. Over and over again, we let go of fearful stories in our minds and contact the fearful feelings in our bodies with acceptance and compassion. Gradually we can wear out our resistance and aversion to our fears – our fear of our fear - and move into the House of Love, even when we're triggered.

Self Inquiry & Practice

What kinds of people and situations are you afraid of? Make a detailed list. Doing this exercise may provoke some anxiety. That's alright. Some anxiety is okay, just remember not to overdo it; relax and breathe when needed. The purpose of this exercise is to learn to face your fears without adding aversion or self judgment to them. Just gently leaning towards them and inquiring into their nature instead of avoiding them is a big step in learning to deal with them in a healthier, more skillful way. As you review those things you fear, you will see patterns in them such as fear of failure, fear of abandonment, betrayal, being shamed, etc. The big fears will touch on your very survival; those fears are better worked on with a counselor or spiritual guide.

See if you can come to a place of acceptance inside yourself that you have these fears. For example, say to yourself, "even though I am feeling afraid of being embarrassed in this social situation, I accept myself just as I am, anxious, feeling awkward and all."

Explore what judgments you hold against yourself for having these fears. Write these down without believing them. See if you can forgive yourself for having these fears. For example (putting your hand on your heart) say, "I forgive myself for judging myself as being unworthy of respect when I feel fearful of being embarrassed. I forgive myself for judging myself as looking ridiculous when I feel afraid of being embarrassed."

Go down your list and keep working on accepting yourself and letting go of any self judgment you have against yourself for having these fears. This can be one of the most liberating things that you can do for yourself because you will no longer be adding insult to injury. You will no longer be adding the pain of resistance and self judgment to the discomfort of experiencing fear. The interesting thing is that free of the resistance and judgment, you will be much more able to work with the fear.

IMPORTANT PRACTICE

Become mindful immediately when you get triggered into fear by a situation. Gently notice where in your body the fear resides. Move towards these feelings in your body where they are held: your neck and shoulders, your heart space, your gut, etc. Remember to breathe gently into these feelings in the body to gently soften them and aerate them so they aren't as intense or heavy. See if you can be curious and empathetic towards these feelings in your body and stay with them. This is challenging work but incredibly valuable. Put your hands tenderly over the places in your body (usually your heart and gut) where you feel the fear, gently holding the fear as a loving parent would a frightened child. This is indeed a kind of re-parenting of your fearful places inside you, sending them compassion and warmth

Work with one of your fears that has been freshly triggered in your body in this manner: let yourself be in an open aware state of mind. Let the fear be as it is and continue to breathe gently into it, exhaling any tension that will release with the outbreath. Remember: avoid any strategy that tries to resist or get rid of the fear. Your ego will probably attempt this as you are experiencing the fear in your body. It can do this by tensing up the body to resist the feelings or by causing you to become very mental and start obsessing about things. Just notice this if it happens and gently come back to the feelings in the body. Don't fight the resistance or try to make it different. Just allow and be aware.

The ego's whole job could be said to protect you from experiencing fear. If you keep allowing yourself to experience your fears without resistance and feeding them with more stories, then the ego's grip on your consciousness is being loosened. While you are engaged in this challenging work, your ego will probably say things like, "This isn't working. I'll die! This is too much for me to handle. I can't do this, it's too painful." It will raise doubts about your ability to handle the pain and doubts that this is a viable way to freedom. Our culture is avoidant of unpleasant experiences, promising us quick fixes, pills and other panaceas for all ailments. So your ego has plenty of company to back its doubts up!

Watch for when your mind darts into the future and starts to play out various negative scenarios. Bring it gently back to the present moment. Breathe more slowly. Use your breath to breathe gently into the fearful feelings and to keep your body open and less reactive to the fear. Especially use the outbreath to relax and breathe out any tension. If you sense any tendency to dissociate, come back to your body and breath. Come back to awareness of the inside of your body and notice your grounding on the earth. Imagine yourself deeply rooted into the earth, feeling gravity pull you towards the ground beneath your feet.

It is important that you do this work with love and patience. Aggression, impatience or any effort to push away the fear only feeds it and stops this process of healing. You may have realizations as to the source of your fears as you stay with the experience. These can be very valuable for learning more about your fears, where they come from and how they are triggered. However, these insights are better put down in a journal and then left behind in this particular process. More about journaling later on in this section. The most critical part of this experiential process is allowing yourself to just be present in your body with the fear, not identifying with it, not pushing it away.

The fear may show up in your gut, solar plexus, or heart space. These are the most common areas of the body to hold the fear. To stay with it, you feel into the fear and become intimate with the sensations of trembling, burning, constriction, etc. that you feel in your body. One typical experience in the heart space is to feel the fear there as a painful tightness. As you stay with it, the tightness might start to become a flaming ball of energy in the heart space. Or it may soften and you drop into a quiet peaceful open spaciousness. You will more than likely have to work with the fear many times. Don't expect that it will take only one experience to heal your fear. It might, but be willing to do whatever it takes to heal and complete your work. Don't put a timetable on this work!

Being with the feelings of fear in our bodies is one of the most challenging and useful spiritual practices we can engage in. It requires a willingness at times to be present with very difficult and unpleasant feelings. Yet when we make this effort, we are liberating ourselves from the most pervasive and limiting impulse we have: avoidance of fear. And when we are willing to move into the demon's mouth, we are no longer constrained by it. We can move forward even when we feel afraid.

Another practice you can try when fear shows up is to let yourself relax and expand out, opening to the presence of Spirit, God, the Divine Union, however you picture it. You might try letting your heart space open up to let the Divine energy in. Often then you will encounter what Christians call Grace: you find yourself opening up in love to the Divine Presence in the face of your fears and they vanish. As it is said in 1 John 4:18 "Such love has no fear, because perfect love expels all fear. If we are afraid, it is for fear of punishment, and this shows that we have not fully experienced His perfect love." There is great wisdom in this; much of our fear derives from old memories of punishment and hurt we suffered in our past and we still look at the world out of the fearful eyes of our childhood. When we experience this unconditional Divine Love, fear has no foothold to stay.

Make a list of the incidents that have happened in the last couple of months that have caused you to feel afraid. Try going back into one of them experientially in your mind's eye and feeling the fear that comes up for you. Remember to do this with compassion and gentleness with yourself. Inquire of your fearful part what was most upsetting about these incidents. Being with these feelings, Let yourself drift back to times in your memory when you felt this way as a child. You may want to journal about this process. If this work is too hard to do alone, by all means do it with a counselor's or spiritual guide's support. With this work you will gradually become clearer on what your fears are really about and how to heal them.

If you frequently have trouble with fear, this may be telling you something important. Maybe you have trouble setting limits with other people. Maybe you were forbidden to get angry as a child and you don't have an Inner Guardian to hold the line for you. Perhaps you take on too much responsibility for other people's upsets. Possibly you experienced trauma in childhood that keeps surfacing when triggered by events in your life today. This is where engaging with your fears becomes critical for your healing and empowerment. Engage with (befriend) your fears and inquire into exactly what your fears are about. With this comes deep insight into what unconscious programming underlies your fears and points the way to liberation.

With traumatic memories, it is very helpful to do some healing work with EFT tapping and Self Forgiveness. This energy work helps to reduce the fearful emotions attached to traumatic memories. See Appendix # 4 on EFT. With the EFT process it could be helpful at this point to make a list of fearful memories that have shaped how you see your world. This is called your Personal Peace Process. You could use these memories to do a series of healing exercises with the EFT method. The EFT basic protocol is detailed on the free website www.emofree.com.

With intense fear, it is important to engage with the feared experience in gradual increments. Approach your fear gently, lean into it just enough to be able to bear it but not enough to be overcome by the fear. Then relax and back off, giving yourself a break. Then address the fear again, perhaps moving in slightly closer to it. Thus you progressively engage your fear and reduce your reactivity to it.

If you have a current incident that is triggering considerable fear, know that you are being given a great opportunity to practice with fear! This is not to sugar coat the difficult and challenging nature of your experience, but it may give you some encouragement to realize that there is something to be gained out of your struggles to work with your fear. Be as willing as you can to stay present. Watch for any temptations to space out or avoid your fear by addictive or repetitive compulsive behavior.

It is so important with a fear inducing situation and any other emotional upset to inquire deeply into its nature and cause. Rather than seeing the upset as something to get over and done with and forget as quickly as possible, use the experience to find out what old limiting beliefs and painful memories are hiding below it. When you do this work, the upset actually serves your spiritual path!

Try dialoguing with your fear to find out what it is afraid of. Before doing this, meditate and center yourself in Love, then use your Loving Self to dialogue with the fear in written form. Let your Loving Self ask the fearful part of you what it fears, while reassuring it that it is safe. Then let it reply back in writing. Putting it down on paper instead of keeping it in your head leads to more clarity and thoroughness. Eventually in this process you will become clearer on what is at the root of your old irrational fears and be able to heal it!

When there are practical matters to attend to, face the fear as directly as you can and make a realistic plan of action to address your real life concerns. But watch for fear to want to get involved in this process. Don't let fear make the plans! Keep your head.

Invitation

Be friendly with your dear old companion, fear. Don't push him away or drown her out with all the things you have done in the past to escape. Invite her in, give her drink and something to eat. Listen kindly to his story. You don't have to believe it, mind you, but don't argue with him. It's probably a very old story that you know so well; one that you have been hearing inside yourself since you were very young. So remember, fear often speaks in the voice of your child self and needs a compassionate hearing. Put him on your knee and hug him and kiss his booboo.

Aren't you tired of the narrowness of your life? Of your boredom and the sameness of your life? Remember that your fear is the ultimate barrier to moving beyond your familiar (and boring) comfort zone. Fear will show up when you step beyond your familiar sense of self. It is your ego trying desperately to protect itself. Just be willing to feel the fear – and to step out beyond the barriers it has set up in your mind.

When you allow yourself to feel fear, this is an opportunity to shed some resistance to Life. Probably your ego is freaking out over some old hurt and wants to retreat inside. Remember to breathe deeply and gently allow these feelings to arise and to pass away. Gradually you will learn to relax instead of fighting against the fear and you will step past it into the larger life that is calling to you. A strong guardian figure may arise in you that'll put an end to the nonsense others are trying to pull you into!

Your fear of Fear has tried its best to keep you safe all these years but has only caused you to shrink inward and limit yourself to a dull and uncreative existence. You don't need to wait for Fear to go away before you step out into the unknown, which is your freedom. Just take Fear with you and keep walking on with acceptance and open awareness. Ultimately, you will walk far past the walls that you created within you to keep Fear out. Now Fear is just a companion from time to time on your journey and you do not turn away just because fear shows up.

CHAPTER 10

Accepting and Loving Ourselves Just as We Are

I find that when we really love and accept and approve of ourselves exactly as we are, then everything in life works.

- Louise Hay

Good Work

There is a good and patient work to be done,
hoeing out the weeds of our discontent
with ourselves and our lives.
Weeds that have choked out so much
of the fruit of our labors
over these many years of toil and trouble.
Here are the self loathsome burrs that stuck
to our shirts and dug into our flesh,
which we spent much effort pulling off, one by one,
sometimes with them sticking to our fingers
before they would finally let go.
There are the tick weeds of dejection
that burrowed into our trouser legs so deep
we despaired of ever getting them out.

Now we are done with them.
The weeds have been pulled out with love and song
and we can rest in the joy of what we have planted
in the hearts of ourselves and others.
Each has to pull out their own heart weeds
that can fester in one's soul for far too long.
It is good not to delay from this task,
before the evening comes and the night settles in.
Good to know as the light dims that your heart is at peace
and you have done your work, good work
that was given to you alone to do.

- Robert Cornell

Introduction

For so many of us, it is a struggle to accept ourselves just as we are: fallible, human, but mostly well intentioned and good hearted. What a sad state of affairs this is! And pretty much this is how our Western society sets us up: to judge ourselves solely upon the basis of our performance, our possessions, our physical appearance and other external attributes. We are then often anxious about whether we meet up to these standards and feel depressed over our perceived failings. Some of us come to believe we have no intrinsic self worth at all. Every bit of our self esteem has to be earned through making money, being successful, having power over others, being famous, having an attractive physical appearance, and on and on, an impossible Sisyphean task.

It is deeply significant to me that the ministry of Jesus starts after he is baptized by John the Baptist. When He comes up out of the water, God says, "This is my Son in whom I am well pleased." For me, this was the basis of Jesus's deep faith and the power of His healing charism. If we could experience that we were as well loved as Jesus was, we would be free of so much insecurity, fear of failure, envy, shame and self rejection. From the Christian standpoint the most important thing we can receive is this fundamental experience of being accepted and loved unconditionally by God.

This unconditional unearned love is what in Christianity we call "Grace" and it is one of Christianity's great gifts to the world's religious traditions. When I was a Buddhist monk, I had little self acceptance and my self doubt drove me to constantly try harder to prove myself to myself and to my Zen teacher. I would meditate with great effort, which would only make me feel more strained and uptight, even more separated from Source. It was only when I gave up being a Zen monk and came back to Christianity that I began to open up to the possibility of being loved and accepted as I am. This was an amazing turning point for me: to allow that I could be loved by God and that I might accept myself as I was, warts and all. Yes, Amazing Grace how sweet the sound, that saved a wretch like me.

There is something in our Western mentality that needs this possibility of unearned love, acceptance and forgiveness. The shadow of our Western culture of self made men and women is that we are focused on our individual accomplishments and personal attributes to the point that many of us feel hopelessly deficient. If we know that God loves us unconditionally, we can then begin to let go of our obsession with personal success and all of the external attributes to which we have clung for our poorly based fragile self esteem.

Our Eastern brethren don't seem to need this in the same way that we do. If you look at traditional Buddhism and Taoism, the Christian Gospel notions of grace and forgiveness of sins do not show up in their scriptures. There is an oft-repeated story of when a group of American Buddhist teachers were having a meeting with the Dalai Lama, his Holiness could not understand the kind of self hatred that the American teachers talked about their meditation students having difficulty with. Tibetans might have their own craziness, but self rejection was not one of their problems.

So for us Westerners, it is a good thing for us to wean ourselves from our culture's toxic over focus on individualism and to rediscover our value in loving connection with Spirit and others. We can learn to find satisfaction in the intrinsic worth of our work and set aside extraneous considerations like fame and fortune and power. This takes much letting go of what we have absorbed unconsciously from our culture and our families. And when we let go of self centered ambition we find that there is another motivation which will keep us growing and achieving things: the sheer joy in the process of what we do and learn. And we find out the true meaning of enthusiasm, which comes from the Greek, En Theos, which means "of God."

Self Reflection & Practice

Where in your life do you find it hard to accept yourself as you are? Do you struggle with workaholism? Perfectionism? Envy of others? Depression? Hyper dieting & exercising? Performance anxiety? Feeling like you are never enough? Write about it. Let yourself free form write about this issue in your life. (Just write without being concerned about punctuation, grammar, etc.)

Usually, when we begin to think about letting go of an obsessive or compulsive pattern that has been part of our life for a long time, we are ambivalent about it and will waffle back and forth. For one thing, there is often a secondary gain that we get from our addictions to performance. Write about what kinds of things you get from your compulsions. For example, if you are a workaholic, journal about your addiction to performance as your source of your self worth. Do you get admiration from friends and colleagues for your work ethic? Money? Possessions? Status? Reputation? Pride in yourself for your hard work ethic that keeps you from feeling guilty and worthless?

IMPORTANT PRACTICE

In the practice called Biospirituality, we place our hands on our heart center and our gut center. These are areas in the body that have rich neural networks that are highly interconected with the brain. They are also the most common areas in the body where we feel our strong emotions. Because most of us in Western culture are to some degree alienated from our bodies and our emotions, this is a very important practice for learning how to be with our emotions in a grounded way.

In doing this practice we place one of our hands over our heart and the other over our abdomen. When we do this, we are bringing more attention to these areas and it says to whatever we are experiencing, "I'm here for you." It is a very body based way to learn to be with ourselves compassionately in the present moment. Our acceptance of our feelings then becomes not a head trip but rather a very grounded experiencing in our bodies with whatever feelings are arising.

Reflect in detail upon how your own fixations on your personal performance and your personal attributes have undermined your connection with Spirit. Name each fixation and specifically reflect on what that has cost you. For example: "Because of my workaholism, I rarely have time in my life for spiritual practice and I always feel rushed and off center." Or: "Because I value success so much I am always ill at ease with myself and with God, for I never think I have done enough." Reflect upon what it has costs you in your personal life and what costs there are for those you love for you to be this compulsive. For example: "Because I am preoccupied with my compulsive exercising and dieting, my spouse and I have become estranged." Or: "Because of my preoccupation with how I look, I never feel entirely unselfconscious when I'm trying to connect with others."

Which of your compulsions are you willing to let go of? How would you go about letting go of them? Practice letting go of a compulsive performance pattern and see what comes up for you. As an example, if you are a workaholic, cut back your work hours and see what patterns of thought and behavior come up around self criticism, self doubt, fear of other's judgments about you being a slacker, fear of not having enough money or status, not getting ahead, getting fired, etc. You may become anxious or depressed; don't buy into the story behind these feelings. These beliefs and emotions are what drive the compulsion. Learn to accept these feelings and to befriend them instead of rushing headlong back into your compulsion. This is the beginning of recovery from a compulsive pattern.

What support would you need from your family, friends, loved ones, and counselors or spiritual guides in your effort to accept yourself for who you are? Who can you enlist to hold you lovingly accountable for your progress and be supportive and encouraging when you fall back in fear?

How might you go about learning to accept yourself without the props of your accomplishments and personal attributes? Who do you have in your life that will love you just as you are? If you don't have any such people already, start to look for some, for it will be difficult to learn to accept yourself as you are if you don't have people on your team who can reflect back your intrinsic goodness until you can see it for yourself. See if you can find some other healthy satisfactions to replace your compulsion: friends, family, pets, hobbies, charity work. But don't make them another kind of compulsive prop for your self esteem.

Sit or stand in front of a full length mirror, clothed and then naked. Notice any self-judgments and acknowledge them and gently learn not to buy into them. See if you can accept your appearance just as it is. And gradually learn to love what you see. Yes you can do this, and it may take awhile, especially for women! Learn to lovingly care for your body in little ways. For instance, notice when you have hurt your body and tend to it with a Band Aid, some lotion, or a hot bath. Yes, this is for you men too! Take good care of your body and it will take good care of you!

Look at older people and begin to see their beauty. Practice seeing the inner beauty of people that you would not ordinarily see as beautiful; and practice seeing it in yourself! Smile at yourself in the mirror. Send loving thoughts towards your image in the mirror. If in the past you judged and rejected your physical appearance this is hard work- and it is very worthwhile! Practice letting God love you just as you are. In daily prayer open yourself nakedly to God's loving presence and wait patiently for Him/Her to show up. And if She/He doesn't show up perhaps ask for their love! Open your heart gently and be ready to receive Grace.

Daily practice accepting and loving yourself just as you are. If you have a harsh critical Inner Voice, practice letting the critical thoughts go. Don't fight them but don't believe them either. Notice good things about yourself and keep a daily log of them as they come to mind. So when bad thoughts come to mind, you can put them in perspective. Think kind thoughts about yourself. Remember your essential goodness. Remember to practice daily being your own best friend. In all the ways stated above, self rejection and self criticism can gradually be replaced by kindness towards and acceptance of yourself.

Invitation

What would your life be like if you no longer judged yourself harshly? How much joy might you feel without the constant fear of failing to meet impossible standards looming over your head? God constantly sends you love messages in the blooms of flowers, beautiful sunsets, playing children, shading trees and singing birds that invite you to slow down and enjoy what is present right now. You needn't rush around so frantically trying to do so much.

Learn to love the one who has accompanied you all your life. Who is more worthy of your love than yourself, who knows you through and through? You may have done things you regret and have not accomplished what you thought you set out to do in life, but that does not mean you are unworthy of self acceptance and love. You are human and, like all of us, imperfect. Accept that and open your heart to yourself.

Keep close to your heart. You are part of God and God is love. To judge yourself as unworthy of God's love is a sad blasphemy and you deserve better than that. You are a hair's breadth away from God and if you relinquish your self judgment, you will find yourself resting in His / Her arms. So just let go and fall into the bosom of Love; this is your true home, my dear.

Enjoy your work for its own intrinsic value, for the connection with co-workers, the joy of daily jokes and caring for each other. Enjoy serving customers and clients and knowing that you make their lives better. Be honest in your dealings with others and enjoy knowing that you make the world a little better each day by what you contribute. And at the end of the workday, go back to your loved ones and spend time with them, and let yours and their reservoir of love be replenished.

If you have children, enjoy their presence in your life. They are God's gift to you, even when they try your patience. Practice loving them as best you can. And remember to keep refilling your heart with God's love every day so that you may have enough love to give to them. Remember, you are the conduit of God's love for your children. And remember that you don't have to be perfect!

Find time to spend in Nature, which does not judge you or demand anything from you. Perhaps by a stream or next to kindly trees are the places you feel God's embrace. Or perhaps it is with music. Remember to feed yourself to keep your soul nourished, my friend. Life is a long walk without food for the journey.

Growing Up

There is a necessary growing up that we humans need to do if we are to truly appreciate our lives. It is more than most people are willing to do and it is not something our culture particularly commends, except when the person is safely dead and no longer challenging the culture and its values. This growing up means a kind of dying to our old selves. And a letting go of our "personal salvation project", the agenda that we thought would make us whole through success, fame, wealth, power, security, social acceptance and all the other chimera of the ego's wishes.

CHAPTER 11

Being Willing to Pay the Price

The kingdom of heaven is like treasure hidden in a field. When a man found it, he hid it again, and then in his joy went and sold all he had and bought that field

Matthew 13:44 NIV Bible

The Pearl of Great Price

Looking outside ourselves,
we grasp after any shiny thing
other than what is present,
in front of our very nose,
within our very heart.
When pain arises, we run from it
as from an enemy, too horrible to face,
and numb ourselves from our aliveness.

Gradually, at times painfully, we realize:
the treasure resides within.
This moment. This encounter.
This sorrow, this joy.
Nothing more. Nothing less.
Little by little, we give ourselves away
to the Beloved,
to this breath,
to this loving heart.
And we get back in turn the whole world!

-Robert Cornell

Introduction

In the previous section of this book, I emphasized the need for letting love into our lives, to learn self acceptance and to stop berating ourselves. In this section we explore the other side of spirituality: our need to grow up as spiritual adults. This is not about self judgment but rather clear headed neutral self evaluation and a commitment to ourselves to be honest and to be in integrity. As we become more self accepting, it is easier to be more honest with ourselves as to where and how we are falling short of our aspirations. This honest self evaluation is critical to the spiritual path. Without it, we are in serious danger of deluding ourselves and avoiding seeing where we can improve.

Lack of self awareness and self examination would be like an airplane not having a onboard guidance system to let it know where it was on its flight path. Without the feedback from taking our personal inventory from time to time, and asking the frank advice of others, we are likely to wander off the correct path. Because we cannot see ourselves completely accurately and without bias we will always need the counsel and feedback of others and it is important to be willing to take to heart what they say to us.

The spiritual path can be pretty pricey at times. If we are to grow spiritually, we must be willing to face the truth of who we are, even when it is uncomfortable. And then to be willing to let go of what in us is not aligned with Spirit. As we travel along the path of liberation, we will be called upon more and more to give ourselves away to the world that is in need around us. But what we get back in return is so much more valuable than what we have sacrificed! We find a life full of meaning, deep satisfaction, joy and love. And we live in the present, in the truth of what is.

There is so much false spirituality for sale in the marketplace these days, promising that we can have material things effortlessly, that we can have anything that we want: fame, fortune etc., if we just think positively. This is such blatant nonsense! This prosperity gospel, as it is sometimes called, is part and parcel of our self centered capitalist culture where the focus is always on "what do I get out of it?"

To become a spiritual adult, we must be willing to forgo the often seductive appeal of a spirituality done without any effort or sacrifice on our part. If we think about the great spiritual teachers, we see that they all paid a high price for their holiness, their wholeness. They had a deep willingness to surrender their self centeredness in service to the Beloved. Any spirituality worthy of our respect asks a great deal from us and, at the very least, asks us to let go of our bottomless desire for ease, security and comfort.

However, there is something different about the effort expended on the spiritual path in comparison to the ordinary effort we exert in our everyday life. Effort is ordinarily expended in order to satisfy personal desires and usually comes from a place of ambition and fear. Spiritual effort, sometimes characterized as "effortless effort," has a different quality to it. Spiritual effort lacks the drama of self involvement seen in ordinary effort and is motivated by love and compassion. It does not seek its own glory or gratification. Spiritual effort also does not struggle so much as move gently with the force of Love.

Mature spiritual effort isn't done from a place of grim self denial or ambitious grasping, but rather from the vantage point of calmly taking responsibility for our own lives and wanting to be of service to others. And, as we practice, we experience greater joy and deeper meaning as we learn to align ourselves more fully with Spirit. We let go of our stubbornness to have things go our way. We let go of our fears and narrow concerns. Our hearts awaken to the needs of others. We move into a loving service orientation to Life. Then joy naturally appears in our hearts for we are not so much concerned about ourselves and what we can get out of Life as taking pleasure in being there for those we love, which steadily encompasses a larger and larger circle.

As I have gradually matured over these many years, I find I take great pleasure in being there for others on their spiritual journeys. There is for me no greater joy at this point in my life. And if I had not worked steadfastly for many years on spiritual practice and being of service to others, this joy would not have come to me. I would still be the anxious, self centered workaholic focused on personal success that I used to be. I have to admit, if I didn't serve others in my therapy practice and have the ongoing heart connection with them, I could easily fall back into my old fearful patterns. I have to keep connecting to God's love and giving it away. So this heart work is a pearl of great price and a treasure trove of countless blessings that I am sharing with you in this book.

Self Reflection & Practice

Enlightenment is not something you achieve. It is the absence of something. All your life you have been going forward after something, pursing some goal. Enlightenment is dropping all that. Enlightenment is not something you do. But to talk about it is of little use. The practice has to be done by each individual. There is no substitute. We can read about it until we are a thousand years old and it won't do a thing for us.

- Joko Beck

Reflect honestly on what motivates you on your spiritual path. Is spiritual practice a means to an end, of getting what you want such as better health, enlightenment, peace of mind, less stress, etc.? Don't be tempted to embellish out of embarrassment or guilt. Be honest with where you are on the spiritual journey! We grow when we admit and accept where we actually are-not where we think or somebody else thinks we should be.

What would your spiritual practice be like if it were an end in itself –not something you did to get something for yourself? What would it be like to just meditate without concern for any goal outside of the meditation itself? One breath after another breath, just being present with what is? Try meditating with no goal in mind, no criteria for whether or not your meditation is "good" or "bad." See if you can accept your meditation being just as it is: sometimes restless, sometimes tranquil. Do you notice any change in the quality of your meditation when you have this attitude?

How would your spiritual life be different than it is now if it were focused on opening your heart to everyone around you? What would it look like if it were a way for you to give yourself more fully to a world in need? Reflect on this in some detail.

What price have you so far been unwilling to pay for your spiritual journey? Not been willing to engage in regular daily spiritual practice? Not been willing to stay mindful during the day? Not avoiding gossip? Not stopping the habit of putting others down to make yourself feel better? Not been willing to care for others? Not been willing to give up a harmful habit? Not been willing to put yourself at risk or inconvenience?

What have you not been willing to do? Reflect on this honestly without self castigation or guilt or feeling unworthy. What fears or reservations do you have that keep holding you back from giving yourself more fully, to Spirit, to Life? Write these down and keep them in mind for further work in this book. Also, you might feel moved to pray to your Higher Power to release you from your fears and your withholding yourself.

What beliefs about your spiritual life prevent you from committing more fully to it? Beliefs such as: I don't have the time or the luxury to be spiritual? I have let God down in the past and I have too much to make up for to approach Him/Her in my life now? I have to be perfect? I'm just totally afraid of making a mistake? A person like me can't be a spiritual person? That's for other people; I'm just a _____? What?

Do you see yourself as "just a layperson" so you think it isn't possible to be fully committed to spiritual practice with work and family obligations to be concerned about? How could such a viewpoint be self limiting as to what your spiritual practice could actually be?

Take stock of your life and appreciate how spiritual practice could be integrated into every aspect of your so-called secular life. Raising children. Driving to and from work. At your place of work, dealing with your fellow workers, clients, and superiors. Relating to your partner at home. Dealing with money and possessions. Keeping priorities straight and not letting yourself be overcome with busyness and distraction. Loving and serving your family.

Just as a concrete example, I use my car time to practice being with myself in the present moment. I often don't put on the radio or let my mind wander too much from the present. I keep my focus on being in my body, driving the car, noticing the changing traffic and road conditions and enjoying the view around me of sky, trees, etc. For me this is an excellent opportunity to bring meditation into my "real" life. Take an inventory and look at how your so-called mundane life has many opportunities for spiritual practice. Journal about this.

See if you can look upon all the aspects of your Life as essentially spiritual practice. How would they be different if you saw every aspect of your life as spiritual, even going to the bathroom? Be honest and down to earth! The purpose of this self examination is to generate a list of possible intentions for spiritual growth, not a list of your shortcomings to beat yourself up about! An intention is a gentle aspiration to move in a particular direction, not something where you grimace and try to make it happen and then beat yourself up when you fall short!

Choose a couple of places in your daily life where you could practice more intentionally. Daily meditation practice? Learning to be more present with the people in your life? Letting go of negative thoughts about yourself and others? Slowing down a bit when you catch yourself feeling rushed? Keep your list of intentions about practice in a place where you can see them daily to remind you to practice them. Appreciate when you make small incremental improvements. Avoid 5 Year Great Leap Forward plans!

You might support and grow your spiritual intentions by creating a list of affirmations that have energy for you. It could be a collage of great sayings of famous leaders that inspire you. You might find quotes through reading books written by great spiritual men and women and soak up their words in your heart. It might be in allowing their lives to speak to you in your own life situations– but not making comparisons with them.

And remember: this is not a spiritual To Do list! It is something that invites you to rest more fully in your Being.

Invitation

Everything in your life belongs in Spirit's realm: the sometime drudgery and heartache of child rearing as well as the joy. The happiness of communing with your partner as well as having those difficult conversations with them. The discipline of learning and studying. The long hours at work. Being an adult and facing reality. And being a playful child with your children and partner. Being a good friend to others. Doing your best to love and to serve in whatever opportunities your life presents to you; it all belongs in spirituality. It all belongs, every last bit of it.

Nothing is left out or excluded. If you are leaving something out, then you do not fully understand yet what Spirituality is all about. We are made to live Life to its fullest, to show up for our lives every day as best we can. To be responsive to our families, communities, and our nation. Not perfectly. As best we humanly can. And if you are human it is guaranteed that nothing you do will be done perfectly!

And in our showing up for others, we gradually grow beyond the confines of our own narrow wants and preferences. Over and over again we give ourselves to Life so that others may live and flourish, so that our children may inherit a better world because we cared enough. Your Life is waiting for in your bank account and your recycling bin, at the voting booth, at your job and in your close relationships- and in your love and your caring for our earth home and our human family.

CHAPTER 12

Healing & Letting Go of Childhood

When I was a child, I talked like a child, I thought like a child, I reasoned like a child. When I became a man, I put the ways of childhood behind me.

1 Corinthians:11 NIV Bible

The Child

The Divine Child lives within us all.
Joyful and playful, she knows no cares.
She lives in love, joy and the magical now,
has no concerns for past, nor worries for the future.
We grow up (or suppose we do.)
and we forget this one,
becoming preoccupied
with past and future,
with getting and keeping,
with attaining and protecting.
Texting, Twittering and Face Booking
and busying ourselves endlessly
with all sorts of things that mean so little.
But the past of our Inner Child often haunts us
and we have so little insight into why this is.
This child withdraws inside us, mute and hidden.
Go find this child and take them out of the shadows.
Heal and nurture and love them.
And then, call them to maturity.

When we love and heal this one,
She comes back into her divinity.

–Robert Cornell

Introduction

There are wonderful things about children: their spontaneity, joy, playfulness, innocence, their full presence in their bodies. But there are also other traits not so pleasant: their selfishness, greediness, obstinacy, emotional instability, etc. The reality is that most of us carry some of these traits into adulthood and so we have to learn to discipline ourselves and let them go. Some of the best ways for us to learn these lessons are having children of our own, going into military service or going into a demanding vocation and being of service to something greater than ourselves.

Each generation has to find its own way out of childhood. In earlier generations, children were expected to be productive parts of the household and had important and demanding chores at an early age. Now with technology and urban life there are not nearly as many opportunities for children (and even young adults) to take on the responsibilities that begin to wean them from childhood. The current Millennial Generation has the challenge of having been greatly supported by their parents and now facing a very difficult work environment. Some of them may have a hard road ahead in growing up. And adversity can either embitter us or cause us to grow. It is always our choice.

My own childhood I can say truthfully, in many ways, lasted into my mid twenties when I found myself a father and needed to put aside some of my dreams and bring in a regular income for my family. Having been rather spoiled in academia where I had a full National Science Foundation scholarship for my studies in graduate school, this was a big wake up call. That would not be the end of putting away my childhood; in some ways I am still dealing with the old patterns of childhood when I still have to let go of old feelings of being overlooked, not seen, not feeling important.

If we use as our models of true adulthood the examples of great spiritual teachers such as the Buddha and Jesus, one could say that our whole human life is a journey towards true adulthood. And if we are honest with ourselves, we can see some part of our not so pleasant childish behavior showing up in our so called adult lives: a certain stubbornness, a need to be right, a bit of histrionics when we don't get our way. So it is important from time to time to take stock of our behavior and reflect upon where we still have some growing up to do. And here's a hint: there is ALWAYS more growing up to do even into your last years of life!

As we let go of the traits of childhood that we call "childish," we find a well-earned equanimity; we no longer have to have things always go our way. We can let go of disappointments without making a fuss. We become much more generous with both our time and our material possessions. We no longer need to blame others for our shortcomings but can soberly admit our responsibility and can learn from our mistakes and improve. Our lives become more and more about others and less and less about my things and my desires. Over time we take on a service orientation to others and to Life itself.

There is another aspect of growing up and that is about healing old childhood wounds. Some of our "retarded childish" behavior has to do with unhealed trauma and wounds from growing up in less than ideal households. The woman who was parentified as a child, the man who was abused and vilified by both of his parents, the woman who was sexually abused by her father, the man whose mother emotionally fed on him as a child - all these adults have wounds from childhood that need healing. And in some way they are stuck in their past roles until they learn how to heal and re-parent themselves.

This work is often not easy: it requires insight into the source of one's patterns of thinking and behavior. It involves repeated efforts to heal and change one's perceptions and patterns of interaction with others. And for those who have been abused, it also entails the healing of old traumatic memories. While we have more psychological techniques such as EMDR and EFT now to help heal the emotional charges of traumatic memory, this is still often a long and challenging journey of healing for those who have suffered this fate. There is an odd and wonderful sort of recompense for this hard journey, though. Those who make it are often the best equipped to help others on their healing journeys. And being of service to others in their healing gives us much inspiration, joy and gratitude and helps us on our own journey.

Self Reflection & Practice

Remember that it very important to deal with this exercise from a place of self acceptance and self forgiveness. If in doing any of this work, you feel yourself slipping into self judgment and depression it is important to stop and do some work on Self Acceptance and Self Forgiveness. It will do you no good to do this work feeling awful about yourself. To balance this work out you might also want to make a detailed list of your good qualities. Incidentally, if you find it difficult to make a list of the things you like about yourself, that task would be the far better practice for you now rather than finding more ways to dislike yourself!

What are some of your personal patterns that are left over from childhood that no longer serve you? Make a list and be specific. Examples: impatient, short tempered, easily hurt by other's comments, etc. constantly needing validation and attention, etc.

What behaviors of yours get negative comments from family and friends or bosses at work? Granted, some of these criticisms may be entirely off base and really about the other person, but have you ever taken any of this feedback to heart rather than beating yourself up about it or resenting your critics? If not, this is a really good place to start! Make a list of criticisms that others have made of you that you admit, even if reluctantly, might have some basis in reality. Try to do this as if they had been talking about someone else to maintain some kind of distance and objectivity about this inventory. In other words, you would talk about yourself in the third person: for example, he/she is often late. He/she hems and haws and beats around the bush a lot, etc.

See if there is any consistency to the criticisms and if there are, try to see this as constructive feedback from the universe. Then see if you can find ways for you to become more aware of your tendencies and come up with some plan of action as to how to improve your behavior. This probably means facing some fear, awkwardness and moving out of your zone of comfort.

Do your childish behaviors serve you in any way? Is there some secondary gain that you get from maintaining them? For instance, if you play helpless or clueless, can you get others to pick up your responsibilities for you? If you are stubborn and dig in your heels, will others relent to your demands? If you get angry, will others back off and let you have your way?

Where in your life today are you feeling called to grow beyond old ways of being, doing and thinking? Make a list and keep it somewhere in your living quarters where you can consult it from time to time. But don't use this as a way of beating yourself up and feeling bad about yourself!

Work on just one "character defect" at a time and hold a gentle intention throughout your day to improve upon it. For example, if you find that you have a tendency to be stubborn, try to be gracious when others want to do things differently. This may just mean being aware of your irritation when someone suggests something different and refraining from refusing to consider it.

Rejoice when you catch yourself doing something you are less than proud of. Be grateful for every sign of progress on your part and give thanks to your Higher Power for guiding you.

Rejoice when someone else notices that you have made some improvement in your former not-so-desirable behaviors. It is good to have some validation of our efforts to improve. After all, we're not totally indifferent to other people's opinions of us!

Invitation

There is a time and season to be a child and then there is a time to let go of childhood and grow into adulthood. This is hard work. Growing up has always been hard work and it will ever continue to be. Growing up requires us to loosen the grip on our demands that Life be there just to please us. There always will be temptations to want things to go our way, to hold onto toys of some kind, even if they are fancy "adult" toys. There is nothing sexy about growing up; the real growing up process occurs offstage in most Hollywood films. It's time consuming and not much fun for the ego. But it develops great gifts of character.

You can stay a child if you wish, but it's not very pretty at age fifty. There are some Puers and Puellas that have successfully avoided the responsibilities of adulthood, any long term commitments and the raising of children. Who mostly have managed to have their life their way and to play at things. They have chosen never to truly master anything - for that would require far too great a sacrifice of their personal pleasure and freedom. But Peter Pan doesn't look so good in midlife and Wendy was right to leave him to go back to her real life. Peter can stay on his little island forever and play at his little imaginary life chasing pirates and rescuing maidens.

To be a truly good man or woman comes at considerable personal cost. Wisdom and integrity can't be bought but must be paid for by continually living beyond oneself. Abraham Lincoln personally suffered greatly from his leadership in the Civil War and led our country out of the blight of slavery. Nelson Mandela spent 27 grueling years in prison and came out of that experience a great man who could lead his country out of apartheid. Martin Luther King died for his convictions and is still a voice of conscience for us fifty years later. One thing common to all great spiritual and political leaders is that they were willing to grow beyond their personal agendas and serve something larger than themselves.

Life is calling to you. It needs you to be the adult that has grown beyond your old self, beyond the confines of narrow and selfish ways. Are you going to answer? If you do, a great adventure awaits you!

CHAPTER 13

Letting Go of Victimhood

The man who can articulate the movements of his inner life need no longer be a victim of himself, but is able slowly and consistently to remove the obstacles that prevent the spirit from entering

- Henri Nouwen

The Road out of Victimhood

You have been down this road before.
You know how it turns out, but you go anyway.
Now comes the opportunity:
Do you see that it was your choice?
That your finger was on the trigger,
That it was your mouth that shot off first?
That you were looking for a fight
and you conveniently found one?
If not, then play it again Sam.
Play the whole damn drama through again.
And again. And again.
Until you are really sick and tired
of being sick and tired.
And you can finally admit to yourself,
"Yeah, I did it. It was my choice."
"I can't blame anyone else for it."
Then my friend you have an opportunity to choose
a different way down a different road!

- Robert Cornell

Introduction

If we are unwilling to take responsibility for our lives and our experience, we will never grow up. For then we will always see ourselves as the victim in our lives and hence can never take the ownership that gives us the freedom to choose differently. Many of us spend a great deal of time blaming our circumstances and other people for our problems in life. Then we are unable to put the focus on seeing what we could do to solve the problem that resides inside of us, not out there in the world.

Dr. Ron Hulnick, one of the wonderful teachers at the University of Santa Monica, used to say that people go around complaining "I'm upset because." Fill in the blank-- she said this, he did that, they didn't do this, I didn't get that, etc., etc., etc. When we orient ourselves to Life in this way we are unknowingly saying to ourselves that our unhappiness comes from the outside and we have nothing to do about it within ourselves. As they used to say in the old days at EST, this puts us "at effect." In other words, when we are at effect, our satisfaction in life doesn't come out of ourselves but rather from what we expect to get from other people and outer circumstances. Then we are thinking like a gambler waiting for his lucky night. And we should know already how that turns out for the gambler. Hint: it doesn't turn out so well like it sometimes does in the movies!

Sadly enough, many of us get great comfort and satisfaction from blaming others and venting to friends about how badly we have been treated - at least in part because it lets us off the hook for looking into what we might have contributed to the situation. We fear being in the wrong because we ourselves judge those who are wrong as being bad people. And we certainly don't want to judge ourselves as being a bad person!

The more rigid and black and white our moral judgment is, the more we are afraid of admitting our wrongs and so any doubts about it are pushed from our awareness. This is why so many fire and brimstone preachers are caught in disgrace. Indeed, they have no sense of grace and forgiveness for their shortcomings and so they must wall it off and deny it even to themselves until it all comes out in glaring and painful scandal.

There is often another thing that can keep us from taking responsibility for our lives: toxic shame. There is the healthy remorse that we feel when we come to the painful realization that we have done something wrong that we need to put right. But some of us harbor an habitual toxic shame that takes us down into depression and self loathing rather than energizing us to show up and make things right. Addicts are drowning in toxic shame; it is part of what keeps the cycle of addiction turning over and over again in their lives. They act out in addictive behavior to try to relieve the pain of shame and self-loathing. Then they become deeply ashamed of the consequences of this addictive behavior, can't face it and numb out with their addictive behavior and thus start the whole cycle again. And again.

Those of us who can forgive ourselves for our mistakes and shortcomings have a lot easier time admitting our part in some issue and can then let go of blaming others for our situation or getting mired down in toxic shame. When we can forgive ourselves for our mistakes and shortcomings, we actually give ourselves a great gift: we can much more easily take responsibility for our situation and learn from it.

The person who insists on blaming others for all of their problems will never be able to see how to improve their life by making different choices for themselves. Because they don't see how they are choosing bad things they cannot see that they can chose better things. They doom themselves to a life of perpetual victimhood and ignorance, repeating the painful patterns over and over again. And those addicted to toxic shame just stew in it and cannot find their way forward.

There is a more insidious version of victimhood. It comes from believing that we have no power over a situation in our life and we cannot see that we are contributing anything to create this problem, even when we try to. These situations keep repeating themselves like a theme and variations and we just don't see what we are doing to deserve such a fate. It might be a difficult boss at work, a quarrelsome spouse, being taken advantage of by relatives, etc. In such cases we are quite likely to fall into depression, frustration or anxiety as we feel hopeless, confused and overwhelmed. As long as we cannot see what we can do to work with the situation we find ourselves in, then we have a victim mentality.

When we feel powerless over a repeating pattern of events in our life, say being fired again and again, or feeling taken advantage of by many people, there is some kind of unconscious process going on that leads to these outcomes. But we just can't see it. Freud talked about this over a century ago and called it the repetition compulsion. In this frame of reference, we keep trying to work out old childhood wounds by repeating them in the present.

The man who had an abusive father keeps fighting with authority figures in his life today, trying to get even or protect his rights. But often this person is tilting at windmills and perhaps unconsciously seeking out abusive bosses or abusive spouses to replay the pattern with. The unconscious hope being that they will finally get satisfaction this time around. What they can't see is that they are being run by old, unconscious scripts that are not based on present-day reality.

The way to freedom from such repetitions of experiencing victimization is usually through some kind of insight into the patterns we are stuck in and working through the automatic emotions that arise so that we finally can choose to respond differently. I remember a client who had anger problems with his ex girl friend. He was reared by his Black American single mother, who had nothing good to say about men, especially his father. He sorely missed his father growing up and was determined to be there for his kids when he became a father. When I met him, he had two young boys by his on-again off-again girlfriend and he desperately wanted to stay connected to them.

But his ex didn't want him to have anything to do with them as she and my client got into one fight after another. Finally, as I helped my client to control his anger and inquire into its origin, he began to see how his anger stemmed from his feelings of helplessness as a child. He started to do things differently, owning he was now a grown man who could manage his old angry emotional outbursts. He got legal help to win equal access to his children and he stopped the fighting with his ex. He stepped out of the repeating cycle he had lived with as a father hungry child himself and could now be there for his children.

In some cases, of course, we may be able to right what has been done to us in a court of law or by some other means. But we should inquire carefully if, in the greater scheme of things, it is worth it in terms of the time and energy we would need to expend to see justice done. Sometimes, it is indeed worthwhile to see justice done. But again we have to ask ourselves: at what cost to ourselves and to others? If we are to go through with the effort to gain satisfaction through the law, we will need to regularly relinquish our anger and resentment, for legal proceedings can bring them up again and again.

Self Inquiry & Practice

Life will keep sending us the same problem again and again until we see our part in the pattern! If Life keeps sending you the same difficult problem, it is trying its best to get your attention!

Before doing this section, you might want to meditate and come to a place of self-acceptance and equanimity. When we begin to take ownership of a painful pattern in our life, it can take us down into self-rejection and shame if we aren't prepared to give ourselves empathy and support. Engage in this work in your sacred space perhaps with music and incense or anything that might help you to stay in a peaceful state of mind.

Remember: This is some of the most self liberating work that you can do for yourself! And it is difficult. You will be so tempted to blame the other party – and may have good reasons to do so. And the self righteous anger feels so very......gooood! But, if you can see anything that you are doing that contributes to these situations happening again and again, then you have things that you can do to prevent them from happening to you again! It is your taking responsibility for your part (not blame and self rejection) that will give you your freedom!

What painful situations in your life keep coming up again and again? List them at length. Do you see any patterns in their repetition? Can you see what you might be doing or not doing that leads you repeatedly into these painful places?

A very important question to engage with: is there anything about a current situation that reminds you of a painful event in your childhood? An authority figure you have difficulty with now, somehow resembling a parental figure? A situation with a colleague that resembles a problem you had with a sibling? If you have repeating patterns happening in your life today that are harmful in some way to you or others and you cannot figure it out yourself, by all means find a good counselor!

Here is a by no means exhaustive list of traits and behaviors by which you might be contributing to painful repeating patterns in your life:

Procrastination or avoidance.
Not setting healthy limits with others.
Not listening to your inner intuition about something.
Being uncertain, doubting your own wisdom.
Not valuing yourself, your feelings or needs.
Never considering other people's needs and feelings.
Needing to control the situation or other people.
Needing to be right. Being stubborn and belligerent.
Being unreasonably demanding of other people.
Being self indulgent. Feeling entitled.
Not standing up for yourself.
Focusing on others' needs, not your own needs.
Letting others tell you what to do.
Always looking to others for advice and confirmation.
Always expecting a negative outcome.
Distrusting others' motivations and agendas.
Seeing others generally as hostile and undependable.
Seeing intimacy with others as dangerous.

Journal at some length about how you could be setting yourself up for these negative repetitive experiences. Some of our traits and behaviors that lead to these undesirable experiences are very hard for us to see in ourselves. We are simply blind to them. That is where good friends and counselors who aren't afraid to give us kind and honest feedback are so very useful. And our so-called enemies who criticize us can be incredibly valuable! Ask for feedback when you feel your behavior may have been problematic! Listen carefully to any criticism you get or negative reactions to something you do. And be ready for when you slip into self-judgment and self-rejection to practice Self Forgiveness! If you can see the patterns then you can free yourself from them!

These self defeating patterns of thinking and behavior can eventually lead us to engaging more and more deeply with the underlying issues. Usually we begin to see what we are doing that causes us to experience painful outcomes but it takes some time before the patterns will be completely eliminated. This takes a lot of patience and persistence with ourselves as we keep the faith and continue to work on our issues, even though we are still screwing up. And after many years of self work, the repetition of patterns will be seen by us as the need to focus more carefully on the underlying issues. There is less drama and self recrimination and more inquiry into what is happening in our consciousness.

Invitation

Where does it still burn inside you my friend, when you think of the wrongs you have suffered? How many sleepless nights have you had, tossing and turning, thrashing around in bed planning how to wreak revenge? How often have you marched the offender to the gallows in your mind, lowered the axe, pulled the rope, seen the body drop? And how much peace has this given you, chewing your own wound open again and again? What would it feel like to let go, to forgive, and to release yourself from the pain of holding this anger and judgment inside for so long? And that doesn't mean you just forget and invite your abuser back into your life!

And what if you finally realized what your role was in this sad drama you have found yourself in so many times before? Persecutor and victim might find their roles hopelessly confused. In the case of adults, every abuser needs another who will tolerate the abuse. Everyone who needs to be right needs someone to relent and give in. Everyone who needs to have control needs someone to be subservient. And so the dance goes, until we see our part and we can then decline the invitation of certain partners whose dance steps we no longer enjoy. Step on my toes? No thanks. I'll pass this time. Make derogatory remarks about my agility? Find someone else to dance with. Even if you have to dance alone for a while it sure beats this unpleasantness!

Do you repeat the same dance steps and fall down again and again no matter who your partner is? Don't blame your partner then! Perhaps it's time to learn a new dance step. Perhaps it's time to dance solo for a while. Perhaps it's time to learn to dance with God and let Her call out the tune. If you have been ignoring Her and insisting on dancing with others who bend to your will, it's high time you let Her lead!

CHAPTER 14

Letting Go of Grasping

One thing to deeply ask ourselves when we find we are stuck with something is this: are we grasping or being grasped? The answer often comes from the pain we feel in the grasping.

Letting Go of a Thing

Whoever has caught a butterfly knows:
how gently you have to hold it
by its pulsating body
so as not to dislodge its scales,
while enjoying
its admirable sheen.
And then to let it
fly off, unharmed
Or else, someday,
there won't be any more.

- Robert Cornell

Introduction

If you realize that all things change, there is nothing you will try to hold on to. If you are not afraid of dying, there is nothing you cannot achieve.

— Lao Tzu, Tao Te Ching

There is an old Zen parable about how hunters used to catch monkeys. The hunter would hollow out a coconut of its meat, using a small hole in the one end that was just large enough for a monkey to get its empty hand into. Then the hunter would put something the monkey would like to eat inside the coconut, place it on the ground tied to a bush and wait for a monkey to show up. The monkey would stick his hand into the coconut and grab the treat. The hunter would then make his sudden appearance, but the monkey would not let go of the treat and so its hand would be stuck in the coconut. In that way the monkey would be captured.

And so, the parable goes, this is how we are captured by the various things of the world that entice us and often enslave us. There are all kinds of things that beckon to us and seduce us, some of them obvious and some not so obvious. Most of us that consider ourselves spiritual know about the obvious pulls of fame and fortune, sex and materialism. Then there are the less obvious enticements that Chögyam Rinpoche called "spiritual materialism." These are what I'm going to focus on in this chapter.

One of the most common inclinations in human beings is our tendency to want to hold onto pleasurable experiences. With spiritual practitioners, this shows up in the desire to hold onto pleasurable states of consciousness. It's not that there is anything wrong with these experiences; it is simply that they are not the ultimate goal of spirituality. They're wonderful when they come to us and at times they encourage us to remain faithful to our spiritual path. But, like all experiences, they don't last.

The goal of spiritual life is to accept with equanimity what comes to us, good or bad, and to focus on being courageous, loving and in service to others. This means being willing to face into difficult experiences at times; and in point of fact, it is our engagement with challenges that helps us to grow. If we are looking only for pleasant experiences in spirituality, we might as well be doing drugs!

Another way that spiritual seekers limit their spiritual growth is by seeking enlightenment for themselves only and ignoring the welfare of others. Enlightenment then becomes some kind of merit badge or prize that validates you, boosts your self esteem and elevates you above others. This spiritual perversion is potentially deadly in many ways. If the practitioner has any kind of enlightenment experience this can become the support for pride and arrogance that will end any kind of genuine search for the truth. It also puts the emphasis on the over individualized self which is the problem we are trying to free ourselves from in the first place. Finally, if you make Enlightenment the goal of your life, you have just eliminated from your concerns all of Life which is process, not goal.

For those of us who have obsessive-compulsive tendencies there is a tendency to grasp onto some idea of what the enlightened state is and then to follow a set of rigid rules to try to become enlightened. I did this for many years as a monk, not realizing what I was doing. I would try harder and harder to be PRESENT, but what I didn't realize was that I was becoming fixated on some pretty rigid rules of how to be present and was becoming more and more stiff and inflexible. And.... not present!

I remember coming home from a week long sesshin (Zen meditation retreat) in which I had intensely tried to stay present every minute of the retreat. I felt strange and rather disoriented. I happened to pull down off the shelf a little book of writings by Brother Lawrence called *Practicing the Presence of God*. The simplicity of this lay Brother's faith life and how he did not worry or effort as he went about his daily routine hit me like a thunderclap. I started to laugh uncontrollably as I had a taste of feeling free.

And then the controlling part of me would freak out about this and shut me down. For several days after this breakdown / breakthrough, I would seesaw back and forth between my compulsive control freak self and the part of me that longed for freedom. Gradually in my practice, I became more and more willing to give up my efforting and control in meditation and find Presence by simply and gently abiding in the present.

For those of us spiritual seekers who are intellectually oriented there is a tendency to grasp after information and to relate to the world mostly on the mental level. We try to understand how the enlightened state works so we can think our way into it. The belief underlying so much of our mental fixation in relating to the world is this: if I can understand something then I can control it; I can make it happen. But this is not how the World actually operates, spiritually speaking. We do not think our way into Enlightenment; we let our focus on thought and its duality fall away and gradually we come to realize the suchness of our life in many small graces: the smile of a baby, the happy bark of a dog or the rustle of leaves in the wind.

When we are relating to our life mainly through our thinking mind, we are most likely in some way afraid of our bodies and our emotions. We are using our intellectualism as a protection from experiencing our life. We would rather analyze our life or be detached from it from a mental stance than engage it directly, in the moment, in our body with its uncontrollable sensations and emotions. As Dogen Zenji so eloquently states, "Not knowing is most intimate." By being spontaneously and intimately living in the moment, we do not relate through our thinking mind primarily but rather through our whole heart / body / mind / world. When we try to live Life through our minds only, we dry up and become brittle; we lack the savor and spontaneity of the living moment.

One place that mental level religion can take the spiritual seeker is to a kind of nihilism, a suspicion of human nature as inherently sinful and a hatred of "the world." We can see this tendency in all the world's religious traditions in the more extreme ascetic fundamentalist versions that reject human desire as sinful and usually burden women with the weight of this opprobrium. If this world is inherently fallen and evil, then the only thing to focus on is release from this earthly prison. Then we grasp after release and transcendence and we have no caring for our mother earth, no concern for "worldly issues" and a devaluation of all that is feminine and sensual. This is a male perversion of religion that occurs when the mental level and a kind of pseudo hyper-transcendence are valued over living in deep connection to our mother earth and our incarnation.

Another temptation on the spiritual path is getting caught up in a certain "brand" of practice or teacher. When we are not confident in ourselves, we are inclined to "buy into" a particular teaching, a particular church or training center, a particular teacher. Then we defend them to protect ourselves from own self-doubt and uncertainties. It is a rather dreary and self-congratulatory conversation to talk about how this teacher or that school of meditation is "the best one or the only one that is really enlightened" or some other such self-limiting and self congratulatory nonsense. While we may find a particular teacher or a style of practice a really big help to us, to limit ourselves to just one perspective and to make others wrong for their different ideas and practices borders on idolatry. The world is so wide and people are so different. How could any teaching, no matter how profound or complex, capture all of Life?

Self Reflection & Practice

There is no better way of keeping on the right track than developing the ability to see when you are going off track.

This takes a kind of sensitive awareness towards your states of mind and attitudes. For example, being able to see when you are getting self satisfied, a little over confident in the way you see things. Or when you are being too uptight and critical. Here are some things to practice being aware of:

Are you always looking for ways to get "high" with your spiritual practice? Do you need the constant high to escape your regular life? Is it to escape from pain, from boredom? Would it make sense to begin to practice with pain and boredom?

Are you envious of others who have ecstatic experiences? Why does this matter to you? Would it set your doubts to rest about whether or not you are on the right path? Are you always standing in judgment of your life, as it is, as being not good enough and you need to look elsewhere for that "certain something" that will fill a hole in you? Perhaps it is time to investigate intimately this sense of a lack in your life. Explore when you sense that lack what it feels like in your body. Where does it reside? What does it feel like, look like? Feel into it and befriend it.

Do you tend to be boastful when you have some kind of opening or enlightenment experience? Do you tend to get argumentative about your practice being superior to another style of practice? Do you tend to look down your nose at other practitioners and their teachers? Do you like to tell others how great your teacher and your practice is? Are you close minded about how others engage in spiritual practice?

If you find yourself very satisfied with your spiritual practice and rather judgmental of other people's practice, make it a point to try some other practice for a time. For example, if you are attached to sitting in silence, try participating in groups where there is a lot of deep and intimate sharing. You may very well find this both a bit challenging and quite a wonderful cross fertilization of your spiritual work that will bear good fruit!

Learn to listen carefully to the experience of other spiritual practitioners who have very different types of practices than your own. Ask good questions of them and look for what you can glean from their traditions that might open a door for you that you otherwise might never knew was there.

Do you get tunnel vision and find your practice is getting rather dry or rigid and effortful? What ways have you found so far to ease up, step back and allow yourself to take a broader view? When you find yourself getting rigid, look for ways to ease up on your beliefs about getting somewhere in your practice or doing it right and widen your focus. Find ways to soften and melt both mind and body, to let go, to not effort so much. If you are always getting uptight when you meditate, try lying down to meditate. Just don't go to sleep!

Do you tend to read lots and lots of books on spirituality but rarely sit down and practice with your heart and mind? If so, stop reading for several months and just let your mind clear of all your ideas about spirituality. Just be present in your life as it is: no big agenda, no constant trying to figure out how your life should be more spiritual. Then notice any difference in your ability to just live your life without a lot of thinking and analyzing and trying to make it something it isn't. If you have trouble with this you may be barking up the wrong tree with all your intellectualism.

Do you devalue work to improve our world? Do you think that people who are politically active are naïve and their work is ill founded? Is your focus always in transcending the material world, thinking that it is nothing but an illusion? Be very careful about these attitudes; this is a kind of spiritual nihilism! It can lead to a solipsistic view that overcoming Samasara should be your only focus. And how my friend is that really so different from those who just give up and space out, being only concerned with their own well being?

Become aware of your mind states and energy states when you are practicing. Is it effortful and striving after something? Is it dull and unfocused? Do you separate yourself from your practice and keep judging and analyzing it? Do you practice with impatience? Doubt? Begin to just notice without judgment what your ego brings to your spiritual practice. Notice in your body whether there is a sense of grasping after something, a sense of something lacking, a sense of urgency. All of these suggest a deep and incorrect belief that resides below your practice. Become very curious about this and see what it is about. You may find out something that will redirect your practice in healthier ways.

Invitation

Oh you travelers on the Path, there are so many potential snares on the Way. And yet it is so wide and inviting! How do you walk straight on this winding Path? Just listen more and more deeply inside of yourself, beyond your limiting beliefs and fears. Listen to Love for She is trustworthy and true.

If you are constantly looking for spiritual highs, my friend, you are treating spiritual practice like a drug. You may have times of elation and great clarity, but these are states that will come and go. Keep coming back to the practices of Love, Presence, and Service to others; they will serve you well in the long run.

If you are completely focused on your own liberation, consider that such self-focus is probably part of the disease of self- centeredness you are trying to cure yourself of. Open your eyes to how you might be more connected and engaged with others and how you might be of service to them. Then you are treading on the well worn path of the Bodhisattvas and Saints.

If your spiritual practice is always rigid and painful, ease up on yourself! Relax. Breathe. Rest. Abide. You are trying too hard! Let yourself fall into the Presence of Love. Don't make the spiritual path too difficult; Life has enough challenges for you so don't make it any harder than it already is!

If your practice feels easy and a sure thing for you, perhaps you are too self assured and a bit lazy. Go beyond your comfort zone. Look for ways to be of service. Question your motives and aspiration. Ask others for their feedback on how they see your practice, especially practitioners that you respect for their diligence and sincerity.

The brilliant Diamond of Presence does not effort but it is not to be confused with laziness. It is like a cat resting effortlessly but quite awake by the mouse hole. It is like a mother lovingly attending her child. It abides with Love in its heart and great curiosity about the suchness of the world. It dwells in the present and plays as needed in past and future.

CHAPTER 15

Letting Go of Aversion

The more we resist, the more it persists.

-saying from the Twelve Steps Programs

In The Field of Whatever

When we fight with our pain, we are split
and our suffering gets worse.
Besides the pain, now we suffer a war
between we who resist- and the one that feels:
our faithful body with no other choice
than to feel what it feels.
Feel what you feel, pain or pleasure.
Your dear body will lead you
into the suchness of yourself.
Resting in this Field of Whatever,
pleasant or painful, it is all of one piece.

- Robert Cornell

Introduction

There is an old Chinese toy: a woven bamboo tube that you put on opposing index fingers and then try to pull off. The harder you pull, the tighter this toy tightens around your fingers, more and more strongly resisting being pulled off. But when you push your fingers towards each other, the trap loosens and you can ease your fingers out. This is rather like our experiencing of things we dislike and resist. If we fight with our experience, our bodies tend to tense up and resist more and more. As we do this, our awareness narrows and becomes even more focused upon the experience we are resisting. Then we can find ourselves trapped inside of a prison of our own making.

This is particularly true of "negative" emotions such as fear, anxiety, anger and unpleasant sensations such as pain, itching, etc. When we experience these, our immediate default impulse often is to stiffen our musculature against the experience and to hold or tighten our breathing. These reactions tend to solidify and intensify our resistance to the unpleasant experience even more. And our resistance reinforces the energy of these emotions and sensations and we become more and more stuck in them as we fight against them. Paradoxically, the best way to "get rid" of what we dislike is to accept it as it is and not make a fuss about it when it shows up in our awareness. And then, to let it flow through our bodily experience and out of us as it surely will if we do not resist it.

One of the most common experiences in meditation practice, particularly when we first begin, is struggling with an itch. The sensation of an itch when you are sitting formally and intending not to move can become overwhelming and seem incredibly unpleasant. It can blow up into a maelstrom of suffering that you can barely tolerate with the greatest of effort. But when the bell sounds to end a meditation period it is not uncommon for that same itch to suddenly and mysteriously disappear! The mind has this incredible capacity to make a sensation or emotion seem unbearable in one moment and then for the difficult experience to just be gone in the next.

We resist so much in our lives: we are unhappy about our jobs, our relationships, our health and our life in general. When we let ourselves stay in the mode of resistance and resentment, we have no positive energy available to move us forward. We are putting all of our attention on how much we don't like our experience of these things and no energy into how to flow with our life as it is. This is often how the mind operates until we find ways of working with acceptance and nonresistance.

So when we find ourselves complaining about some aspect of our life, it behooves us to give open, accepting attention to it, to allow it to be and to be intentionally present with it. From this stance we will very likely find the constructive way to deal with the issue or situation we have hitherto been stymied by. When we are finally willing to stay with whatever it is we are resisting, often something will open up in us, something will soften in us and what had been repugnant or so difficult to bear no longer seems to be. And we may find some meaning in what was distasteful before. We have come out the other side of our discontent and found something of value in it.

As a teenager I spent many long summer hours sweating and mowing our steep hillside lawn at our home in Indiana. I didn't enjoy it much then, sometimes even resenting it. But it eventually led me to running a landscape business where the work was physical and at times hard. I had been well prepared for this by my previous hard physical work at home, so for that I can be grateful. Not many white middle class kids have that opportunity these days. Now I really enjoy mowing our little front lawn in Pasadena with an old fashioned hand push reel lawn mower. What was once resented has now become a subtle pleasure and healthy exercise: the smell of fresh cut grass, the sound of the mower blades as they cut through the grass, the visceral enjoyment of exertion, the satisfaction of a job well done.

Self Reflection & Practice

To be Awakened by all things is to be intimate with all things, including our resistance to such radical intimacy.

- Robert Augustus Masters

IMPORTANT PRACTICE

Pay attention during the day to the quality of your experience. Notice when your body tenses up. Notice without judgment when you tighten or hold your breath. These things typically occur when you are averse to your experience. Notice without judgment where in your body you are tensing up and consciously breathe gently into that area. On the outbreath, breathe out the tension and allow the area to melt, to relax. Notice when you space out or get sleepy during the day. This is often another way that we deal with experiences that we don't like, that bore us or we subtly dislike. Find some way to engage more with the experience, to become more present. Drink some coffee or tea and wake up! Be present with what is!

Noticing when you tense up or space out as a daily practice, you will soon find patterns in your resistance to things. Based upon this practice, what in your life do you dislike, resist? Do you resist intimacy? Conflict? Boredom? Detail work? Chores? Public speaking? Deadlines? Following orders? What? Make a list. Keep it someplace where you can consult it from time to time, perhaps in your journal. This can be a great source of growth opportunities for you! Remember if you want to grow you will need to overcome your resistance and open up to doing new things that initially may be outside of your comfort zone. What does this list suggest to you as a possible new way forward in your life now?

Perhaps you would like to set some intentions about working with your resistance to specific aspects of your life. For instance, suppose you are strongly resisting some detail work on a project you have to do and you are avoiding and procrastinating. Then set an intention to do some detail work on the project for a fixed amount of time each day until the project is done. You may want to place your progress on a calendar where you mark off that you have done what you set out to do each day. Show your progress chart to others. That way you have some support and also some accountability.

Take one of the experiences that you resist and practice being more present with it. Remember to breathe if you are highly resistant to the experience; this will help soften your tensing your body against the situation. Especially be attentive to your outbreath and lengthen it slightly to help release tension in your body. If you would begin to disassociate (feel dizzy, unreal, detached, numb) this work might best be done with a therapist or spiritual teacher familiar with trauma work, because you may have tapped into some traumatic memory.

As you work with an experience you have in the past resisted, be aware of any negative thought patterns that show up as you think about engaging with the experience and then as you actually engage with it. Also note any negative stories you may want to buy into later after the experience such as " see, I told you it wouldn't turn out well."

Remember that what you don't treat as an impediment, even when it seems to you scary, unpleasant or difficult, is always going to work in your favor spiritually! What is considered by your ego as an impediment is often the gateway to your spiritual unfolding.

Invitation

There it is: the one thing that you most dislike, showing up in your life... again. You have fought it, avoided it, resented it, dreaded it time and time before. And yet it keeps showing up as if to torture you. You want to reach for the bottle, the anesthetizer, the club. But wait! Stop a moment and reflect. How many times have you resented and resisted this visitor's presence? And how many times has your resistance made the situation worse for you and for everyone else in your life? Perhaps it is time to try another tack entirely. Try allowing the experience to flow through you and not to resist it!

Stay present, breath, melt and soften and you will pass through the straits of resistance. There is no need to fight with the headwinds of your experience. They may seem frustrating and even fearsome, but they are some of your very best teachers! Perhaps you would do better to tack back and forth with your resistance, giving ground here and still moving forward there. Ride on your breath, your own wind, right through the narrows of resistance. Watch the stories you tell yourself and don't turn your life into stone!

Often as you let go of your resistance what was once your bugbear, your bête noir, your personal demon turns out to be an abandoned part of yourself. And when you finally give it your attention, your acceptance and your love, it quiets down and no longer blocks your way forward. When you don't resist, Life is good. When you accept a situation, it becomes more workable.

CHAPTER 16

Going off Autopilot

Whenever we are on automatic pilot, we are not learning anything new. We are just following things we have learned long ago that take no awareness or self reflection. The spiritual path is all about waking up from this trance and seeing things anew.

Automatic Drive

I was drivin' all night through the dark 'n the air.
There was booze n' the radio, but I wasn't there.
Behind the wheel must've been somebody else,
'cause I was in another time and another self.
Looking out the window past the roadside view
Seein' what I dreamed of and nothin' new.
'bout things I'd already seen,
time and time again- if ya know what I mean.

- Robert Cornell

Introduction

We human beings have a strong tendency to solidify, to color, and to prejudge our experience. We pigeonhole our experiences as "good" or "bad" and ignore those that are neutral. We do the same with people that we encounter, deciding whether they are "good" or "bad," and ignoring those who are just neutral. This is the way the human mind works: it wants to know first and foremost if a situation or person is safe or dangerous. Are they safe (good) or a threat to us (bad) or just boring (neutral). Do they meet our needs (good) or do they take from us in some way (bad)?

We reify our stories about our experiences and our interactions with other people as we repeat these stories, mulling them over in our own minds and in our sharing them with others. We like everything wrapped up and explained like in a good murder mystery. We want to know clearly who the good guys are (usually us) and who the bad guys are (usually them.) Yes, it all makes perfect sense that the butler did it. Case closed.

This is our evolutionary heritage of having a brain that contains primitive parts focused on survival issues. In our lives we often need to make snap decisions and we have an emotionally based system that can quickly decide "friend or foe?" However, our lives today are often much more complex than this system of assessment can ever encompass. Plus, this survival-based system is inherently dualistic. To put it in a nutshell, it basically is set up to decide whether we can eat something or if we are in danger of being eaten ourselves.

If we look at the world, we see that so many people are caught up in this simplistic and polarized world of me versus you, us versus them, our religion versus theirs and our country versus their country. And the more polarized a society is, the more conflict, violence and malfeasance there is in that society. Because there is little trust of others, most people in such a society are in survival mode most of the time and are looking out for number one. The fear-focused mind of duality is always looking for potential conflict and ways to protect itself; it has little room for empathy, generosity or even integrity.

To free ourselves of this strong tendency to see things from this dualistic framework of the me versus you, zero sum game mentality, we need to stay aware and to be grounded in our hearts. For we are wired by our biology to think in these dualistic terms much of the time. You will probably notice that, if you stay aware of your reactions, several times a day you feel threatened or vulnerable in some situations. When this happens, your survival system kicks in and there is a strong tendency to use your automatic coping mechanisms that are all based upon your pre-programed survival programing.

For instance, when someone appears to us to be angry or aggressive, we have a tendency that, if unchecked, would instantly size them up as a difficult or even a dangerous person. Then our survival programing will kick in. We retreat or we attack, we lie or we appease. All of this, without self- awareness, can be automatic, unskillful and preprogramed patterns of perception and reaction. Then later we tell our side of the story, making the other person wrong and getting sympathy from our friends. Unfortunately during this whole episode we were likely to be running on automatic pilot and we have not seen how our own perceptions were distorted and our reactions unskillful.

With compassionate awareness, we have the opportunity before we go on automatic to see our unconscious programming: our strong emotional reactions and our ingrained tendencies to follow certain impulses. When we develop this heart/mindful awareness as part of our daily spiritual practice, more and more we give ourselves the opportunity to go off of automatic and to let our hearts and minds come up with better options.

I had an example of this in my own life when I was working as a landscape designer for the producer of a TV show who had a rather tough New York exterior. One day my secretary called him at the studio and he chewed her out royally for bothering him there. She was so caught off guard that she burst into tears and went into the restroom to recover. We were just getting ready to present him with the contract for the landscape construction and this incident made my heart sink. My personal programming was that I feared conflict and avoided it as much as I could. But I realized I had to confront this issue with him in order to decide whether or not to continue to work with him.

The next day, I showed up with my heart in my throat for the contractual meeting with him, his wife and the general contractor. I fully expected that this was going to be a difficult and contentious meeting and I dreaded it. As the meeting progressed, I finally stated how I was very uncomfortable with how he had treated my secretary and that I was uncertain about whether I could work with him. Instead of a huge fight ensuing, he dropped his rough exterior and reached out to me. If I had not been willing or able to drop my negative prejudgments of him and my desire to avoid conflict, I could have ended the relationship then and there. But fortunately I was able to let it go and respond positively to him and our working relationship was very warm and positive from then on.

Self Reflection

Can you remember situations where you have caught yourself starting to put someone in a pigeonhole of good (or, more likely, bad) and you decided to stop thinking in terms of that kind of categorizing? Reflect on what helped you to stop that automatic pigeonholing process.

Remember situations where you got triggered and overreacted. See if you can find out what set you off. Was it a particular type of personality that you had to deal with? Was it a situation that you often find yourself in, such as being evaluated or potentially rejected? Is it a pattern that shows up with your close relationships or in work situations with peers?, with authority figures? Or perhaps a situation that is slightly threatening and uncertain? What patterns do you see?

When you overreact to a situation, what do you do afterwards? Do you feel ashamed and try to put it all behind you? Do you make a case for being right and the other person being wrong? Journal about this.

Do you rehearse a situation over and over in your mind trying to figure out what you should have done and what to do next? What might be a more constructive approach for you to take that is outside of your usual repertoire of behaviors?

Are you aware of particular triggers – sights, sounds, smells, etc. that set you off? These might suggest a prior experience that felt upsetting or threatening to you, perhaps was even traumatic. See if you can follow the triggering situation back to a memory that is disturbing. If so, this could be something to work with the EFT tapping process described in appendix #5.

Invitation

Being on automatic may seem the easy way to deal with Life at first but this strategy has its hidden costs! Automatic pilot likes to stay on the same path, but the path soon gets rutted and narrow and there is no way off. The path of least resistance goes downhill – and it never takes us back up. Nothing is learned, and our life gets more and more constrained and other ways to explore disappear from sight.

When you take the dirty goggles of habit off from your eyes, there is opportunity everywhere that you did not see before. Yes, it seems harder to steer and you have to push down on the gas pedal harder but there are a lot more ways up the hill than down. And as you go uphill the view gets more and more enlivening. Let yourself take in the scenery: was it not worth the effort?

When you presume to know, step back and question. When you project out into the future, go back to not knowing. When you are triggered into old familiar ways of thinking and reacting, be vigilant. Chances are you have gone on automatic again! Go back to manual stick shift and be aware of every move your mind and emotions make. Question it all. Get out of the rut you have been driving in for so many years. If your story is an old tape, buy a new MP-3!

Hold to old self centered ways of seeing and reacting to things and your world will shrink and grow dark. Stay awake, let go of old assumptions, and the world will look fresh and new.

CHAPTER 17

Letting Go of Security

"When you feel the mist in your mouth
and sense ahead the embattlement
The long falls plunging and steaming-
Then row, row for your life toward it."

From West Wind II - Mary Oliver

Introduction

One of the things that keeps our lives small is our obsessive need for security. We can see this in our own country, the United Sates, as we have spent our treasure and the blood of our young men and women to bring terror and ruin to other countries in the name of ensuring our own security. It is very doubtful that the second war in Iraq did anything to make us more secure. In spite of all of the security measures that we have undertaken here at home, it would be foolish to think that we have solved the problem of terrorism and it would be even more foolish to insist that we have to spend our resources and give up our personal privacy until we are perfectly 100 % safe. Sad to say, it would be sudden political death for one of our political leaders to talk completely honestly to our country about this and what our inordinate need for security causes us to spend our money on rather than the real needs of our communities and people.

There will always be this tension between the need for security and predictability playing out in our lives against the desire to follow our own inner prompting and to take risks. Sometimes we are open to taking a risk and at other times, perhaps because of family concerns, we are less willing. That is why it is important to take some big steps into the unknown in our youth for then we don't have the concern for the welfare of family to balance against our desire for finding our calling and taking big leaps of faith.

And let's face it: the great discoveries and inventions have often been the work of young people confident enough in their own passions to go off the beaten path. If we are to add something to any area of human endeavor we have to be willing to take risks.

I was fortunate when I was young to not give much heed to financial security. That allowed me to follow my sense of calling even when it led me into and out of the most seemingly random and nonsensical choices: giving up a full scholarship for graduate school in Physics and Philosophy of Science to study Indian classical music. Giving that up to study Zen Buddhism. Giving up Zen after fifteen years of practice, going into the unknown and starting a landscape design and construction company from scratch. Sorting my way through my confusion about spirituality until I could find another way to practice that would be right for me. Becoming a therapist at age 50 to follow my unrequited passion for spiritual growth and helping others. And I am deeply grateful to myself for having had the courage to make such leaps of faith into the unknown so that I can now be where I am.

And I still feel the Call nudging me along today, now to become a spiritual teacher of some kind. What that will look like, I don't exactly know, and it has already taken me to places where I am not at all as certain of success as in other areas I have already explored and mapped out. In order to do something new and meaningful, I always have to give up some bit of security, to let go of the comforting sense that I know the road ahead so well. If I were not willing to do that, I would stagnate.

The secret to staying young as we age is to be willing to move into new areas with a beginner's mind, a heart and mind that are open to the unknown. All of us need some level of security to function. After all, it is not the homeless or the indigent that accomplish great things in society. They struggle just to find a place to lay their heads at night and to gather a meager amount of food to eat. But beyond the basics of survival there is a wide disparity in what we think we need to feel comfortable and secure. Some of us sacrifice our authenticity for the seeming safety of a loveless relationship or the financial security of a meaningless job.

Others of us chase after power and possessions to have a sense of security and being in control of our lives. Those who are creative and true to their own nature will always face more risks and uncertainty than those who play it safe. That's inherent in life. But playing it safe has its own hidden costs. When being secure is uppermost in our mind, we will then face boredom. Boredom usually arises when we do not take on sufficient challenges. When we stay in the area of the predictable and the safe, boredom will be there to prod us on. When we don't let boredom egg us on, then resentment will surely follow, resentment that we have an uninteresting job, that our life is so bland and meaningless.

Or we just allow something vital to die within us. We have all seen such people who have in some way died but they are still alive. It is a sad sight. We would best be honest with ourselves that we have created this boredom, this deadness by our own choices to play it safe. If we can do this, instead of complaining about everything else but our own responsibility in the matter, then we have a chance to get out of our rut and accept the risks involved in truly living. What we have to face then are our fears of failure, of not being good enough, of there not being enough money, etc.

If we think that spirituality is something to just make ourselves comfortable and to make our troubles and challenges go away we are really devaluing the spiritual journey, which is one of the greatest and most challenging endeavors we can take on as a human being. Spirituality is not here just to comfort us and make us feel good about ourselves. No, in many ways it encourages a creative discontent with the lack of depth in our current life experience. The degree to which we can be truthful, to be present and open, to listen to and honor our inner promptings, to that degree we are taking the vital and necessary risks and moving forward in our spiritual lives. To the degree that we hang back, dishonor our truth, and deny our inner voices, to that degree we have wandered off the spiritual path.

Self Reflection & Practice

Life is either a daring adventure or nothing. Security does not exist in nature, nor do the children of men as a whole experience it. Avoiding danger is no safer in the long run than exposure.

— Helen Keller

In your life now, what is your relationship with risk? Think about activities and goals that you identify as some things that attract you but you believe are too risky for you. Not just whimsical things like bungee cord jumping but real world situations that have meaning for you but seem just too risky for you at "your stage in life," with your "lack of resources," or whatever reasons you dissuade yourself with. Allow yourself to look at these with new eyes: is there something you might be willing to venture into? What are the things you need in order to feel secure? Make a list of what you feel that you need to feel secure. Examine your list and look inside: what would you be willing to give up to have one of your dreams come true? What are the things you need for security that are non negotiable?

Do you feel a bit stale in your area of expertise these days? Have you had thoughts about some new area of endeavor? If so, what might be a new direction that could interest you, give renewed zest to your life? Can you allow yourself to be a beginner again in some new area? What in your old mindset would make you feel uncomfortable about starting over again in a new area? Can you let that go? Can you see the risks in staying where you are? Journal on these subjects.

Do you tend to hide out in your spiritual community in order to feel safe and you don't want to make a commitment to spiritual adulthood and giving back to your community? Do you use your spiritual practices as a way to escape from life rather than increase your ability to step out of your comfort zone and serve others? Do you hold back from taking any risks in your spiritual life for fear of failure and embarrassment? If so, this is an important come-to-Jesus moment for your life to admit this to yourself and pray for guidance to move you forward!

Try something new in your life today. Say hello to people you wouldn't ordinarily greet. Plan a visit to a place or group unfamiliar to you where you might volunteer your kind of expertise. What does your voice of curiosity and passion say to you about taking a certain risk for a new endeavor? Is there something that has been nudging you for some time? Perhaps now is the time to heed its push! Journal on a regular basis about what it is that's calling to you.

In thinking about a new endeavor, clarify what holds you back, what old fearful, self limiting voices are present in your thoughts and feelings. Acknowledge them and learn to work supportively with them while not letting your fears hold you back. Affirm what calls you forth into this new adventure. Share this with significant others both for support and for accountability. Take the risk and you will never regret it!

Invitation

People sometimes settle for a little bit of novelty to spice up their lives: a vacation to a foreign country, buying a fancy car. Your soul is far bigger than that! It is calling to you to let go of the familiar, to let go of security and to take the plunge into something deeply meaningful to you: to be of service, to do something of significance with your life, to be creative.

Yes, row your boat out into the center of the flowing river and let it move towards the rapids ahead. Sure your heart may come up in your throat as you give your first talk, or you may have sweaty armpits taking a public stand on an issue or be sick at your stomach confronting an abusive boss. You may feel scared you are going to fall flat on your face or be humiliated. But you can feel that you are ALIVE.

You can feel the quickening pulse as you go down the chute into the thrashing water and you feel alive and excited. So row towards your heart felt goal even if there be big rocks ahead, for the journey is well worth it. And remember, staying on shore and playing safe, you could regret for the rest of your life. You will not live forever. There will be only so many opportunities for you to take chances. Let the voice within that beckons you forward speak to you. And listen. Listen.

CHAPTER 18

Letting Go of Judging Others

Remember that when you point your finger at another person there are three fingers pointing back at you.

-Anonymous

Introduction

When we judge or criticize another person harshly we are rarely being direct about what is happening within us. As Marshall Rosenberg says in his teachings on Non Violent Communication, or NVC, what we really need to be talking about, instead of reading the other person's pedigree, is what is going on inside of us. What are our needs and feelings that we are expressing indirectly in the violent language of judgment and attack? For instance, if someone has demeaned us, what we are really feeling when we call them names back is hurt, perhaps embarrassment and shame, and we have a need for respect, acceptance and safety.

But we usually don't want to share our vulnerability with others, particularly if they have hurt us. There it is again: vulnerability. We often don't want to acknowledge even to ourselves our being hurt or to open ourselves to being hurt again. And of course, if someone has hurt us we certainly don't want to expose our vulnerability to them! We would rather hurt them back behind our armor of anger and self righteousness. So often this just escalates the conflict and misunderstanding and everybody loses. Nine times out of ten, the issue could have been resolved if each side was being honest about what their real needs and feelings were.

Of course, there are other reasons we judge others: Sometimes we are jealous or envious of what others have and this triggers our feeling less than them. Sometimes we stereotype them into a group that we dislike. Other times we judge them for a trait we don't like in ourselves. And frankly, sometimes we are prejudiced against them from the very start: because they remind us of someone, we find something about their appearance or behavior that we dislike. In any case, to overcome our unaware reactivity, we have to be willing to be dead honest with ourselves as to what is going on inside us.

The vital question to ask ourselves whenever we judge others harshly is, what is behind it? When we are harsh in our judgment of someone else, most often there is a deep hurt or fear occurring inside of us. We have felt demeaned, criticized, shamed, betrayed, deeply disappointed or threatened by what they have done or what they represent to us. And what complicates it even more is this: what part of it do we carry from our own past that may have made this episode even more painful than it might have been otherwise? Almost without exception, the angrier, the more fearful, the more hurt we are, the more likely it is that this has something to do with an unresolved issue of our own. Sure the other person may very well have their own issues, but from a spiritual standpoint, our work is to see what in us is not serving our true selves and needs healing.

So when we have the urge to judge someone harshly, there is invariably underneath our anger and judgment, fear, deep hurt and disappointment. But we don't want to acknowledge and feel this fear or hurt because that would make us feel more vulnerable, while our judgment and anger give us a sense of power and protection. Paradoxically it is by exploring our fears, hurts and disappointments (but not buying into them) that we begin to mine a rich vein of gold and come to a deeper understanding and healing of our own issues. To do this we allow ourselves to touch into the painful feelings in our body and ask, "Where does this hurt come from? What is this situation really about?"

As we inquire, we may find ourselves going back to an incident in our childhood or adolescence that resonates with what we are feeling now. This is almost always the case when someone's actions frighten us or hurt us deeply; there is a carry over from old wounds that are triggered by the current incident. If we want to heal these old wounds we would do well to stay compassionately present with these feelings and let Love enter into the wound. And breathe and let the hurt pass through our body without developing and solidifying a story about how bad the other person is, how they had it in for us all along, etc., etc. If we can learn to stay with (not repress mind you) our feelings in our bodies and let them be, we will always become less invested in making the other person wrong and bad.

This doesn't mean we let others walk all over us. It means we process our feelings until we have clarity on what is going on inside of us. And when we are clear on that, we can decide wisely what actions to take with regard to the other person. Even if we had a childhood wound triggered by their actions, it doesn't mean that we excuse their behavior. It just means that we will now engage them from our adult self, not the hurt and frightened child part of us that has been triggered. We can then decide what consequences and what boundaries would be appropriate to enforce with the other person, not reacting out of fear or anger.

Then there are those judgments that we make of others that do not come from hurt feelings or fear, but rather from other needs of our egos: to feel better than, to focus on differences, to make the other person an object not a human being. And some of our judgments are just the automatic kinds that our egoic minds make all of the time. If we notice our minds' chatter for any length of time we will see a lot of adventitious judging going on like a stream of consciousness: "Oh, look at his nose; it's so big. Wow, she has a fat ass, etc., etc.

This is what the egoic consciousness does: it judges. I like this, I hate that. I like him, I dislike her. She is pretty, he is ugly. On and on and on it goes. When we look at the world from the egoic mind this is what it does: pigeon holes, stereotypes, judges and jumps to conclusions. It is always making other things and other people into objects separate from us to be judged as to how much we like or dislike them, how they can be of use to us or not, deciding how to get our needs met through them.

And there is no love in this. We can see the world in another way, though: from the heart. When we see through the eyes of love, we do not make objects of other people and things. The mind of the heart is only interested in connection, not in separation and judgment. Much of spiritual practice is involved in learning to see the world around us from this place of the heart. We see the random judgments that the egoic mind is churning out, but we see through them with our heart space open and connected so that we can see past this judging mind.

Another thing that we can see when we become more aware of our judging mind is that it can turn against us as well. It is an equal opportunity offender; it judges one and all the same way, even ourselves. So that when Jesus said, "Judge not so that ye may not be judged," he was talking about this egoic mind. If you give this mind permission to judge others, it will most likely turn on you before long. Some of us live in this judging mind and we know how painful that is. Others of us know from being with judgmental people at home or at work how toxic that can be, both for them as well as others.

Self Reflection & Practice

Beyond ideas of wrongdoing and rightdoing there is a field. I'll meet you there.

- Rumi

Practice watching your mind make judgments. Don't judge yourself as bad because your mind makes these judgments; this is just the function of the egoic mind. All of our minds do this; it is just a matter of whether you buy into the judgments or not. Take a day and from a place of neutral observation, make a list of the judgments that you see yourself making about others such as: They are fat, ugly, losers, stupid, selfish, vain, mean, etc. etc. And also make a list of your self judgments!

Look for the patterns in your judgments of others. Are these judgments your egoic mind makes against you as well? See if any of these patterns have a purpose in your life. Are there sometimes judgments your egoic mind makes against others to feel better about itself? Does it prejudge people in some way to provide protection? Does it have patterns of predicting certain negative outcomes that it believes will happen if it doesn't keep watch and criticize?

Now see if the judgment has to do with how the person you have judged may have hurt you. For example, you judge him to be a "wise ass" because he is always making fun of you. Now see how you could put in Non Violent Communication to them how their words and actions have affected you. For example: I felt hurt and angry when you said _____ because I have a need for consideration and respect from others.

When they did what they did, how does the hurt / fear / disappointment you experienced seem similar to something that happened to you in your childhood that was painful? How does that give you a way of working with yourself before you confront the other person about their behavior? Journal on this.

Invitation

Up and down, up and down I will lead them up and down
I am feared in field in town. Goblin, lead them up and down.
                    - Puck in Midsummer Night's Dream, William Shakespeare

The little mind prattles on and on about this and that, good and bad, me and mine. Just watch this little Goblin prance around on the stage of your mind, giving you its opinions on everything and everyone. It's a narrow minded little thing, so lacking in perspective and humility. A rainbow, a child's smile, a sunrise will cause it to fall into silence, for it is such a tiny thing that it cannot hold these sublime things inside the cramped dimensions of its realm. Let the right and wrong mongering little beastie go; most of the time he's of no use to you anyway, only making the seeing and sensing of things more convoluted and distorted. Look out from your heart's eyes and you will have a more direct and clear way of seeing things in their true nature.

This little Goblin will keep whispering in your ear. Just notice him and ignore him. He will eventually go away when you don't play with him. At play in the fields of the Lord, you can heal hearts and minds that have been led astray by this little rascal. Spring up as a beautiful poppy; smile a baby's smile at everyone. There is no one who isn't you and you can play funny games with yourself! Be the hole in Hafiz's flute that the Christ blows through. Then you will be a Pied Piper that leads others to the land of bliss and love.

CHAPTER 19

Letting Go of Anger & Resentment

Resentment

Resentment's like a dog, gnawing on a bone:
The bone tastes so good,
      and the dog chews on and on,
          until the bone is gone.
But resentment finds a new bone
      and gradually the pleasures dim
          as it eats inside your bowels
              and chews you up within
Resentment doesn't chew up
      the one that you despise;
          no, it chews you up and spits you out
              with no relief in sight.

- Robert Cornell

Introduction

Anger is fear with enthusiasm.

- Werner Erhard

Anger can be a very useful emotion. It can tell us when our boundaries are being inappropriately crossed. Anger can activate us into action when something of value to us is in jeopardy. It can keep us from imploding into guilt and shame when someone is attacking us unfairly. Our anger can be a warning sign to another person that they are stepping on our toes and should back off. The energy of anger can provide the spur to us overcoming our resistance and moving ahead with something. (Alright, let's get on with it already!)

But some of us are addicted to our anger. We all know a person who seems perpetually cocked and ready to go off when they are affronted by something and they take exception and defend themselves at a moment's notice. It seems that they are always on the look out for something to be offended about and to protect themselves from. As a therapist I know that this is often caused by the abuse or trauma that they suffered as children and now they are constantly vigilant to defend themselves from potential abuse. The sad thing about this pattern is that, without healing it, the abused child may now become the abusive adult.

The seductive thing about anger is that it can allow you to feel invulnerable, in charge, righteous, on top of things. The angry person can feel their energies being summoned to repel the wrongdoer and they don't need to fear that they will be overwhelmed. Underneath this veneer of supposed strength however is the same energy as fear: the fight or flight mechanisms in our consciousness have been activated and our loving nature is nowhere to be found. Chronic anger takes the self-righteous position "I am right and you are wrong and you are bad! You have hurt me and it's all your fault." It leaves little room for subtlety and dialogue. Chronic anger clouds our judgment, creates distance from others, and is physically, psychologically, and spiritually toxic.

When we are triggered into anger, it can be very useful to look inside and see what is going on with our own issues. Recently when dealing with a program important to my role at church and someone didn't take care of an action in the way I thought they had agreed to, I confronted them angrily in an email. Later, what I found when I looked inside regarding my reaction was that I personally had a lot riding on the outcome of the workshop and underneath my anger was my fear of failure. It would have been more skillful for me to notice and work with this fear earlier on. Then I would have been less triggered and more able to ask the person whom I felt dropped the ball to clarify with me what they thought their responsibility was.

Then there is resentment, which is truly an addictive feeling. Because we have felt we could not resolve the issue with the one who offended or hurt us, the feeling of anger keeps coming up again and again. And we chew on it – or more accurately – we let it chew on us over and over again until it gnaws a deep hole in our soul. Resentment is toxic; it literally can destroy our peace of mind and drain our energy for moving on with our life. Instead, we circle around and around the painful incident again and again replaying what we could have said in return, what we could have done in retaliation, imagining all kinds of things we could do now to get revenge with the wrongdoer....

This is truly bondage – a bondage that feels so self-righteous, so delicious and consequently is so insidious. We cannot see that we are the one holding the key to our own hate filled prison cell. And often we could have said something or done something to hold the one who hurt us to account. But some fear inside of us disempowers us and holds us back from taking appropriate action. And perhaps because of this, some of our anger is in fact directed at ourselves, but we can't acknowledge it.

Resentment has a disempowered feeling about it. It feels like the only outlet for the defeated that they can rehearse over and over again: the just punishment they will mete out to their enemy in the future. There is a way out of resentment. It starts with us taking responsibility for our feelings and realizing that we can deal with the situation constructively and in an empowered way or we can stay in our victim role. It's our choice. And so often what we need to do with our resentment is to get past our fears and speak out. Or take action and get our needs met in another way.

To avoid resentment in the first place, we need to be able to listen to our anger when it is indicating that our appropriate boundaries are being stepped over (or on.) Our anger is indicating that we need to speak up and do something! This is healthy anger. If we cannot access our feelings of anger we will find that we are taken advantage of again and again. It is even more useful to us when we can firmly and calmly speak about the inappropriate behavior and ask for a change in attitude or behavior on the part of the transgressor. And if this is not forthcoming, healthy anger knows what to do to take care of the situation.

Many spiritual people are afraid of their anger and think anger is "not spiritual." In reality, many of us who consider ourselves spiritual were raised as "good little boys and girls." We were raised to be "nice", non confrontational and to get along well with others. But this is a false conditioning that isn't our true Self. It is missing something vital about being a whole robust human being that can, when needed, defend him/herself and others it cares about. Those of us who labor under this false kind of belief are unequipped for the inevitable conflicts and confrontations that life presents us with. And if we have no access to our authentic and appropriate anger, we can't rise to the occasion. We will wimp out and try to withdraw or placate, losing the precious opportunity to stand up for what we really care about.

Another way that the good girl and good boy miss out is that they lose the activating and empowering aspects of anger. If we are used to habitually disowning our anger, there are many ways that we may shut down and feel stuck in potentially conflictive situations, unable to move ahead or resolve the conflict we are in. Anger can jostle us into a wakeful state where we have our wits about us and we can ask incisively, "what the hell is going on here?!" Anger can cut to the chase, doesn't put up with bullshit and gets quickly to the point. Anger is impatient with wishy-washy evasions of responsibility. Anger is clear about boundaries and not afraid to set them and defend them. This healthy kind of anger comes out of a passion for life and life affirming values.

And anger has an ability to shake us out of our immobility and to move us past our hesitation and self doubt. It motivates us to stand up for ourselves and not to let anyone push us around. Without our being able to access our anger, it is as if we had pasted on our backs: "here is a victim; do anything you want with them." I once had a client that was clearly developmentally delayed. Even though he was in his fifties, there were many life stages he had yet to pass through. He always had a shit-eating smile on his face that said to the world, "Please don't hurt me. I'm a really nice guy and I'll be really nice to you, so please don't hurt me." It was sad to see how this stance had cost him so much in his life. My hope was that he would eventually be able to allow his anger to surface and then begin to own his power.

Self Reflection & Practice

Anger is a signal, and one worth listening to.

-- Harriet Lerner

Against whom in your own life do you still harbor judgments, anger, blame, and resentment? Make a detailed list. Probably exclude childhood abuse for this is usually work to do with a therapist. Look at each person on your list. Write down what you think they did to you and how it affected you. Remember, to the extent that you still harbor anger, resentment or blame you are not free, so be honest and thorough. Let your angry self speak!

This is part of the Step Four in AA of making a fearless moral inventory and an excellent way to become more aware of yourself and your issues. What is the judgment, anger, resentment based upon? Did their behavior trigger some of your own issues? Do you feel you need to let go of your resentment or do you feel that you want to confront the person with the issue that stands between you? What has gotten in the way of your resolving the issue previously? What might your part be in your holding onto this anger/ resentment and how might you get past this?

Carefully look inside and see what your part might have been in the hurtful situations that you hold against them. This can be very hard, but remember, if you see what part you had in it, you will be able to choose differently the next time. And believe me if you don't see your part, there will be another time in your life where you will get another chance to experience this situation again! And where you can see your part is exactly where you have an opportunity to grow and not repeat the cycle again.

Especially where you feel the strongest anger/resentment, look to see how these people may have hurt the soft spots in your psyche, those places where you are easily hurt by other's actions or comments. When someone has made hurtful comments about you, can you see where some part of your own mind agreed with them? If so, forgiving yourself for making these same judgments against yourself may very well be the way out of resentment, for when you release yourself from self judgment, others have little sway over your own self acceptance.

What is your relationship with the energy of anger? Do you stuff it down because you think it is wrong to be angry? Do you try to put it behind you; do you try to let it go but in reality are repressing it? Do you avoid conflict for fear of getting angry? Are you a person with a short fuse and easily get angry? Notice what commonly triggers your anger. What issues are hot buttons that set you off? How does this relate to hurtful issues from the past?

Notice carefully and with as much dispassion and compassion as you can muster what happens when you get angry. Where in your body do you hold the anger? Are there habitual patterns of thinking and judging that show up with the angry feelings? Do you blame, think of ways to reap revenge, savor a certain kind of simmering resentment?

If you are a person with a short fuse learn how to contain your anger (not suppress it.) Use the breath, especially the outbreath to release tension and anger. Watch out for the patterns of thinking that accelerate your anger. Learn to detach from these thought patterns. Look at what the payoffs are for you for having a short fuse: you can make people afraid of you and you can bully them into giving you what you want? You like the sense of power and protection it gives you? Be aware of the payoffs then also look at what the costs to you are in terms of broken relationships, lost jobs, etc. Make a thoroughgoing list of the costs of your having a short fuse. Then see if you would be willing to let go of your habitual patterns of thought.

If you are a person who tends to placate and avoid feeling their own anger, look at how this works for you – or doesn't. What are the payoffs? You get to feel safe, keep on people's good side, feel good about how "nice" you are, etc., etc.? What are the downsides for you? You feel pushed around, feel weak and ashamed of yourself, you don't get things you really want from others? What? Journal on this.

If you are always playing nice guy or girl, look for opportunities to begin to feel your buried anger and to give it appropriate expression. One way to do this, when you think you might be angry about something, is to give yourself permission to free form write about it. Write without editing or concern how others might react to your writing (because you keep it private). Let your anger speak. When you get in touch with your anger this way, invite it to speak, let it hit cushions. You may have been holding this anger in for a long time so give it a voice and don't expect it will calm down right away. It may have a lot to say!

Consider what it costs you to still hold resentments about what this person or situation did to you. Reflect on how much energy you still give these stories in your life. What would it take to let them go? What would YOU need to do to resolve old situations where you did not take care of yourself? Would confronting the perpetrator help? Would self forgiveness be an appropriate part of that process – forgiving your self for not standing up for yourself? Would changing the pattern as it plays out now in your life help? What is the most important thing for you to do right now? Do it!

IMPORTANT PRACTICE

When you are triggered into anger, let your awareness go to the places in your body where you feel it. Be compassionately present with these angry feelings in the body as you refrain from acting out. Notice where in your body the anger is manifesting. In the Heart area? Then the issue may be about connection. Gut? It may then be about survival. Solar Plexus? Maybe it's about will, volition, autonomy. Head? Probably you are giving yourself a headache trying to figure it all out or tell the offending party what's so. Put your hands on the areas manifesting the anger so as to bring more perceptual awareness to them.

Avoid the temptation to conceptualize at this stage; we are far too given to analysis that prevents a deeper connection with and healing of the emotions. Stay with the feelings in the body; let the body speak, not in words but in the felt visceral sense. Explore with curiosity this angry feeling: what is present in terms of energetic pattern, color, weight, movement, texture, shape? Let the anger be; don't try to change it, transcend it, spiritualize it. Just sense what is present in your body from a visceral standpoint, not in an analytical sense of trying to figure it out.

Breathe and soften below the anger and sense what might be there. This is where the work often becomes very valuable to getting out of the rut we have been in for so long. Below the anger is almost always a part of us that is shaky, immature, fragile, fearful, hurt, vulnerable. Can you feel it, make contact in your body with it? If so, stay present in your body with this vulnerable part.

If not, know that there is some resistance to being present with your vulnerability; this may be work to do with a therapist. This can be challenging; many of us do not want to stay in this vulnerable shaky place where the work of transformation happens. You may find your mind wanting to wander off in all kinds of directions. Into pity party stories, angry stories, "coulda woulda shoulda" self recriminations stories, etc., etc. Don't let your mind feed on this!

Bring your awareness gently back to being present in this shaky, vulnerable place you so don't want to be present with. This is exactly where healing happens. This is where God can get to you with the Balm of Gilead. Release angry thoughts, let angry feelings be, staying present with them in the body. Do this again and again and you will gradually release your bondage to anger and what underlies the anger. Afterwards, journal on this process and what insights you have gotten from it.

Invitation

To hold onto anger is like holding a burning coal in one's hand, thinking it will hurt the person we are angry at.

- The Buddha

Get to know your anger, better; it is your familiar protector after all. It is trying its best to defend you even though you may not need defending anymore. Watch it out of the corner of your eye as if you were watching it make a scene across the room in a bar. See what it does with your body and mind...and remember to breathe. Breathe in cooling air to bring down the emotional temperature inside you. Breathe out the cramped energy of resentment, judgment, and the desire to do harm.

Let go, let go, let go, even if you have to do it a thousand times and the anger sticks to you like flypaper and insists on coming back again and again. Anger can be like a mad dog, slavering with spittle and frenzy that has to be gently leashed and pulled back from battle. Calm down, calm down and breathe in, breathe out. Let your body loosen up; unclench the tight fist and grim visage. You can sit this fight out.

If resentment comes back in your thoughts like a dog chewing on a bone, look at what you might be called to do to appropriately set things straight with your transgressor. Then let the thoughts go and set about doing this! Your continuing judgment and anger are of no use to you for they only painfully burn in your own body/mind and no one else's. If the mad dog of your resentment then still insists on chewing on the bone, try to take it from him with the gloves of compassion on. Ask your anger what it needs from you. Listen carefully, for you will probably hear an old story from your past. There is healing work to be done here!

Let yourself gently sink below the surface of your anger into the darker cooler waters below and contact what might rest under the angry waves above. Down here what is present? Is there hurt? Is there possibly even sadness? Is there a sense of vulnerability, fear? Let yourself sink into these feelings and embrace them. They may be the truer story hiding beneath this torrent of anger.

CHAPTER 20

Letting Go of Control

One of the greatest and most unnecessary struggles we have as human beings is trying to control things we cannot control and have no business trying to control.

The King of Tides

There was once a King who believed he was meant to rule over everything in his kingdom, which bordered on the sea. One day he got it in his mind that he should show the sea that he was its ruler and had dominion over its tides. So he instructed his retainers, against their protests, to carry him in his throne down to the sea's edge so he could oversee the tide, which was out at the time. The King sat in his throne there on the shore with his scepter, and commanded the tide to remain out. His attendants pleaded with him to let them bring him back from the water's edge, but to no avail.

The waters started to lap up against the king's throne, but he would not move and instead stood up on his throne and imperiously commanded the tide to retreat. The tide paid no attention to him and came in, finally drowning the King as he raged against it. The townspeople when they heard about this sorry episode were neither surprised nor dismayed, as the King had burdened their lives for a long time, demanding exorbitant taxes, costly festivals, and other things with which to bolster his grandiosity. At the King's funeral they secretly celebrated his passing and dubbed him humorously the "King of Tides."

Introduction

Sometimes we act like this king, wanting to have far too much control over things that by their very nature we cannot and should not try to control. This happens far too often in families, where parents try to control their maturing children, causing unnecessary and fruitless battles and eventually alienating them. Both in my extended family and with my clients, one of the most painful things that I have witnessed are adult children struggling with differentiating from parents that will not let them lead their own lives. And the more control the parents try to exert, the more inevitable is the eventual alienation and distance they create with their children.

Another place where control battles take place are in addictive processes and our desperate and futile attempts to control emotions that we find intolerable and frightening. When we feel these difficult emotions arising we are tempted to reach for the bottle, the pill, the bong, sex, or food to drown it out, numb it out, and to escape. In doing this we don't learn how to embrace and work with these feelings that are there to be healed. Others of us so called normal people try to control our difficult feelings with compulsive work, people pleasing, buying stuff we don't really need, zoning out with TV and the internet, or just pushing the feelings down and "moving on."

Then there is the compulsive, practically obsessive thinking we do to prepare for some situation that we are anxious about. We will play out the future event in our minds, rehearsing over and over again what we will say if they say that and on and on and on... Of course, there is some use to thinking out carefully what to do in a difficult or complex situation, but so often we spend an inordinate amount of time and energy uselessly worrying about a future event that doesn't even happen the way we feared it would. All we have succeeded in doing is stressing ourselves out by projecting our worst fears onto the future.

Underneath our excessive and obsessive attempts at control lie our fears: fears of being overwhelmed by feelings we dread, fears of losing, being ridiculed, proven a failure, or being hurt, rejected, abandoned. We struggle with these our worst nightmares trying to wrest victory out of what we fear will be our impending defeat. What would be far more effective would be for us to see clearly that our compulsive struggles are against projections in our minds that are based on old negative beliefs that were generated by our early traumas and hurts. If we can own our vulnerability and move towards it and be compassionate with our fears, we would be far less likely to act out as control freaks.

The solution to all unnecessary control battles is to.... surrender. To let go of our desperate attempts to stave off what we fear will happen and to simply and compassionately face our fears. This is not psychological work done solely on the mental level; it is an emotionally challenging working through of our worst fears and self limiting beliefs in the body. Allowing the dreaded emotions to wash over us and to see that we do not die from them. Letting go of trying to control our loved ones and to feel the vulnerability and fear of abandonment and betrayal that come up when we do let go. Dropping the obsessive planning and strategizing about a feared upcoming situation and being willing to be with the feelings of fear and uncertainty as they arise.

We could say that the ego is largely a defensive structure that we develop over time to protect us from imagined harm. Initially, these defenses are unconsciously adopted in childhood to fend off potential abuse, punishment, abandonment, shame, betrayal, etc. Then as we mature, this ego structure takes on more and more protective layers and more and more stifles our authenticity and spontaneity. And it cuts us off from intimacy with our Self, others, and God/the Beloved.

Spirituality is all about letting go of this need to control, this need to defend our false self that feels separate from everything else, needy, and inordinately in need of protection. This is the path of surrender, the way of unilateral disarmament. We allow ourselves to drop our ego defenses and to feel the wounds that lie vulnerable underneath them.

Self Reflection & Practice

But he said to me, "My grace is sufficient for you, for my power is made perfect in weakness." Therefore I will boast all the more gladly about my weaknesses, so that Christ's power may rest on me.

- 2 Corinthians 12:9 NIV Bible

Make a list of all the things that you struggle to control. Here are a few of the things to give you an idea of the possibilities:

Your emotions – such as feelings of emptiness, loneliness
fear, anger, guilt, shame and depression.
Your body - weight, signs of aging, your appearance.
Your spouse so they don't hurt, betray, abandon,
disappoint, enrage, scare or embarrass you.
Your children so they don't do the same.
Other people so they don't do the same.
Your finances, status, power, possessions.
Your freedom and independence from others.
Having to know things that gives you the illusion that you
are in control.
Your being right in any difference of opinion.

Then look at your list and decide which ones you have some chance to control or at least to influence and which ones you most likely cannot. And those things it would be better if you did not try to control. (Hint: your spouse and adult children.) If you could be honest with yourself at this point you could probably save yourself a lot of trouble!

On this list, look honestly at those situations that, when you tried in the past to control them, the outcome was even worse than had you not even tried. Where do you find yourself continually frustrated by outcomes you don't want? Could this be a clue that you might want to learn to accept something you haven't wanted to accept? Journal on this.

What are you trying to avoid experiencing inwardly in trying to control this outer outcome? Let your imagination play out what you fear would be the outcome in some situation where you are fighting for control. For example, If you let so and so win an argument how would you feel? How do you fear others would see you after that? If you let your responsible child(ren) do what they wanted to, what would you fear happening? If your spouse did what you insist they not do, what do you fear would happen?

Write down the scenarios where you fear losing control and allow yourself to imagine what you fear happening, actually happening and just sit with the feelings that arise, in your body. Notice how your mind may struggle to find a way out. Just notice this and let go of the desperate thoughts and breathe. Being compassionately with yourself, continue to let yourself feel what you feel; paradoxically this is the way to inner freedom.

If you let fear or depression (or some other emotion you try to avoid or shut down) bubble up in your awareness, are you afraid that they would overwhelm you? Just try an experiment when one of these feelings shows up again. Try your best to welcome the feeling into your body. Observe all of the fear based thoughts and beliefs that may flood in when one of these feelings shows up. Perhaps they tell you that this will never end, that you will be overwhelmed and destroyed by these feelings. Or some such feared scenario. Can you begin to see through these thoughts, not take them quite so seriously?

Notice how in real life situations, your mind will hash things out over and over, rehearsing what to do in a situation to try to control the outcome or avoid what you fear will happen if you don't. One way to know when you are turning into a control freak is when you think obsessively about a situation. That in itself is a sure litmus test! Hint: thinking of something a dozen times a day is probably obsessive. Remember to not beat yourself up: your ego is working overtime trying to protect you the best way that it knows how. It's just operating on false information.

When you have an obsessive run of ruminating about a situation, feel down into your body and see what is present there. Most likely you will find there what your mind has been running away from and trying desperately to control. Let yourself be with these feelings even when they are challenging, for this is the gateway to your liberation from being a control freak!

Once you see clearly what you are trying to control and the hopelessness of trying to control it, practice letting things be what they are. Let others do what they will instead of guilt tripping and harping on them to do it your way. Just allow yourself to feel whatever you feel: anxiety, anger, abandonment, hopelessness, despair, etc. But don't believe the stories these feelings tell you. And don't rush back to regain control.

The Invitation

If you are trying to control the universe, God may get tired of you trying to do Her job. So don't expect to get any help from Her if you should run into trouble from being a control freak! You don't need to try to control your emotional weather. Your emotional weather flows and changes without any effort on your part. So enjoy it and let it be what it is: blue skies and now and then clouds of sadness and the joy of sunshine that pass through. It all passes through, clouds and sunshine and you don't need to control it. When you do try to control it you get stuck with it! Let the feelings be and they will float away on their own.

When flying, your desperate attempts to keep the airplane up in the sky by gripping your chair armrests and pulling upwards aren't really necessary. And besides, the other passengers on the plane will not applaud you as you get off the plane.

You don't have to rescue your children or spouse from their mistakes; this is how they will learn. Let them make mistakes and suffer the consequences without angrily lecturing them to make sure they get the lesson. They actually learn faster this way! You don't need to control them or try to enlighten them or help them see the error of their ways. If you try too hard they will only resent it and put their focus on resisting you. Just work your own side of the street. And if they are impossible for you to live with, leave them. I know, easier said than done but in reality that is mostly how it turns out in the long run!

If you fail at something you will not die from it. The whole world will not stop to ridicule you for screwing up. Other people will hardly notice. After all, they're too busy worrying about their own necks.

You don't need to please everyone; some people are really hard if not impossible to please. And you won't get a Greatest Martyr in the Whole Wide World Medal for it anyway.

You don't always have to be right. You won't die from admitting that you made a mistake. In fact you will probably have much better relationships with those you have been arguing with over who is right.

So why are you holding on? Aren't you tired of gripping the steering wheel of your life so grimly? Don't your hands hurt from the effort? Aren't you tired of trying to get people to do what you want them to do? Isn't this all just so tiring? Smile. Breathe. Let go. Loosen up. Regain a sense of humor and perspective. Your world will not end. In fact, your life will lighten up and begin to flow. Who knows, you might even be happier. You will certainly be more at peace!

CHAPTER 21

Letting Things Be as They Are

The Perfect Way knows no difficulties except that it refuses to make preferences; Only when freed from hate and love, It reveals itself fully and without disguise.
"On Believing in Mind" by the Third Chinese Patriarch of Zen

- Translated by D. T. Suzuki

Introduction

It is easy to believe from a kind of general philosophical point of view that it is good to accept "what is." It sounds very "Zen" and cool and we like to somewhat facetiously say, "It is what it is." However, when life gives us something we dislike, that we find really challenging and uncomfortable, even downright scary, then it becomes far harder to actually accept what is. One of the Buddha's great insights was that pain is inevitable in life but suffering is optional. (He discovered this before the Twelve Step Programs did.) We will inevitably grow old (if we're lucky) get sick and die. And before that many things will happen to us that we won't like and that there is not much we can do about.

This could be a difficult boss at work, a chronic illness, or even unpleasant weather. But as someone once pithily said, "If you argue with reality, you always lose." Suffering is what we experience when we resist what is actually happening in the moment to us. And what I am specifically talking about here is our direct inner experience. This is what we need to learn to accept and to engage constructively with in order to grow spiritually.

So for example, when a boss speaks to us in a meeting and we feel embarrassed, we are talking about dealing with our inner experience of feeling embarrassed. This is the thing to be worked with first, before we react automatically and unconsciously to the situation. It is better to process our feelings of embarrassment, hurt and anger before we decide what, if anything, we want to say to the boss. And in that way we could do what was in our best interest, not just reacting out of our immediate upset.

Accepting "what is" does not mean we just passively accept whatever happens in the world around us and that we do nothing about what we perceive to be unjust or destructive. We admire leaders who have stood up for the rights of others and sacrificed their own comfort and even their lives so that others might have a better life. And in our own personal lives there will be people and problems that we need to confront and correct. Accepting "what is" means that we look inside ourselves before we react and see if what we perceive as unacceptable is based on our own biases or clearly is something that needs redress.

All too often our upset is because one of our own old issues has been triggered and we need to deal with our reactivity and gain clarity before we engage a problem, because it may only be a problem in our own mind. Recently someone shared with me how he had been given constructive feedback about how he was resistant to authority. As he reflected on this, he had to admit to himself that all too often he had tried to undermine those above him because he perceived that they were being abusive with their authority – and this was his distorted perception- not "reality." If we are more discerning about whose problem something is, we are less likely to tilt at windmills and we will also make fewer enemies.

And when we don't resist what is, what our experience is in the moment, life is more enjoyable, even when it is not what we might have wished for ourselves. For the last two months, as I was working on this section of this book, I have been sick with a recurrence of Mononucleosis. I have not been violently ill but rather chronically tired with no reserves of energy, so any exertion would leave me flat out exhausted. For a recovering workaholic, this is a great lesson in learning to listen very closely to my body. If I do listen, I can go on with many of my usual responsibilities, albeit more slowly and with rests in between tasks. But if I tax myself at all, my body goes on strike. It gives me quick feedback to stop pushing and resisting my condition.

This afternoon, being a Sunday and a beautiful sunny early spring day, I went out into my wild back yard to do a bit of garden work. Being very weak, I lay down on the ground and slowly dug out the clumps of weedy grasses that were sprouting up through the native sedges, which act as a ground cover in my garden. Because I knew I had to slow down, (two months of chronic fatigue is really good training!), I found I had more patience than usual to sort through the sedges to find the weeds intermixed with it.

The gift of this patience and acceptance was that I enjoyed the whole process and I was actually quite effective at getting the weeds out and not removing a bunch of the sedges with them. Illness is not something you would think could be enjoyable, but oddly enough I was happy out in the garden, pulling weeds. I was not pushing my body; instead,

I was listening to it and accepting it as it was – not as I wanted it to be. With the gift of acceptance of my condition came a kind of grace and pleasure. Perhaps I will have more to learn from this guest of illness before it leaves me.

More precisely, there is much to be gained from being intimate with our own inner bodily experience as it happens, moment by moment. So many of us are up in our heads at a remove from our direct experience and somewhat at odds with it, resisting it in subtle or not so subtle ways. When we are alienated from direct, moment to moment experience in our body, we have cut ourselves off from our aliveness and much of the truth of our inner knowing. We often dissociate from this direct somatic experience in childhood because of some difficult experience that we could not handle and unfortunately we continue this process into adulthood. This is by and large a completely unconscious alienation that we can only undo by becoming gradually reacquainted with our inner experience through gentle awareness practice.

Reflection & Practice

If you try to change it, you will ruin it. Try to hold it, and you will lose it.

-Lao Tzu, Tao Te Ching

What in your life right now is hard to accept? What is this thing that you resist and would like to be rid of as soon as possible? How has this resistance worked for you in the past? Does this thing that is so difficult to accept have anything to teach you? If so, what? Journal on this.

Perhaps it is something that shows up in your life on a pretty regular basis and you just cringe when it does. How many times have you resisted it, cursed it, resented it, wished it would go away, seen all kinds of doctors, self help gurus, therapists and healers so you could "release it" or "transform it" or "quantum heal it?" (Perhaps not-so-subtle forms of resistance in New Age clothes?) How has resisting what you dislike or fear worked for you so far in your life? Has it made your life easier or harder?

What exactly is your inner experience of this situation that you find hard to accept? Would you be willing to befriend the feelings inside you that this situation brings up? If so, relax as best you can and become present to the feelings in your body as you think about this challenging situation. Be sure to breathe and not hold your breath; this will help you to release resistance to your experience. Often as you do this, your resistance will lessen and the problematic situation will appear more workable. The less we resist, the less our problem will persist.

IMPORTANT PRACTICE: TAPPING ON YOUR RESISTANCE

Try this experiment in gently Tapping into your resistance to your experience. When you sense that you are not connected to your inner experience, that you are experiencing some inner resistance to it, try Tapping with it as follows. (See Appendix 5.) Start with a set up statement about what you are struggling to experience, let's say sadness. As you tap on the side of your hand, you say, "Even though I am feeling resistant to feeling my sadness, I deeply and completely love and accept myself." Then go through the full protocol. Afterwards check in to how you are feeling. You may find yourself yawning and relaxing and perhaps getting more in touch with what you are feeling. This is what I experience with my clients: they begin to soften and let go of their resistance and connect to themselves. You can do a number of rounds like this to get deeper into your experience.

How do you discern when something is a problem that can be fixed and when it is a situation to accept? What aspects of the situations in your life right now might indicate to you that acceptance is the better option? Fixing is the better option?

What is missing in your life now that you have yearned for prayed over, complained about, resented God for not letting you have? Would accepting the "suchness" of this situation for at least the present moment be tantamount to defeat in your view? If it would be, why do you think that is so? If this resonates with you, journal about it at some length.

Whenever you want to "let go of something," first look carefully inside and see what resistance might lie there. Notice if, when you experience this thing, you feel your body tensing up. This is a sign that you are not accepting the situation as it is in the moment. Your body does not lie! Before you can let go of anything, first you would do well to deeply accept your experiencing of it, in your body, emotions, and mind. Letting go is not a thing you just do mentally. Otherwise you are just continuing your resistance, not letting go. The key to letting go is that there is no inner resistance to the experience and you can let the experience move through and out of you. To let go you first have to let be.

Invitation

What would it mean to accept that for now, this experience is with you? You may not like it. Accept that. You may fear it. Accept that. But gently, oh so gently see if you can open to this very experience, even if it means just opening to experiencing your resistance to experiencing it. See if you can soften the tension in your body with which you try to resist experiencing it. Breathe into the resistance and breathe out. Allow. Acknowledge any tension in your body that is resisting the experience of this thing. Soften. Surrender. And again…and again, each time softening a bit more, surrendering a little bit more.

Don't ask when it will be over; just surrender to it for this one moment and leave the future to take care of itself. Let the mind go with its judging and its stories of how bad this experience is and how much you don't like it. The mind just perpetuates and accentuates your misery. So let go of its stories of it being unfair that you have to suffer like this. Let go of the horrible scenarios in your mind and your judgments of how terrible this situation is. Or judgments about how weak and pathetic you are.

What would it be like to let go of what you keep yearning for, pining for, putting your life on hold for until it shows up? Let it go. Let it slip out between your fingers like water and hold your hands open down beside your body. It doesn't mean that you will never have this thing that you ache for, but for now, let it go. And perhaps God will surprise you someday when you least expect it. Or perhaps She won't. But at least you won't have lived your whole life through waiting just to have this one thing you have put your life on hold for.

When you feel that horrible abyss of loneliness, emptiness, fathomless hunger and dread arising again inside you, try just a little bit to befriend that hole instead. That hole in you that you have been avoiding your whole life. That hole you keep trying to fill up with something outside of yourself. Try walking gently over to the edge of the abyss and peering ever so kindly down into it. It may look so hopeless down there – and frightening. You may be afraid that there is no bottom to it and if you let yourself down into it you would fall endlessly.

Perhaps take a little bit of this black hole away with you to a safe place and put it by your heart and try to love it as a mother would her infant. Remember that your darkest demons are only your own scared inner children trying to get your love. Your darkness just needs your gentle and patient love to light it up. Your darkest fears will abate with your acceptance of all of yourself. Spend time with yourself. Spend time with your darkness and your light. Someday they may all seem to be made of the same light of loving awareness.

CHAPTER 22

Letting Go of Our Personal Plans for Enlightenment

That you carry yourself forward and experience the myriad things is delusion. That the myriad things come forward and experience themselves is awakening.

- Dogen Zenji, Shobo Genzo,

Introduction

Dogen Zenji was responsible for bringing the tradition of the Soto sect of Zen Buddhism from China to Japan. In this pithy, deep comment above on what is genuine enlightenment, there is a deep caution to us about taking our Western worldview that we are individuals separated from everything else and moving by our own understanding and will towards our own realization. Master Dogen invites us to realize a world where everything is a seamless whole and that whole moves in harmony with itself.

There is such a temptation in our culture to manage our spiritual path in a way that reinforces our ego rather than lessening our attachment to it. Time and again I see offerings that will help you achieve a "quantum leap" in your transformation, or that will "turbocharge" your spiritual unfolding. Or some charismatic figure or guru will zap you into spontaneous Nirvana and then you can flaunt your newly gained enlightenment to all your friends! This plays right into the ego's desire to do everything its way, to make enlightenment happen fast and without any effort or sacrifice on our part. By all means, our culture says: let's invent an easy spiritual path so we can have instantaneous ego gratifying enlightenment!

Sometimes a person will have a great letting go experience that will transform their whole lives. For most of us, this possibility of a great enlightenment experience early in our spiritual life is more of a temptation than a real possibility. Fastening onto the possibility of achieving great changes in our lives early in our spiritual practice leaves us open to our ego's ambition directing our choices rather than being led by Spirit.

Probably most of us, left to our own desires, would rather choose what we habitually choose: a boosting of our self esteem, a false security, a painless realization, bliss and consolation without personal effort, enlightenment without true surrender. This is what Dietrich Bonhoffer called Cheap Grace. Let's face it, most of us would rather not face our worst fears - or even to be forgiven for what we cannot forgive ourselves for.

Spiritual practice involves the gradual reorienting of our self centeredness into an open hearted concern for the well being and growth of others as much as for ourselves. The reality is that many of us are too stuck in our self centered dreams (and nightmares) to be able to make wise choices as to what would be best for us, spiritually speaking, at least until we have had some years of dealing with the ups and downs of spiritual practice.

Then we have some basis for our being able to discern what works for us or not. This is why the great traditions of spiritual practice are important for channeling and directing our efforts at Self Realization- at least in the beginning. We need wise teachers and healthy spiritual communities to provide the framework for our spiritual work. Without this we are likely to be led as much by our egos as by true spiritual desire.

It is also the reason why crises that come upon us unbidden and unexpectedly are so often the impetus for our genuine spiritual development. They take us out of our usual comfort zone and plunge us into what our ego defenses have been trying so hard to protect us from. The people pleaser is brought face to face with another's anger and disappointment with them. The spiritual addict, looking for spiritual highs is brought down to earth with the practical issues of learning to support a family in the material world. The ambitious one using accomplishments to ease their sense of unworthiness is brought low by failure. These are not the things that we would have chosen for ourselves, but so often they are exactly what we need to grapple with and eventually surrender to in order to heal the unconscious patterns running us.

Awhile back I had an extremely upsetting situation with a client that lined up with several other challenging experiences in my life at that point. This chain of events took me on a very dark journey to meet my deepest fears. The journey took most of a year to traverse as fear showed up in my face almost every day for me to finally accept and come to embrace and work through. Facing my deepest fears was the last thing I wanted to do and I realize that I have many times resisted facing this fear in my life. I would never have wished this for myself but, in retrospect, it was one of the most valuable learning opportunities of my life. Now I can face my fears with more ease and I can truly be with others who experience terror and I know the feeling from the inside out without myself being frightened of their experience.

Self Reflection & Practice

Cheap Grace is the grace we bestow on ourselves. Cheap Grace is the preaching of forgiveness without requiring repentance, baptism without church discipline, Communion without confession... Cheap Grace is grace without discipleship, grace without the cross, grace without Jesus Christ, living and incarnate."

-Dietrich Bonhoffer

What do you feel you need now to grow spiritually? Reflect carefully on this and journal about it. Use the following questions as a jumping off point. These are not easy questions and there is no right answer to them. In some cases, they cannot be answered outright but rather lived into.

Will what you think you need now in your spiritual practice stretch you or just keep you feeling safe in your usual comfortable spaces? Do they meet a deep longing in you for God or will they just give you some familiar consolation?

Or perhaps you cannot accept yourself as you are and are always looking for further ways to push yourself to attain something? Do you see spirituality as a never ending series of efforts to attain something that seems to perpetually lie outside of your reach? What would it be like to let go of your ambitious goals and to learn to just be with your life, as it is?

What life situations do you tend to avoid out of concern for your spiritual growth? Having children? Engaging in challenging work? Social action? Are your concerns well founded or do they reflect your unconscious conditioning that would be better for you to question and overcome? This is something to keep reflecting upon. Because Life is the greatest teacher and engaged spirituality is probably the best way for you to practice. (It certainly has been for me! Much better than monastic practice was.)

What experiences have been the most impactful for you on your spiritual journey? List them. Which did you have some control over and chose for yourself? Which happened to you unannounced and not chosen and, in wrestling with them, led you to a new understanding? Which gave you the deepest wisdom and compassion? Reflect on this at some length.

Try some spiritual practice that lies outside of your usual comfort zone. See what comes up for you. Welcome whatever shows up and engage with it. This may take you beyond your ideas of who you are and what you need.

Invitation

Let go of trying to maximize your spiritual growth like some kind of investment portfolio. This can be just more of your old self centeredness and more efforts to control your experience the way you want it to be. And anyway, you cannot be sure of what will benefit your growth as a spiritual being. Sometimes hard blows of fate will do more to crack open your hard shell than anything you would have chosen yourself. Other times you are too hard on yourself and letting in the gentle acceptance of yourself opens more doors than all of the discipline that you could possibly impose upon yourself. Let go of trying to make enlightenment happen on your own terms and be open to learning from Life itself.

Of all of the teachers, unconditional, compassionate, wise Love is the best teacher. For with Love as your guide you will be less likely to either play it safe or to abuse yourself. Love leads us out of ourselves but it does not lead us to abandon and abuse ourselves. After Love, Life itself is the best teacher for it will take us to places we otherwise would never think of going, left to our own devices. Life will, if we open to it, take us beyond the confines of our small minds and our limited sense of possibilities.

Show up for your life with Love in your heart and pray to be of service to others. When life presents you with great challenges, surrender (don't give up!) to the Way that will lead you forward, not by your own will, but rather by the intimations of your Soul that is informed by Love. As difficult as your life may be at times, there will be gold in it as you develop deep compassion for others in your own suffering. There is no better way, for suffering, besides Love and Life, is one of our greatest teachers.

And you don't need to go out of your way looking for suffering. If you are encouraged by Love to move outside of your comfort zone, there will be plenty enough of suffering (and adventure and joy) for you. This suffering is not meant to destroy you; it is meant to open your heart and strengthen you spiritually as almost nothing else will. You don't need to play the martyr, either; just show up and do your best.

Do not despair when suffering visits you as it does everyone; it is the great equalizer and the one that teaches us equanimity and compassion. Don't close off to joy either! Some of us believe that we have to cudgel ourselves into submission to the Divine. And that is just as wrong headed as insisting that the path only lead us to continual happiness. As your heart and mind open, there will be more and more joy; that is the gift of Spirit.

You will go through dark times and times of joy on your spiritual journey. These times are all valuable; they will all teach you something. In the dark times you may be tempted to despair and doubt that you aren't following the path correctly. If you are following the path of Love, you are not amiss. And it is when you come out of the darkness that you will begin to appreciate what you learned there; it is hard to see it when you are in darkness. And that is why faith is necessary for your journey, my friend!

Loosening The Grip on Who We Think We Are

One of the greatest challenges we have is to let go of how we see ourselves and the world around us. We are often so deeply conditioned by our childhood experiences and our cultural biases that we are compelled to repeat the same mistakes over and over again in our lives. When we begin to inquire deeply into the nature and truth of our perceptions and reflect upon our behavior, we begin the journey to freedom.

CHAPTER 23

Letting Go of How We See The World

The way you see one thing is the way you see the whole world.

- Richard Rohr

The Mirror	**rorriM ehT**
What you see in the world is you.	WORLD
The world is a mirror that reflects	REFLECTS
back to you who you are -	BACK
or at least who you think you are:	YOUR
good, bad, story and judgment laden.	STORY
But in moments when	MOMENT
the old thought/emotion waves	WAVES
are stilled, you can see clearly.	STILLED
And then what you see IS the world	WORLD
And it is who YOU really are.	IS YOU
	- Robert Cornell

Introduction

The Gates of Perception

Once a long time ago there was a wise old man who sat at the entry gates of a walled city. Each day he would greet visitors who were entering the city and they would ask of him "what are the people of this city like?" And he would reply with a question " What were the people like in the city you have come from?" If they would answer, "Oh they were really bad, selfish people," then he would say to them "Well the people in this city are just like that." When he said this, the visitors would sigh and head off away from the entrance, looking for somewhere else where people were good and trustworthy. If the visitors would reply, "Oh the people in that city were really good people," he would then say, "welcome, you will find the people in this city as good as in the one you left. Please enter."

As a therapist, it never ceases to amaze me how differently we each see the world. It reminds me of the Akira Kurosawa movie *Rashomon* in which a noblewoman, her retainer and a robber each recount the fateful encounter they have with each other in a forest. Each one retells the story of their encounter from their own distorted self centered perspective and you are left to wonder where the truth lies, because their stories are so radically different. You can hardly believe they are talking about the same encounter in the woods. In my therapy work, one of my primary goals is to assist clients in letting go of their limiting interpretations of their lives and to open to more positive and flexible ways of seeing their experience.

In my own life I can see all too clearly at times how my personal mishegas shows up to try to lead me astray. Whether I have a "good" day or a "bad" day is mostly contingent upon which parts of myself I choose to listen to and believe. If I believe the voices of old fears, I will experience a closed off, unhappy, fearful day. If I open myself to the part of me that is Love, I will have a rich and meaningful day with many satisfying connections with my wife, other people, playful pet kittens, singing birds, clients and beautiful flowers. It is my choice! And as I have practiced over the years I can see more and more clearly that I have a choice, day by day, moment by moment as to how my life will unfold.

We think that the way we ordinarily see the world is the TRUTH, that what we see is an objective picture of REALITY. Unfortunately for us, this is seldom so. Far too often we do not see how our way of looking at the world has been distorted and we end up feeling like victims in our own B rated old movie. Our perceptions have been colored and conditioned by our past experiences and by the very structure of our brains. From an evolutionary standpoint, our brains are biased towards remembering negative experiences and protecting us from imagined harm, because that is what would have kept us alive in times past.

In today's world, this bias does not serve us well, for we as a species need to become much more focused on our connections with each other and our connections to the natural world if our civilization is to survive. The time for our living in either our modern individualistic or ancient tribal consciousness with their partial, prejudiced worldviews must come to an end if we are ever to resolve the great problems of our times. Our self centered thinking, be it on the individual, tribal or national level is too limited to solve the problems of world peace, global warming, over population, resource depletion, mass extinction and pollution. Indeed this kind of limited thinking IS the source of our problems.

Vipassana or Insight Meditation is one of the profound spiritual practices that can help us to become increasingly aware of how we distort our personal reality – and to detach from it. In this Buddhist meditation practice, which today is often called "Mindfulness" we develop and strengthen the neutral witness awareness that lies behind all of our experiences, "good" and "bad." As a thought, feeling or perception arises in our consciousness, we simply note it neutrally in our awareness. We don't argue with or buy into it, we just acknowledge it gently and allow it to move on through and out of our consciousness. Over time, this kind of practice begins to free us from our over identification with our all too subjective interpretations and reactions to what is occurring around us.

The value of a practice like Vipassana meditation is that we have a means of developing ongoing, moment by moment awareness of our core beliefs, emotional reactions and impulses as they arise and we gradually increase our ability to note them, not buy into them and not automatically act them out. As we practice seeing and detaching from our habitual patterns of thoughts and feelings, our old defenses and negative ways of seeing things gradually dissolve. We practice day by day, moment by moment being awake and present, watching over our consciousness. There is a good reason why wisdom is called the "Pearl of Great Price." To gain this wisdom, we have to practice diligently and meticulously in each moment if we are to disenthrall ourselves from our old narratives about the world and our life.

I remember my Zen teacher saying that experiences of unitive consciousness are fairly easy to come by but that integrating that experience of oneness with our everyday consciousness was like cutting through the root of the lotus, which is many stranded and difficult to cut. Many people who have meditated for a long time can still have serious character defects. This is one of the problems with an over focus on absorptive types of meditation practices that develop Samadhi (concentrative powers) or bliss states. These practices do not develop the ongoing witness awareness practices that are emphasized in Vipassana Meditation that lead to seeing clearly what arises in our mind when we are not meditating formally.

Self Reflection & Practice

The way we chose to see the world creates the world we see.

- Barry Neil Kaufmann

In answering the following questions for self reflection, try to write them from your gut - not from your head. Your intellectually based answers may very likely be different than your emotionally based answer. The answer that matters in this work is the emotionally based answers, because our emotions are what color our experience and are the real driving force behind so much of our behavior. In journaling an answer to the following questions, you may expose some of your core beliefs that limit you from seeing the inherent beauty of your one precious life:

Journal on the following questions, choosing those that bring up the most reaction in you. Answer from your gut and heart by feeling into these spaces in your body and noticing the visceral reaction going on as you engage the question.

Is the world a safe place for you?

Why is it or why is it not a safe place for you?

What is the biggest fear in your life?

Do you believe you are worthy of love or not? Explain

Are others worthy of your love? Explain.

Are others generally trustworthy and good to cooperate with?

Whom specifically can you trust and can't you trust?

Are there discernable patterns here?

Who are your "enemies"?

This includes people you don't like to be around, people who threaten you in some way, not just the people you hate or fear.

What kind of characteristics do your enemies have in common?

What do you reject in yourself, hate about yourself?

What do you hate or reject in other people?

Is there a connection between these two things - what you dislike in others and in yourself?

What makes you feel uncomfortable around some people? When you feel uncomfortable around someone it can be quite subtle. It could be that they talk too much and you feel stifled. Or they tend to think highly of themselves and you feel insecure. Or for many other reasons. Be astute in looking into what underlies your feelings of discomfort around other people.

Take time to look at each of the people currently in your life and the feelings they bring up in you. Rather than looking at what it is about them that is wonderful or awful, generous or selfish, clever or stupid, etc., look at what feelings they bring up in you. This is what it is valuable to investigate. If you spend your time working their side of the street all the time you will learn little about yourself. And there is much to learn about yourself here!

What do you need to have control of? Make a detailed list. Looking carefully at your list, what on your list is within your reasonable locus of control and what is not? What do you feel responsible for that is outside of your locus of control? What feelings and thoughts come up for you around the issue of control?

IMPORTANT PRACTICE

For a day, go around watching your mind as if you were watching a movie, without getting so engrossed in the action. Gently and without judging yourself, note the judgments your mind makes about people and the situations around you. If you notice how judgmental you are, simply note that without judgment! Notice how much of the time you are judging in your mind (either praising or criticizing) rather than directly perceiving. Remind yourself that any judgments that you make are NOT reality. They are just thoughts.

Watch carefully for what expectations or assumptions come up about people and situations in your daily life. For example, if you meet someone frowning, do you assume they are angry with you? If your lover doesn't call you, do you jump to the conclusion that they no longer love you? If you pay close attention, you will see an almost constant dialogue occurring in your mind about what is going to happen in this circumstance and what is going to happen in that one. Realize that your expectations about what is going to happen in upcoming situations are so often pure projections of your old habitual views that are deeply entrenched in your consciousness. You don't have to argue with them, you merely have to see them for what they are: illusions generated by your survival based mind.

Invitation

When we look through the lens of Love, all is bright, all is joyful, all is compassion. When we look through the lens of Fear and Judgment, everything is distrustful and disturbing.

Love trusts all things. The Universe is its playground. Fear trusts no one and no thing. It is always concerned with its survival.

Love sees everyone and everything as worthy of love. Fear sees nothing to value and care for, many times even itself.

When we see through the eyes of our hearts, there is little that we feel we need to control. Things flow and we flow with them.

Fear on the other hand thinks it needs to control many things and many people in order to satisfy its bottomless need for security.

Love does not shame or try to manipulate. It invites. It makes no demands. Fear uses every weapon at its disposal to get its way.

Love rejects nothing. Fear only accepts that which protects it from its imagined dangers and enemies.

Fear loves to judge and chew on resentment and a desire for revenge, Love will evaluate but refrains from judging, excluding, or retaliating.

Love expands and fear contracts.

Love has no enemies. Fear has myriads of them.

Love sees clearly, Fear is always lost in a haze.

CHAPTER 24

Letting Go of "It's All About Me."

When you're upset, your school is in session.

Dr. Ron Hulnick, University of Santa Monica

Song of the Clueless One

You know how it is. You've seen it before.
You're alright, everything is just fine and dandy-
until some smart aleck comes along and screws it all up.
Just completely screws it up – know what I mean?
I mean, the nerve of that guy!
Who does he think HE is, telling me what to do?
I mean really, who needs some smart ass like him.
I ought to go over there right now and just tell him off.
It always happens to me like this.
I don't get any respect from those types.
What with their superior airs and all,
they just think they're the best.
Oh, hey, where ya going? No, stay awhile.
I've got more to say, see. Lots more. A belly full.
Guys like him have been a pain in my keister
as long as I can remember. Should be a law about them.

– Robert Cornell

Introduction

One of the most useful spiritual practices is the ongoing day-by- day work of watching our reactions to things and containing any temptation to act out unskillfully. Ordinarily we try to do this by being "objective" and trying to keep our emotions under control. We often call this "being professional" or "being an adult" about something that upsets us. This is a good practice, as far as it goes. What we must do if we are to really let go of our self centered viewpoint is to become clearly AWARE of our biases and reactivity, moment by moment and then inquire into what they are about. This is work best done with the emotions as they are experienced in the body.

In the Buddha's story of enlightenment, as he is deeply immersed in the process of attaining enlightenment, Mara the deceiver and creator of all illusions appears to try to prevent Siddhartha (the Buddha-to-be) from overcoming his spell. Mara throws everything he has at Siddhartha to try to distract him from his goal: armies attacking him with flaming arrows, seductive women, etc., etc. And Siddhartha is unmoved by these illusions and awakens through his practice of seeing reality as it is – not as Mara tries to convince him it is. However, throughout the Buddha's life Mara would show up periodically to try to catch him back up in delusion. And the Buddha would see Mara and his machinations and he would say to him, "I see you Mara."

This is exactly the kind of self awareness we need when our own clouds of self centered delusions come out to confuse us. In my own personal life, Mara keeps showing up whispering in my ear the same old, same old, old, old story, "you're not worthy, You're not important. They won't listen to you. They don't take you seriously." This old story from my childhood has caused me no end of pain and vexation in the past and can still trip me up even though by now I have seen this story play out countless times before.

Sometimes my reaction comes out as a kind of anger and arrogance; other times as a fear of being left out, depending upon my state of mind at the time. I find it important to have talks with myself when this happens to "talk myself down." This is critical if I am going to serve others for what is important is not my importance, but those I wish to serve. Frankly, I have to remind myself of this again and again.

It is amazing how deeply seated these old stories from our childhood can be that keep playing out for us in our work places, our families, in our friendships – and yes, even in our churches, mosques, synagogues, dharma centers, etc. Knowing this, it really pays us to be on the lookout to see where Mara is going to show up in our lives. One way that almost never fails in this endeavor is to pay close attention *whenever* we are upset. If we are upset, then most likely we have made a situation into something about us. And if we pay close attention to the patterns of our upsets, these patterns will clearly point out to us where our psycho-spiritual work of inquiry and healing needs to focus.

This work means that over and over again we have to disenthrall ourselves from our melodramas when they are triggered. Sometimes we are blindsided and the old tug of upset feels so real and it is so easy to be suckered in again, even when we know better. I see it all the time in my counseling. Many of my clients are tripped up by their old stories and fall into suffering, anger, blame and judgment. And then they are cut off from the reality that keeps them in touch with their healthy selves. As they gain insight and come to accept themselves more and more, they gradually heal their old soap operas of upset and hurt.

In order to do this kind of work, we need to become aware of how we project our issues onto other people and situations when we get upset. If we are reaming someone out in our mind, then chances are very, very high (like a probability of 99.99%) that they have triggered an old issue of ours that we need to look at. The hotter our anger and judgment, the more likely it is that we have an issue within us to work with. However, anger is a very tempting energy and it feels so good to work someone else's program for them when they have hurt us. But, in doing so we miss the great opportunity to free ourselves from our "it's all about me" stinking thinking.

In Psychology, we study these patterns of projection in much detail. This is one of the places where Psychology has a great deal to offer students of spirituality! What happens in the projective process is that our mind has stored up memories of past hurtful events in what we call implicit memory. When a current situation has some similarity to the past event, it will trigger similar feelings in us.

And the more we react unconsciously to these repetitive events, the deeper we etch the story in our brains and the more likely we will react in similar ways in the future. As we learn to see our old stories and reactions, and as we catch ourselves before we go into full upset, we gradually retrain our brain to be less reactive and more flexible and accurate in its perceptions of things. Life becomes less and less about us and our old stories.

Self Reflection & Practice

You can never know in your mind what you truly want, what it is that will give you release. You can only work to let go, to slough off the universe that you know, the totality of your mind.

Ali Almaas Diamond Heart: Book Four

"Upsetology" – the study of what kinds of situations, what kinds of people upset you and how these are connected to past events in your life - is one of the best ways to gain self awareness and liberate yourself from old wounds and limiting beliefs about yourself and the world. Remember first and foremost that studying where and how you get upset is a key to your own liberation- if you can avoid self judgment! So often what keeps people from focusing on the source of what upsets them is their fear of their own self judgment. So be prepared to offer yourself Self Acceptance and Self Forgiveness when you start being hard on yourself. This will allow you to keep on investigating this vital matter!

IMPORTANT PRACTICE

Keep an ongoing journal of situations that occur in your life that upset you. Usually we want to run past these episodes and put them behind us as soon as we can or we want to go to our friends and tell them how bad someone has treated us and get lots of sympathy. Neither of these helps us to free ourselves from these old stories. Instead, we must try to be as objective as we can as to what actually happened, what we interpreted the event to mean and how we felt. Write down as best you can what in particular was upsetting to you about the events you record in your journal, such as (but not limited to) these issues:

- feeling criticized or ridiculed
- feeling embarrassed or shamed
- feeling ignored or dismissed
- feeling rejected or reprimanded
- feeling threatened or attacked
- feeling abandoned or betrayed
- feeling inferior or unworthy
- feeling ashamed or guilty
- feeling responsible for other's behaviors
- feeling exposed or vulnerable
- feeling sad or depressed
- feeling angry or resentful
- feeling envious or jealous
- feeling afraid or anxious.

As you begin to accumulate information on episodes that were upsetting to you, certain patterns should start to become very apparent. You will have certain kinds of upset feelings again and again. There will be certain kinds of people that tend to upset you. There will be certain kinds of situations that you find trigger you, again and again. Working with these upsetting situations is the very key to your healing and liberation.

If you think back in time while reflecting on a current upsetting scenario, you will more than likely connect that situation up with past upsetting events. Sometimes the realization that you are conflating a current situation with a painful childhood experience is enough to free you from the spell. However, if you find that you often get pulled back into painful emotions with these situations it will serve you well to have a therapist to help you clarify and heal these old patterns.

Once you become aware of the wound in you, it presents an opportunity for you to move towards that wound and to heal it, not away from it or projecting it outward as we usually do. For instance, if you find yourself slipping into depression when someone criticizes you, rather than reacting angrily to what they said to you, start moving towards yourself with loving compassion and being present with the feeling and thoughts inside you. Explore the thoughts that accompany the feelings. With depression, there are almost surely self judgments present regarding (supposed) unworthiness, lack of intelligence, lack of personal attractiveness, etc., etc. As you become clearer about these self judgments, practice Self Forgiveness (see Chapter 5).

IMPORTANT PRACTICE

Practice developing a relationship to a Higher Power, an Inner Wisdom part of you, that you can consult with inside yourself when you get caught up in your old pain. You can do this in a meditative state by going into your loving heart center and consulting with that part of yourself that is connected to Love and clear of your egoic reactivity. Let this part of you lovingly talk you down from your upset. Let it talk kindly to your hurting self. Let it remind you gently of what is important to you in the long run. Let it remind you that your old childhood reactions don't serve you well now. Let your Inner Wisdom encourage you to let be and to let go.

The ultimate healing comes from just being non-reactively present with the upset within you, being completely lovingly present with it in your body. This is the very last thing we humans want to do. We are afraid that, if we don't DO something, we will be lost and swallowed up in the excruciating feelings of rage, abandonment, despair, terror, etc., etc. But if we are willing to just be present with these feelings, they gradually morph into an inner calm, strength and presence. This is complete surrender; this is the Cross, and this is the Resurrection that follows.

Invitation

The price of freedom is vigilance.

-Leonard H. Courtney

Be aware, and you will find your freedom. Never take things at face value when you are reactive. Always question: is this really true for me? Chances are Mara the deceiver and spinner of tales has laid a trap for you again. Old stories lie all about you underfoot but your awareness can show them up. The upset comes and tries to hook you: in your neck, your shoulder, your gut or your heart. And then Mara tries to reel you in and land you in a big net of confusion and pain. But you can finally see the hook and anticipate the pain and you don't let the old story hook you and drag you off into another passion play of your victimhood.

You have seen this One many times before, you know Him intimately. You know this is Mara and you let the hook pass you by. You have no need to go down the slippery slope of believing your feeling/thought patterns and falling into the pain body again. You can let be and let go and swim off to freedom. And you can be grateful to yourself, your teachers and healers and to God or your Higher Power for leading you to this place of freedom and healing. And if you get hooked again and fall into the pain body, accept it and let be and let go again and again, as long as it takes. Do not be discouraged when you are hooked by illusion. It is in the nature of us humans to need many repetitions to fully get the lesson, to heal and let go.

When you finally let go of all beliefs about who and what you are, Mara can find no place to set his hook. Without these old core beliefs, there is no place for the hook to catch and generate more reaction and more stories. In your awareness all experience floats in and floats out without your reaction to it. In this there is profound freedom.

CHAPTER 25

Letting Go. Accepting Change

Surfing the Wave

Surf's up, the big waves come rolling in.
   Paddle out on your board to meet them.
         If you stay on shore you'd be safer,
      but it wouldn't be so much fun!
         When you meet the wave, don't hesitate long.
Turn your board and head down the crest.
   Get up and ride!
      If you hesitate, you'll miss the wave-or wipe out.
            Surf's up! Are you coming in?

- Robert Cornell

Introduction

The fundamental truth about life is that it is constant change.

- the Buddha

Life is always changing for us, whether we like it or not. So...we might as well go with the flow. But when a big change is coming in our lives, so often we start fearing what is going to happen and anxiously plotting how we can stay put: safe, secure, knowing who we are and what is expected of us. Even if we aren't that happy with our situation and our role in it, at least it's familiar and predictable. The devil we know seems so much safer and more desirable than the devil we don't know.

Can we learn to trust that life will carry us forward if we will just let it move us along and we allow ourselves to move with it? So often in my own life things have happened that might seem bad at first but that have taken me on new and wonderful adventures. When I was a young man I went through a painful divorce with my first wife and I was quite depressed about that and being separated from my three year old daughter. I felt like a total failure and wondered if I would ever be able to find another person to love.

At that time, I worked in a talcum powder factory as a quality control technician. The work was dusty, boring and very noisy because, besides the aptly named Hurricane mills and the grinders used to process the talc minerals into powder, the factory was literally situated underneath the overhead intersection of the Santa Ana and Santa Monica Freeways in a very gritty industrial section of Los Angeles. While I disliked the monotony of my work and the noise and dust of the factory, I had formed working friendships with some of the men, including John the stoic old, big nosed foreman who seemed perpetually covered head to toe with talcum powder like a fine snow.

And it was security. At least I had a job and could pay my bills and my child support for my daughter Annalisa. At that time I had really wanted to learn to play classical Indian music on the violin and I would go outside of the plant and try to practice under the freeways on lunch breaks. Then I was fired. It was painful, but I got through it and, in the long run, it was a blessing. While I didn't realize it at the time, the management had put me out of my misery by forcing me out of a job that I disliked and only held onto because of a steady paycheck. Afterwards, I dusted myself off literally and figuratively. I continued my Zen studies, became a Zen monk, and later started my own landscape business. But that's another story!

Without change, our lives would be very boring, but when things change around us we lose the sense of predictability and control over our lives. Our ego sees this as threatening; it does not like things happening outside of its control. It has familiar roles that it plays that are very near and dear to it even if they are no longer satisfying and sometimes even downright painful to us. So often we prefer the familiar to what would be really good for us. We allow safety and predictability to trump something fresh coming into our lives. And then we grouse about our boss at work, our spouse or our lot in life. Dare to live. Dare to grow into the unknown that lies before you. You're going to die anyway so why not take a chance now while you are still alive?

Most of us are aware of the worry wart part of our mind that frets constantly over any change and what it portends. This is what causes many of us to stay in safe but unsatisfactory situations far too long. But sometimes Life does us a favor like it did me in firing me from my talcum powder job and we don't have a choice but to go with the changes. Thank God! But then the ego starts to worry about what it will do and how it will survive. And because the ego is wrapped up in a limiting story of who it is and what the world is like, it only operates out of this very limited stance.

When change occurs, one trick our ego can play on us is to lead us down into self blame and feelings of unworthiness. Perhaps we have been laid off or fired, and then we mope about rather than being open to the new opportunities opening up before us. While we may have responsibility for many events in our lives, and it is a healthy step to look at our part in them, notions of over responsibility are not helpful. This is true in what is called New Age guilt where the belief is that you create everything that happens to you in life. This type of magical thinking can lead us to self judgment but not to constructive action because the cause and effect relationships have been based on false views.

Or the ego may want to blame others and stay in a resentful victim mode. We are then stuck in a low energy pattern of resentment and wanting sympathy from others and we don't want to take responsibility for our life and move on. Without a sense of our agency that comes from a sense of responsibility (literally meaning the ability to respond) we will have a hard time getting out of our victim rut and responding to the changes.

Another thing that can cause us to fight change is our over concern for social status and the approval of others. Sometimes the change we are invited into seems to be taking us into a lower social status. We might have a high paying job that has little real social worth but we really want to do something that makes a difference. Do we hold back and feel guilty for our cowardice or do we buck the common wisdom about money and status and listen to our hearts? Please take it from someone who has often followed his heart and not the need for security and status that the leap of faith is always worth it! Regardless of the outcome, for nothing is guaranteed. By taking the leap of faith you are building your trust in the universe and something good will come of it.

Today there is a great deal of fear about losing one's job and not finding another one. There is so much holding back out of concern for one's survival. But that can kill the soul. Many years ago both my wife and I made choices for new possibilities in our work lives. She became a teacher and I became a therapist. For both of us, these new vocations entailed years of graduate studies while working full time. The price of having newness in our lives is often much extra work in retooling for a new career. The payoff for this may be years away so it is important to have a positive vision for what is possible. It is important to have faith in yourself and to keep in mind the positive outcomes of these changes.

Self Reflection & Practice

Life is a constant invitation to let go and flow with life rather than resist it in all its manifold changes.

What changes in your life do you see you as invitations? What changes do you see as being forced upon you? Can you see how you frame the issue either as invitation or as being coerced makes for a different response in yourself to the changes coming? How could you reframe your perception of the changes you face? Journal on this.

Where in your life are you wanting change but not moving ahead? How are you cooperating with the changes? How are you resisting them? What is the voice of fear telling you about these changes? What is the voice of curiosity / passion / love saying to you in your other ear? Journal on these concerns and issues.

What keeps you holding back from making the changes you need to make in your life or cooperating with the changes coming? Worries about financial security? Concerns about loss of status and power? The fear of uncertainty? The desire for stability and familiarity? Self doubt? What? Journal on this.

What possible good things could come out of the changes coming in your life? Be sure to write them down and keep this list posted where you can see it as you go through these changes to keep reminding you of the good that could come from them.

Journal regularly on what your dreams are for a better future. Let yourself picture in words what you passionately want to do with your life. Let Love draw you forward. Enthusiasm is a far, far better motivator than resentment and focusing on what you don't like about your present life! Let any unhappiness with your current situation be put into your determination to find what will give you satisfaction.

Ask yourself each day how you could cooperate with the changes coming. Keep a list of "To Do" items that could move you forward with the changes coming. Keep this list visible and do something on the list at least once per week. When you accomplish something on your list, check it off and give yourself credit for taking a step forward.

Keep in touch with your resistance. Don't make it the enemy! It is very tempting to want to attack it and push against it. Instead, allow yourself to be present with it. At first this might be on the mental level, where you just spin out in negative "what ifs". Move below this level into the body and into the feelings below these thoughts. Feel into your body where the fear is: the heart and the fear of loss of connection; the gut and the fear of survival. Sense into it more deeply and be willing to be present compassionately. When you are willing to do this the resistance will eventually melt away. But not necessarily on your time table! Be patient and persistent.

Invitation

The price of risk is possible failure; the payoff is aliveness and a rich life. The price of keeping things safe is inevitable boredom; the payoff is avoiding what probably wasn't going to happen anyway.

Perhaps you have been playing it safe for far too long. If you are feeling frustrated, bored and uninspired this is likely so. It would be better to take the steps yourself before Life kicks you in the butt out the door. But if it comes to that, don't try pushing your way back through the door because you will likely then be sorely disappointed. Pick yourself up, dust yourself off and move on. When one door closes another opens; as long as we are willing to go through it, all will be well.

Life sometimes knows much better than we do what would be for our greater good. Trust Life for it will lead you on magnificent adventures! Don't grasp the steering wheel of Life so tightly. Relax and enjoy the journey. Don't be too concerned about status, wealth, security, or other narrow concerns. Life will be far more interesting if you don't attach so much meaning to these things!

Letting go of your old roles: mother suffering empty nest syndrome, longtime employee being let go, spouse leaving a loveless, abusive marriage, expert who knows their field like the back of their hand but is now bored with it. All of your frustrations, unrealized dreams and hopes for the future are your motivators for new growth, new directions in your life. Let them carry you through your fears, your resistance and holding back.

Acknowledge your fears and resistance in leaving the familiar landscape of your life. Don't fight with them, simply acknowledge their presence and keep moving on towards your unknown tomorrow. If they importune, listen more deeply in your body to them, for there is gold in this vein to be mined. You will become aware of the limiting beliefs holding you back so you can work at letting them go. Let yourself go with trust and faith into the mystery of your future; you will survive. And thrive!

And, if you sail with the currents of change and follow the compass of your passions, you will reach the shore of a new land of promise. The landscape on that shore may be less familiar, but the fruit you will find there will be sweeter and more nourishing for your Soul. Do you have a vision of how your life might be different but you have never given yourself permission to pursue it? Well, now is the time! Listen to your dreams, listen to the envy you have had of others doing what you only dreamed of doing. Own your own dreams and give up your envy!

This is your life and the time for action is NOW, not sometime in the future. If you keep waiting, holding back, and resisting, your life will very likely hit you again with more changes anyway. Don't wait like a victim; trust the changes coming and go with them! Trust, trust, ride the currents of change for they will take you to a better place for your soul.

CHAPTER 26

Letting Go of Plan A

To make God laugh, tell Him about your plans.

– Woody Allen

You Never Know

A rabbi in 19th century Russia was crossing the city square on an errand when a Cossack rode up on his horse and demanded, "Jew, where are you going?" To which the rabbi ingenuously replied," I don't know." The Cossack was incensed, thinking that the rabbi was insulting his intelligence. "What do you mean, you don't know, Jew? Do you think I'm so stupid I'm going to believe that?" Then the Cossack got down from his horse, tied the rabbi up, tethered him to his horse and took the rabbi off to jail. And the rabbi said with a sigh as he was being led off, "You see, you never know."

Inroduction

The story above is a dark one, and is based on the anti-Semitic persecutions of the Jewish people in Slavic countries during the 18th and 19th centuries. The Jews have had this gallows humor for a long time to make light of their afflictions. They came from a small country in the ancient world that was the doormat of Middle Eastern ancient history with one empire after another steamrolling over them. And this pattern continued for them in many places where they came to live. So it should be no surprise that a story like this should be enjoyed among them with a certain sardonic self mocking humor. We may ask: isn't this nihilistic, too dark? Many of us now buy heavily into the optimism of "think it to be true and it will be so." But reality doesn't cooperate with this rather naïve view. Perhaps it would be better if we could be a bit more humble and just make plans and not be so attached to the outcome.

Of course, it is good to make plans. We need them to be able to have a life that has some order and purpose to it. But some of us tend to overthink and over plan and then get upset when things don't go the way we thought they would (or should). We get locked into a PLAN for our life, strive to accomplish it and when Life says, "No," or we feel a "No" inside ourselves, we fall into depression, hopelessness, resentment or even rage. If we stay stuck in this place, feeling like we have been betrayed by Life or we have failed at life, we can spend a long time in the darkness. When we can let go of our Plan A and listen more deeply to Life, then we have the opportunity to open our eyes and see other possibilities for our future.

Often when Life says, "No" it is because we are supposed to go in a different direction. We don't see this and we spend a great deal of time being frustrated, angry and resentful. When we stay in the narrow mindset of Plan A, limited by our fixed ideas about ourselves and our possibilities, we find ourselves in a dark place of envying others their success and staying in a victim mentality. If instead we could expand our vision of what is possible for us, we would see that we were being guided in a different direction that is more aligned with who we really are.

In my own life, I had the good fortune at the end of my undergraduate program to earn a full National Science Foundation scholarship to go to the California Institute of Technology to study theoretical physics on the graduate level. After several months there it became painfully clear to me that I wasn't cut out to do that kind of very abstract mathematically based work and I dropped out. I left quite depressed and I went back home feeling like my life purpose had come to an end.

I was only 22 so I had little perspective on life and I was too caught up in issues of low self esteem and self doubt to be able to handle this turn of events with anything like acceptance and openness to other possibilities for my life. Now with almost 50 years of perspective, I can be thankful that my life went in a very different direction that is much more in alignment with who I have become. And I am much more flexible when change comes now.

More recently, I was working at a prestigious design school counseling talented students, which seemed like a great way for me to expand my therapy career. Then my contract was not renewed. I moped and felt bad for about a day and then felt... relieved. I realized in retrospect that I wasn't suited to the kind of brief therapy strategies used at the school and they had done me a favor. A saying came to me that somehow deeply resonated within me: When one door closes, another one opens. That night I sat down and began to write this book. Without the time that I now had I might never have started, for I had no idea I was pregnant with a book. And yet as I have written it, the writing has just come.

Many of us are led to think that we should have a clear idea of what we want to do for work in early adulthood and that we should move ahead rapidly towards our goals of financial, social and marital success. The trouble with this scenario is that we often take time to grow up and, as we do, our vision of life changes and our old familiar goals need to change with these new perspectives and new values. This is especially true when we come to mid life and we find that the work that we chose in young adulthood no longer has the same meaning for us. With growing maturity, our own self importance seems a less attractive motivation and the desire to love and serve others becomes, for those of us who choose to grow up, more of our focus.

It is a brave and important endeavor then to step into the current of change and to move in a very different direction that is not based upon ego. Now that we have the real chance of living into our eighties and nineties in good health, it becomes even more important that we allow ourselves to be open to the question of what would be meaningful work for us in our elderhood. With the wisdom of age comes a much greater opportunity to make a positive difference in our corner of the world. It is not new technology that is going to save us from ourselves, it is the accrued wisdom of our elders that has the potential to lead us in better directions.

Self Reflection & Practice

Never be afraid to trust an unknown future to a known God.

-Corrie ten Boom

In what situations when your Plan A has failed has your mind gone wild with worry, spinning one negative scenario after another about what will happen to your life? In what situations in the past have you rushed to beat yourself up and disparage your ever being successful? Were your worst fears in fact borne out? How helpful was all that worry for you in moving on with your life? Reflect and journal on this.

Are there other kinds of disappointments that you have readily adapted to? What might be the difference between those you can be flexible and relaxed with and those that are challenging for you to adapt to? Are there underlying limiting beliefs that caused this difference in your response? If so, what would they be? Journal on this.

Can you let go of your Plan A and welcome plan B? If not, what are you telling yourself? That you failed at plan A so you are a miserable stupid failure and you won't be able to succeed at anything? That plan B is impossible or impractical? That you would be ashamed of doing Plan B because it has lower social status? That you can't make a living doing Plan B? That your family or friends would laugh at you? Write about what keeps you from accepting Plan B when it shows up in your life. With this written down look at your premises carefully and think with your heart (not your head.) Putting your hand on your heart, ask yourself: is what I have been telling myself really true?

Feel into your body when contemplating Plan B: what comes up for you as you do this? Where is the constriction, the pain, the resistance in your body? Sense into it and tease out its fears, its ambivalence. What old story is it running? Can you find some release of the tension and the story?

Allow yourself to think positively about pursuing Plan B. Be aware of when you start going negative and see if you can persevere, thinking creatively about Plan B until you come to some kind of positive resolution about Plan B.

Invitation

Have you been beating your head against a brick wall now for some time with plan A? Are you being nobly persistent or just plain stubborn and stupid? Sometimes it's hard to tell; one good clue is how much your head hurts from butting against the brick wall! Perhaps it's time to think anew. Perhaps it's time to sit down on the grass, take a breath and relax. Then Plan B may show itself after you become less obsessed with your treasured plan A!

So often, we think we know what we are supposed to do but Life doesn't cooperate with us. It has other ideas for us. We may put our ladder up against a wall and assiduously climb only to find out that we put the ladder up against the wrong wall. How do we know what is the right path for us? It usually takes some unlearning of what has been driving us unconsciously. The more we are able to let go of what doesn't serve us, the more likely we are to find our Way.

Life is a constant lesson if we let go of judgment and are open to learning. There is no ultimate failure, just the opportunity to learn to trust more and more to Life's flow. Listen to your Life and be open to what shows up on your doorstep. It might be a crying child. A grand idea to implement. A melody. A desire for justice. Being fired from a job. A divorce. A death. A business breakthrough. Not getting the promotion you wanted. Being offered another job. A new love. Life is short so please be open to what it offers you and take risks!

CHAPTER 27

Letting Go of Over Responsibility

Some of us feel that we are responsible for holding up the sky. I don't think that God appreciates us trying to take over that job from Her. And if we find we need help doing it, She probably won't be inclined to come to our aid.

Introduction

Some of us seem to carry the world around on our backs. We think that we are the only ones who can take care of things. We lack the trust that others are as competent or responsible as we are so we won't delegate to them. Underneath these beliefs and behaviors there is often another layer: that without our self sacrifice, others would not love us. That there is no one who will be there for us; we are all alone and it is all up to us. Often with those of us who are over responsible, there is a shadow side: an angry martyr that resents others for their lack of support that comes out when we are exhausted by our self imposed exertions.

Typically, the over performing martyr complex is inculcated in a child when they grow up in a family where one or both parents are dysfunctional and incapable of giving their children what they need. It may be a situation of extreme abandonment where the parents are addicted or have serious psychological problems. Or, the parents may just be self involved. It is often the oldest daughter or son who will be pulled in to take care of their siblings to make up for the lack of parental care.

My client Sarah was a person who suffered from this superwoman/martyr complex. Her father was an emergency room physician who worked long hours and when he came home from the hospital, he would pour himself a stiff drink and zone out. Her mother was a socialite who didn't really want to be burdened with caring for her four children and so Sarah was drafted to be the substitute mother for her three younger siblings.

While Sarah has the stamina of an ox, the perseverance to move mountains and is super successful in her career, she finds that she is attracted to needy men like "a whore to crack." As we worked together in therapy, the needy little girl in her could finally come forward and be nurtured. Finally, she could learn to be there for herself and to honor her own needs. Then the dysfunctional men she had dated no longer were attractive to her and she found a real, healthy relationship with a man who could care for her as well as she could care for him.

In other situations, the child learns to feel responsible for the well being of others in the family. Perhaps the father was abusive to the mother and the boy child grew up feeling responsible for protecting his mother from the father. Or the child grows up in a loveless home where they feel they have to earn their parents love through constant performance. These children are all vulnerable to growing up to be caretakers of future spouses and familes and finding it very difficult to honor their own needs and to maintain healthy boundaries with others.

Over responsibility shows up in our spirituality quite often from the standpoint that we feel there is no time for a spiritual life. We are too busy taking care of the needs of others for us to enjoy such a luxury. When we do try to take time out to pray or go on a retreat, we feel guilty and selfish. And our spiritual life, at least what we permit ourselves to have, may be suffused with guilt and a sense of shame for not living up to what is expected of us. Not uncommonly, we are likely to find ourselves in religious environments where guilt and shame are used by the spiritual leaders of the community to maintain control.

I once had a client who worked many hours overtime on her job although that was not a requirement of her work. She felt that she wasn't fast enough in getting her work done, so she would work several hours past quitting time and then bring work home with her to finish for a couple hours more after dinner. I could never break through her sense of inadequacy and when I suggested it would be good for her to have a spiritual life as well as her work life, she told me she didn't have time to pray enough so that she could do it right. This is how badly the sense of not being good enough can undermine any inclination to spiritual practice.

Fatigue and resentment can sometimes be helpful ways to get below the surface of over responsibility and to contact the martyr below who seethes at being asked to do so much. And below the anger may lie the loneliness and sadness of an abandoned child. For those of us who are over responsible, it is critical that we can take time to contact these vulnerable feelings and learn to become our own nurturing parent. We need to learn to pull back from our over involvement and guilt and to feel below the surface of our minds to contact the feelings of emptiness and fatigue residing in our bodies.

Those of us who are over responsible are good at staying on the mental level, always consulting our To Do lists for the next thing that needs to be done. When we begin to feel into our bodies, into the fatigue, resentment, and sadness sitting there unacknowledged, we begin to go below the surface and to get in touch with our real selves, layer after layer.

Self Reflection & Practice

What is your relationship with your self like? Are you kind to yourself? Are you a reliable caretaker for yourself? Or do you have a pattern of burning out and harboring resentments towards those in your life who you feel take advantage of you and don't appreciate you for what you contribute? Journal about this.

IMPORTANT PRACTICE

Take time from your busy life to go on a weekend retreat where you are not responsible for anything. Bring no books to read, no phones, computers, etc. No entertainment and no To Do Lists. Let yourself slow down and reside in your body. Sense any buried feelings that may surface and allow yourself to contact them in your body. Do you sense a deep feeing of exhaustion? A resentment and sense of hopelessness about your lot in life? Feeling put upon by those around you? A deep sadness and a sense of being all alone in the world? Give a voice to those parts of yourself that you probably have not listened to in the past. Invite them to come forward and with free form writing just let them speak of their fears, hurts and concerns.

Keep an eye out for the following issues to arise when you try to cut back on your responsibilities: You have the impulse to step right in and take something over for another person when you perceive them not "doing it right." Watch out when you feel guilty that you are not doing enough. Watch out for the belief that it is all up to you. Watch out for feelings of guilt, unworthiness, inadequacy and shame. They will probably surface as you try to consciously slow down and stay more balanced. Allow the feelings. Just don't act on them. They will not kill you!

Invitation

You are not here to hold up the sky. The sky can do quite an adequate job by itself. And if you try, no one is going to applaud you for trying. Mostly they will think you are nuts to try.

You are not here to rescue others from themselves. Your primary job is to take care of yourself and let others be the adults they should be in their own lives.

You are not responsible for meeting the needs of all the people in your life all of the time. That is actually an impossible task. Not even God does that. Mostly He lets people step up to the plate for themselves. So are you arrogant enough to think that you are better than God?

Your spouse and children will not die if they are expected to do things for themselves. It might actually be good for them. Who knows, they might even come to appreciate you more when you aren't their resentful slave! God did not ask you to be a martyr. You demand that of yourself. And mostly others don't ask you to do it either. But they will take you for granted if you volunteer to be a martyr. And don't ask them for sympathy for your martyrdom. Most likely they already sense you playing a martyr and resent you for it!

You are a human being, not a human doing. Remember that when you are tempted by guilt and fear to rush into action. Learn to be present with no agenda, my dear. Learn to rest without guilt or if need be even with guilt. Rest in your heart and wait for the Lord to enfold you in His / Her arms. You have been far too busy and S(He) has been chasing you all around. Stop long enough for Her/Him to catch up with you! Don't just do something, sit there.

CHAPTER 28

Letting Go of Efforting

I Am Enough

I have my rest in you, my Beloved.
For I know that in your loving I am enough.
There is nothing more that I need to do,
for I am fulfilled today in You, my Dearest
This day has time enough in it
for me to do what I need to do.
Whatever is left undone, can be done tomorrow.

I am enough and no longer need to rush around,
desperately trying to prove myself.
My steps follow each other, one after another
as I do what is to be done today.
And I rest in deep gratitude for the peace
that I have come to in You.

-Robert Cornell

Introduction

There is really no such thing as trying; it is an extra concept that just gets in the way of doing something directly and without making a fuss about it. When doing something, just do it. Don't strain and make a face; that is energy very poorly spent. Just do it.

This is a chapter for you efforters. You know who you are. You get uptight at test time and in other high stakes situations. You often doubt your abilities and you worry about failing. We live in a highly individualistic performance based society that sees personal worth as very much tied to your social status, what you own, what you look like and what you have accomplished. There is something good about encouraging individual initiative and being industrious. But for some of us, this becomes our one and only concern, our sole indicator of self worth and it becomes a heavy burden rather than an effective motivator. It is based on our firm belief in the individual self, which is both an overdone story and a dangerous distortion of the basic reality of our world which is that everything is incredibly and wonderfully interconnected.

For efforters it is common when the stakes are high and we want to concentrate on something and get it done fast, that we stiffen up, frown, and take on a kind of grim visage. This is what I call "efforting." Actually, from my own experience, the most effective way to work is being fairly relaxed and staying present with what I am doing. In so much of life I suspect that many people effort because they suffer under the false belief that it makes them more effective. And this efforting pattern may be completely unconscious and just takes over by force of habit. The more pressure we are under to perform, the more likely we will start efforting.

The stress of efforting shows up in our bodies not only on our faces but also in tension we hold in our necks and shoulders. When we are walking under this stress condition, we tend to lean forward and our head and neck go out in front of us as if we are trying to force ourselves forward into the future in an attempt to go faster. We may also have a sinking feeling or a knot in our stomach as if our future survival rides upon this very project that we are working on.

All the physical symptoms generated by this performance stress, such as headaches, neck and shoulder pain and gastrointestinal problems are our body's way of calling attention to its plight. The body can only exist in the present moment and, as we effort and try to force it into the future, it protests by these very unpleasant sensations. And if we continue to ignore the symptoms, they only get worse. We get better as we attend to the underlying thoughts and feelings of inadequacy and fear and start to let ourselves s.l.o.w d.o.w.n..

We develop tunnel vision as we become more and more focused on our efforting. Then many sources of inspiration, hunches or intuitions, and any information that lies outside of our focus (but nevertheless relevant and valuable) become lost to us because of our over preoccupation and anxiety to "get it done and get it done RIGHT." We become automatons and lose our creativity and ability to think outside of the box. The solution to all of this narrowing and tightening is to stop at some point and allow ourselves to feel our anxiety and to begin to question the overall picture of ourselves and our world that underlies our fixation on performance.

On the mental level, what underlies efforting are the beliefs that we hold about our lack of competence and that our sense of worthiness and acceptance is contingent upon our capability to produce, to be "successful." The more we doubt our competence and the more our self worth is tied to our productivity, the more likely we will be to effort - especially when the stress is on for a test, a big project we are responsible for, etc. The Pusher part of us also may want to show others who have doubted us that we can do what they doubted we were capable of. "I'll show them!" the Pusher says as it determines to succeed.

When we look at the inner voices or parts of our consciousness that underlie our efforting we often find the Child that feels inadequate, the Perfectionist, the Inner Critic, the Pusher, and the Worry Wart at work. The Perfectionist and the Inner Critic are both concerned about getting it right and work in tandem with each other. The Pusher is there to overcome any doubt or other obstacle to attaining the goal. It will often voice things like "You have got to get this done NOW." And the Worry Wart gives voice to our fears and self doubt. All of these voices tend to feed off each other and work together. The Worry Wart fears not getting the project done in time and then the Pusher comes in and pushes us to work faster, harder, and longer past our fatigue and doubts.

What happens with the steely determination of the Pusher, the Perfectionist and other parts of our efforting personality is that the Inadequate Child is overlooked and abandoned, so the wound of inadequacy is never paid attention to and healed at the source of the issue. Thus we can effort and achieve for decades without ever healing the actual issue. Instead we just put off for today our feelings of failure and inadequacy through our over zealous efforts. We will go from one crisis to another narrowly averting the catastrophe of failure and shame, feeling stressed out and empty.

We efforters are big on goals; we like them because they give us something to shoot for that holds out the elusive promise of finally being okay with ourselves. And they promise to fill up the emptiness and inadequacy we feel inside. But for us efforters, once a goal is accomplished, no matter how well done, we will often dismiss the accomplishment and set up another goal to direct our energies towards. And our self esteem is again held hostage to the new goal. Forget the implicit deal we had worked out with ourselves that the last goal would do it for us! Rather than accomplishing the goal resulting in a bump up in our self esteem, it just averts failure this one time. And sometimes, achieving a goal can even feel like a let down if we have been using the goal to motivate and feel good about ourselves.

Quite some time ago, when I passed my licensing test to become a therapist after seven long years of study and internships, rather than celebrating, I went into a long funk, feeling sad and listless. I had achieved a wonderful long-term goal, but now, without another goal to accomplish, I felt lifeless and I slipped into a low level depression. It took me six months to let go of the ennui and to let it be okay for me to just show up each morning in my therapy work with an open heart. Truth be told, I am still a goal oriented person, writing this book being an example of this drive. Perhaps now my motivation has become more organic and I take enjoyment more in the process. I don't hold the jury out on my being okay until the next goal is reached.

For those of us who effort, valiantly trying to fend off our feelings of unworthiness and low self esteem, there hopefully will come a time when we tire of this journey. We become weary of the endless Sisyphean effort to push our heavy boulder of self esteem back up the hill, with goal after goal to reach and never a moment to rest. Then perhaps we will welcome the fatigue and the sense of inadequacy that we have tried to fend off for so long and be willing to mend our relationship with ourselves.

There is a very insidious kind of spiritual workaholism that can drive the spiritual practitioner into more and more difficult and even harmful types of spiritual practices. Underneath this supposed meritorious behavior dwells a deep insecurity in the practitioner about whether or not they are really good enough. If they experience a set back or a rejection in regard to their sense of vocation, they can be thrown into a compulsive pattern of intense efforting to be good enough, spiritual enough, enlightened enough, etc., etc.

This can be very confusing to them as they feel they must practice harder and harder, yet when they do, they feel further alienated from themselves, their True Self and from God. For them, the way back to sanity is to be able to feel the pain they have caused themselves in their misguided efforts and finally to let go of their intense and fruitless efforts to be "more spiritual." And to practice self acceptance and the acknowledgement that they are good enough, though in no sense perfect. And that is okay.

Can we begin to move towards the Child within us that feels so very inadequate? Can we just be with our sense of inadequacy and not be driven on again and again to prove our worthiness and our competency? Can we allow ourselves to feel the depression that comes with letting go, of realizing the futility of our desperate efforts ? Paradoxically, this is the way to healing. And this is how we begin to mend our relationship with God, a God who does not require this endless, exhausting performance from us. God is found in Being, but the efforter has no knowledge of Being.

Efforters know only a frantic doing that is motivated by fear; fear of failure, rejection, and ostracism. Until efforters can let go of their frantic efforts to live up to their internalized expectations of themselves and allow themselves to just sit with their sense of emptiness and unworthiness, they cannot know Being. When they finally allow themselves to rest in this uneasy vulnerable place, then they can let down and rest in His/Her loving arms. And, maybe, cry. Cry out of relief that they don't have to effort so much. Cry out of sadness for how hard the journey has been for them. And final to rest in being itself, just as they are. No more and no less.

Self Reflection & Practice

Faith does not need to push the river because faith is able to trust that there is a river. The river is flowing. We are in it.

- Richard Rohr

Think on times when you have been very relaxed and involved in your work and you found that the time ran by quickly. You were creative, productive, and got your project done with ease and on time. What were the factors that helped you to enter into this kind of easy work flow? How did you feel or think in terms of self esteem, self confidence? What was your prior estimation of your ability to perform the task? Were you doubtful or confident? What was your relationship like at the time with others who love and accept you? What was your relationship with God, the Beloved, True Self like?

On what is your self esteem based? Loving connections with others? A loving connection with God / True Self? On past accomplishments? Status? Possessions? Awards and recognition? A reputation as the go-to person to get things done? Your pride in being a helpful and responsible person? Think about the basis of your self confidence and self esteem and what helps you to avoid performance anxiety. Which of them are most like bed rock, keeping you calm under fire? Which are ephemeral and not based upon reality?

Has the basis of your self esteem and motivation changed over the years? If it has, how so? Do you think the basis of your motivation and self esteem has improved over the years or has it gotten worse? What do you ascribe that to?

What kind of Inner Voices do you have around the issue of performance? What kind of Inner Voices show up when you feel that you are "under the gun?" A Pusher who cracks the whip, telling you what you have to get done and spurring you on and on? An Inner Critic that heaps negative comments on you? A Worrier who is continually thinking about the possibility of failing? A Perfectionist that obsesses about getting it all right? An aware and Present One capable of keeping perspective and overseeing the project and carrying it through to the end? A quiet voice of Self Confidence?

Look inside and see if you have any voices like these or perhaps something similar. Remember that you can become aware of and detached from the negative voices and their stories about who you are and what you are afraid of. This is where awareness practice comes into play. You might want to journal regarding some of these voices that tend to dominate your consciousness when you have a project that is important to you. Try dialoguing with one of these voices in your journal. Write back and forth between yourself and the voice until you come to some kind of resolution.

What kind of negative feelings come up for you when faced with performance pressure? Think about this and list them vertically on a piece of lined paper. Then across from each emotion try to come up with what belief is associated with it. For example, Emotion : Fear. Worry: I'm not going to get this done on time. The boss is going to fire me.

Let yourself be with the negative feelings when you are feeling pressured. Remember to breathe. Watch out for the thought patterns that swirl around the feelings, each feeding the other. Try to come back to the feelings in the body as your touchstone on reality: this is what is happening NOW. Thoughts about future failure or punishment are only figments of your imagination.

Remember to slow down and back off a little when you find yourself efforting. See how it feels to catch yourself efforting like this and to let go of the anxious thoughts and the inner struggle. You might find it very rewarding and self reinforcing. As with any fear based behavior, practice being present compassionately with the fear underlying your efforting when you let go of it. Stop and feel into this fear. Where in your body is it? What texture, weight, shape, color does it have? Stay with the direct sensation of the body of fear. Befriend this fear, this sense of inadequacy and explore them with curiosity and compassion. Work with it as suggested in the chapter on Letting Go of Fear.

Invitation

May what I do flow from me like a river, no forcing and no holding back.

- Rainer Maria Rilke

When we are caught up in efforting, we lose our connection to the Beloved. So be aware and notice, my dear. When efforting comes to visit you, always notice the thoughts, notice the tension in your body and acknowledge them: "Oh, my shoulders are tight. I'm having thoughts about failing. Hmmm." S L O W D O W N. Remember to B R E A T H E deeply and slowly, particularly slow down your out breath. Work out and massage any points of tension in your body as you exhale the tightness out.

If you just slow down and remember to breathe you will be far more effective and creative and - who knows - you might even enjoy the process! Watch out for the terrible trio: anxiety, self doubt and worry. Acknowledge them when they show up but don't believe them. You know them; they are old, old voices, old, old feelings. They've been around in your head and body for countless years trying their best to protect you from failure, shame, etc. All these things have little or no basis in the reality of your life today. Unless you continue to believe them!

Sometimes when you let down and let go of the efforting, sadness or even grief shows up. Perhaps you even tear up. This is all good. It may be a part of you expressing the thought "why do I have to work so hard?" and feeling so very tired of the endless rounds of efforting! Give this part your kind attention, for it is a part of you that has been submerged under so much fear and efforting for so long. This is "the gift of tears" where you finally feel that you can let down and fall into the arms of God. Let yourself rest there for it is a most precious gift!

Then the tears are tears of gratitude; for now you know deep within you that you no longer have to struggle so hard for a pittance of self acceptance, a pitifully short moment of peace. You finally know at least for a moment that you are part of the Beloved and that there is nothing you need to do to earn this. You always have been part of the Beloved; you just weren't in touch with it when you were preoccupied by your fear of failure and your rush to prove that you were worthy and you were competent.

So rest now, in this knowing, in this deep peace. You no longer have to rush, to effort, to worry about failing, about not being good enough. You are part of the Beloved so just do your best and that will be good enough. Have faith in this, once you touch upon this truth, for you will have moments of forgetting it again and again. But that's okay because you can remember it just as many times. Enjoy the peace: this is your spiritual heritage.

CHAPTER 29

Letting Go of Being Right

Would you rather be happy or would you rather be right?

saying from the Anonymous Programs

The Man Who Had to Be Right

There once was a man who had to be right about everything. He drove his family and everyone around him crazy because he would argue with them until they were worn down by his insistence and didn't have the energy to continue. At which point, he would feel satisfied that he had had the last word and had been proven right and he would crow about it in front of them. This of course didn't win him many friends so he was left by himself a lot.

One day he was out walking in the forest, returning home on a pathway he had not taken before. He came to a fork in the path and he could not tell which way he should go. Fortunately for him, another hiker was coming up the path towards him. But he suddenly realized he couldn't ask the other man which way to go for that would put him down in the eyes of the other man for not knowing his way home.

He desperately looked for a solution and came up with a way out of his bind: he would argue with the man about the best way home and then take his advice when the man was out of sight. "Good afternoon sir," he said, "I would like your opinion on the best way back to the village." "Well," the man said, "the best way would be to take the left trail down because that connects up with the trail you must have started out on." So the smart aleck began to argue with the man about how the right fork surely must be the better route and made up all kinds of reasons for his position. The other man began to argue back, but then stopped and smiled, "Well have it your own way." The man left him right then and there, whistling as he went up the trail.

The smart aleck breathed a sigh of relief and felt very satisfied with himself as to how he had been able to get himself out of an embarrassing situation. He waited until the whistling man was out of sight and started to take the left fork. But as he turned to take it, some force came over him that caused him to stumble back in the direction of the right fork. He thought perhaps he had felt faint and maybe that had caused him to stumble to the right. But no: as he tried again and again, he could not move to the left. He tried for hours as the light of day gradually dimmed but could make no headway.

Now it was deep into the night and he began to fear he would never get back home. As he thought about his family, he began to cry. At that point he heard the same whistling coming back down the mountain towards him. "Good evening sir!" said the whistling man, "How come you're still stranded out here?" At this point the smart aleck was so desperate he admitted his situation. "Well" said the man," I guess you would do better to admit when you don't know something yourself and to listen to others instead of arguing to prove you're right. Why don't you go home now?"

So the man went home and from that day on was less contentious and, oddly enough, he found he was a lot happier with his life. His wife and children were happier to be around him, and his fellow workers actually seemed friendlier towards him. Whenever he would be tempted to start an argument with someone to prove he was right, he would hear someone whistling off in the distance. Then he would sigh and go silent.

Introduction

It ain't what you don't know that will get you into trouble, it's what you know for sure and it just ain't so!"

– Mark Twain

Sometimes we are so certain that we are right about something that we won't entertain any question about it. And if what we "know" to be true is in fact not true, it can cause us much unneeded pain. I once had a therapy client who was beginning to open up to the possibility that the way he had seen his life up until recently was not true. He said to me, "how do I deal with the fact that I have been wrong all of my life about what my life is about? How can I forgive myself for having bought into such a negative and self limiting viewpoint for so long?"

This can certainly be a stumbling block for a lot of us as we begin to realize that the way we have been looking at our world and our life has been highly distorted and, in fact, has caused us much suffering and also harmed those we love. But if we cannot allow ourselves to forgive and be forgiven for our mistakes, we will be far less likely to be willing to allow ourselves to change our minds and admit we were wrong.

It is often hard for us to admit that we have been wrong when we have a lot of our own ego agenda tied up in it. Perhaps we have invested a great deal of time in a project only to find we should let it go. Other times we think our reputation may be on the line if we should admit that we have been mistaken. In actuality, we are more effective in our work when we can admit we were wrong sooner and learn from it. A recent paper studying the benefits of meditation for corporate officers said this practice allowed them to let go more easily of projects that otherwise would become black holes, sucking up time and money.

If we cannot admit that we are mistaken, that we have made mistakes, we have no way of learning from our choices and their consequences for us and others. We saw this playing out so dramatically and painfully in the American involvement in the Viet Nam and Iraq wars. Because of their stake in their reputations and their ideologies, the leaders who got us into these wars did not learn from them and we have suffered from this as a country, wasting precious human lives and huge amounts of our country's wealth that could have helped the less fortunate.

In my own spiritual life, I came to an important turning point when my Zen teacher became embroiled in a series of scandals about his alcoholism, his sexual relationships with women students and his problematic relationship with his own wife and children. Beside my feeling betrayed by him, it forced me to look at my own practice and to seriously ask myself if it was helping me to become a better human being - or not. This was no easy question to answer because I had spent almost fifteen years in this practice with Roshi and hoped to become a Zen teacher certified by him to teach.

My answer to this question eventually led me away from the Zen Center because I had to admit to myself that the way I related to myself in this practice was unhealthy. Instead of being compassionate to myself and learning how to let go, I had "white knuckled" my way through many years of Zen practice and I was not that much happier or more flexible from the experience. This kind of practice had brought out a rigidity of thought and an abusive relationship with myself. It was hard to admit to myself that I had been wrong in how I practiced and at the time I seemed to be throwing away a career I had worked so hard to achieve. And now I can see that I am a very much different (and happier) person than had I remained at the Zen Center and continued my abusive relationship with myself.

One thing that is critical to accept on the spiritual path is that it is okay to make mistakes about spiritual practice and in fact, it is inevitable. We make decisions based on what we know at the time, and what we know is distorted by our own biases and is inherently limited. We will never know-it-all and in fact that is the sobriquet we give to those who claim they do! When we move into judgment of ourselves for our mistakes and ignorance, we block off the very opportunity to let go, to learn and to heal spiritually. Self judgment always blocks further growth.

That is why self forgiveness and self acceptance are essential to this process. We all are human. We all have been conditioned by our biological and environmental circumstances to have limited and distorted perceptions about our world. So for that reason alone, we are all entitled to be forgiven for our ignorance and for acting out of that ignorance.

Grieving our mistakes is okay. Grieving the things that we lost because of our inability to love. Grieving our failures because we did not trust enough in ourselves or in others. Grieving the lack of love in our lives as children - and as adults. Most likely there will be some grieving as we realize that so much of what we suffered in our lives was unnecessary if only we could have trusted and loved enough and did not let our doubts and fears overcome us. And we need to forgive ourselves for having been so faint hearted and allow ourselves to move on.

Gradually over many years, as I have become more accepting of myself, I have come to see a lot more of how I have caused my own suffering through the false beliefs that I held. These self revelations have sometimes been painful but they also have been very liberating. The more we are able to have compassion and acceptance for ourselves, the more able we are to see our faults and failings clearly. Without self judgment, self abuse and self rejection, we are less afraid to admit where we have been mistaken and to move on from there.

Self Reflection & Practice

There are no mistakes; only opportunities for learning and healing. We are all doing the best that we can at the time. If we had known better, we would have made better choices.

-Anonymous

Are there any places in your life you are afraid to examine to see if what you think is true is actually not so? Be specific and detailed about your answers. Explore where you think you might be wrong about how you see the world. Remember not to shame yourself for this. To admit that you might be wrong about something is a great achievement on your part and is the doorway to moving beyond the restrictions of your unexamined beliefs that hold you back and keep you small.

How easy is it for you to admit when you are wrong, that you have made a mistake? Is it easier (or harder) to admit when you have been wrong in certain contexts, such as at work? At school? With your family, your spouse, your friends? At your church / temple /

mosque? If it is easier (or harder) in some contexts why is that? Do you have more at stake in some situations? And if so, what is it that is at stake for you?

If you have never made an inventory of important things you have been wrong about, do that now. Perhaps you will find that there are some things you are actually very happy that you found out you were wrong about. And be careful to see that you don't fall into self-judgment. If you get depressed making this inventory, that only means you have some more Self Forgiveness to do! Actually it is cause for celebration that you now know you were wrong about something! That means you finally realized the truth!

And if you fall into self judgment, here are some examples of how Self Forgiveness might go: I forgive myself for judging that I was stupid to make the mistake that_____. I forgive myself that I bought into the belief that_____. I forgive myself for judging that I should have known better. I forgive myself for believing that I deserve to be punished for it. For the truth is, I did the best that I could at the time, knowing what I did then and now I would make different choices."

Invitation

A Zen master's life is one continuous mistake.

-Dogen Zenji

When we are learning anything new we will always make mistakes in the process. And when it comes to learning about Life, no one was ever given an owner's manual at their birth for how to be a human being. As if that would help anyway! We learned many things from our parents that we later in life find do not serve us. By the time we have unlearned some of what created problems in our own lives we have probably already had our own children and messed them up. This is the setup in human life. By the time we find our own way, we have already passed on things that our children will have to unlearn. And so it will be with them and their children. This is the nature of being human.

And even if our parents were perfect (which is highly doubtful!) there will always be things we have to learn about Life that no one can teach you anyway. You have to learn them yourself just as your children will have to learn them for themselves. Life is at times difficult, for everyone. It is difficult and challenging to be a human being. We have to learn to let go of ourselves bit by bit until we die the final death. No one escapes this final challenge, no matter how wealthy and powerful they may be.

So spend as little time as possible castigating yourself for the mistakes you have made. It is just wasted energy. Instead, let your experiences from making the mistakes enter you deeply and humble you so that you will learn their lessons as fully as you can. And who knows; you may need another round of mistakes to fully get the lesson. It is like that for really hard lessons in life! Usually these are like little deaths and do not come easily to us. When it is time for another little death, another letting go of something you thought you could not live without, just let go a bit more easily than the last time.

Is there a belief that you have falsely founded your life upon that is crumbling away under your feet? This can be an extremely confusing place to be. Know this is a huge accomplishment on your part and makes God extremely happy! And thank the world, when you have stopped railing against your fate, that it has conspired with your Soul to bring this about. It is your gateway to your freedom even though it may feel like a death. In the past your ego would have done anything it could to prevent this from happening. And now you're ready. Congratulations!

CHAPTER 30

Letting Go of Over Seriousness

My mashpia (spiritual mentor) Rabbi Jacobsen catches me one day when I'm praying. I'm contorting my face with sincerity, wanting connection so badly that it's like I'm saying, "Pretty please God," and only getting into a frustrated kvetchy place. He gives me a bit of elbow in my ribs and asks: "Did you try already in a nice way and you got a 'no'? So look differently for a connection, maybe an ache somewhere?" - Rabbi Zalman Schachter-Shalomi

How Various Chickens Relate to the Issue of Crossing the Road

The Agnostic Chicken isn't sure there is another side of the road but is willing to engage with other chickens of good will in discussions of whether or not there could be such a thing.

The Atheist Chicken denies that there is another side of the road and engages in fierce debates with believers to prove to them that they are completely deluded.

The Fundamentalist Chicken sees no mention of crossing the road in scripture and thinks any idea of trying to cross the road is blasphemous and to be punished.

The Hindu Chicken, seeing all existence as Maya, understands that the other side of the road is only an illusion created by the mind.

The Buddhist Chicken, deeply realizing the emptiness of all phenomena, knows that the other side of the road has already been reached.

The Jewish Chicken consults the commentaries to the Torah about the matter but ultimately decides that he has trouble enough on this side of the road. Oy vey, so why bother?

The Politician Chicken wants to know what groups are for crossing the road and what groups are against it and which will contribute to his campaign fund.

The Engineer Chicken designs a pedestrian bridge for crossing the road but can't get funding for it because of the federal deficit.

The Scientist Chicken studies the statistics relating to becoming road kill when crossing the road before making his decision as to whether to cross or not.

The Avant Garde Artist Chicken is inspired by the idea of crossing the road and starts a new movement of Performance Art based upon standing in the road, waiting to get run over.

Introduction

A man who cannot laugh at himself is a very sorry sight indeed.

- Anonymous

Some of us make the mistake of being overly serious. This does not bode well for our spiritual journeys where a sense of humor is in order! I know because that was one of my early mistakes on the spiritual path. I would grit my teeth and try so hard to concentrate when I meditated. I was intensely serious in my practice. Once my Zen teacher had me down to his house and he was drunk and getting me drunk with Sake. Then, in a teasing moment he mimicked my overly earnest face. I saw this and fell over backwards laughing at myself. I knew what he was implying and I got the joke. But when I sobered up, unfortunately I forgot the message and got too serious again!

After some Voice Dialogue work, I came to see this serious part of myself as just that: one character among a cast of many in my consciousness. I watch out for him when he starts to get too dominant. I call him the Old Monk; he is something of a killjoy, rather grumpy and judgmental about others being too superficial and light hearted. While he is partly responsible for my long dedication to spiritual practice, I would not be whole if I let him run the show. A little bit of the Old Monk goes a long way!

Life is serious at times, but it can also be very funny as well, especially when it comes to our own benighted human behavior! I often picture God being like George Burns looking down from a cloud in heaven, saying to Himself "Oy! Why do they do that? Didn't I teach them better than that? Hey Jesus, come here! You better go back down there and give them some more pointers." When we humans are not creating tragedies for ourselves and others, oftentimes we are cracking jokes about other human beings. And besides the antics of adult human beings, there are many things in life that are much funnier: the way babies look sometimes, kittens and puppies, and wonderful comedians that remind us of our foibles. I particularly like slapstick comedy, the sillier the better, because it gives me permission to let loose of my (still) rather too serious outlook on life...and to...laugh.

Thank God for laughter! It is life saving. One of the signs of "lightening up," spiritually and psychologically is the ability to laugh. Many of us have carried around for most of our lives a sad story about Me, Myself, and I and finally we get it: this is a story that we have made up. And when we get that it is just a story and not the Truth, sometimes the sudden freedom that brings leaves us shaking with laughter. The joke is on us and what is even more wonderful is, we get the joke! Ha, ha, ha, ha!

Then there is the laughter that comes from paradox, struggling with two contradictory ideas in our minds until we have some kind of breakthrough and see beyond the obvious black and white either / or thinking. Some Zen Koans are like this. Old Zen Master Ma Tzu said to the assembled monks, in holding up his kotsu (a ceremonial teaching scepter) "If you say this is a stick, I will hit you! If you say it is not a stick, I will hit you. Quickly now, tell me what is it?" The mind wants to settle down on one side of this or the other; that is the nature of linear logical thought. But old man Ma Tzu is forcing us to take a leap, and that leap might be into laughter! Or getting hit!

This is true of the dichotomy of effort versus grace. My Zen teacher called Zen meditation "effortless effort." And it can be damned hard for some of us to find this paradoxical place within us where we are very much present but very relaxed in our mind and body at the same time. For so many of us engaging in anything "seriously" implies some kind of heaviness, tension and efforting. Spiritual effort has a very different quality to it; you learn to be very present with a kind of gentleness and openness at the same time.

It usually takes some time for us to get this right in meditation. We want to make meditation into another doing where we use our thinking mind to pursue it. We judge whether or not our meditation is quiet or restless and then we try to quiet it down. Bingo, we set up the dichotomy of good and bad again and we effort towards what we think is "good." Then we are back in the same old game of duality that runs our everyday life.

Spirituality is about Being, not doing. Efforting is all about straining towards some mentally established goal. Meditation is about giving up any idea of a goal and just letting ourselves be. It can take many, many years to learn to let go and let be for us goal oriented Westerners. This is why Grace is such an important part of Christianity. It undercuts the whole idea of the Self and the merit system that our culture is based upon.

Self Inquiry & Practice

Where might you get off track with over seriousness and a one track, tunnel vision mind in your spiritual life? What specifically does your over serious side say to you about spirituality and how you should practice?

Do you have a rather heavy, serious belief regarding spirituality such as "no pain, no gain?" Or that it is about getting everything right? What else might you hold in a heavy, rigid or over serious way regarding your spirituality? Try to imagine that something might come to you easily, spiritually speaking. See what protests your mind might make to such imaginings.

Do you have any Life Scripts that take you down into a pity party or a "life is grim" story? If so, what are they? These are good to know so that you can be on the lookout for them!

Do you have ways of lightening up when you get too serious? What are they? What are your favorite kinds of humor? Can you find humor in your spirituality? How do you do that?

If you find that you get overly grim when you do your spiritual practice, try backing off a little, doing it with more warmth, more perspective.. and some humor.

One way to meditate suggested by Thich Nhat Hahn is to have a slight smile on the corners of your mouth when you meditate. It has been shown scientifically that this creates a lighter mood in the mind when you do it because of feedback loops between the brain and the facial muscles. In Yoga practice they also remind you about loosening any frown or grimace you have when you practice. Try this in your mediation practice if you find that you are trying too hard.

Invitation

You stand there, looking overly serious. Perhaps you have something to grieve about, but if not, then smile. Life is a dance; come to the party. There is always a place for you here in the dance. Yes, there are hardships, and it is okay to shed a tear for yourself and for others. Life can be hard at times. And then the clouds part and the sunbeams come out from behind them. Life is good, the whole of it, beginning to end. Even when Life starts out hard, it can get better as we learn to lighten up and let go of what's heavy and unnecessary. It's a long journey, so be sure to travel light! The less moralism and judgment you pack, the lighter your baggage will be. Forgive yourself and forgive others. Find humor in your situation as often as you can.

Watch out for Chicken Little of the sky-is-falling fame. He has a way of making even good times worrisome. He's never happy unless he can tell you "I told you so" when misfortune strikes. Look out for Green Eyed Envy that always sees the other person's lot as better than hers. Poor thing never knows how to be content! Always sees her glass as half empty when others' are half full. Funny thing: her glass is just as full as theirs - but try telling her that! Look out for the Efforter and Perfectionist that tell you how hard you must work and how you have to do everything right. They can kill the joy in anything!

Standing in the line at the bank, strike up a conversation with the person next to you. Probably you will find something to share with them and laugh about. Yes, I know that Global Warming is a serious threat to all of life on the planet and we must do something! But don't let that keep you from grinning from under your sweat at times and joking about the weather. It's going to take some real discomfort for all of us to do what we need to do about it. Just remember that Republicans sweat too when they're hot! That might give you some consolation.

If you are always frowning, fretting and struggling, where are you going to find the energy to do anything of consequence? To accomplish anything significant takes a lot of work so you're going to need all of the positive forward-moving energy that you can muster! Keep some perspective as best you can and daily do things that bring a smile to your face. Pet a dog, kiss a baby, tease your spouse! Enjoy the trees, flowers, sky and all the beauty that is this world we live in. They are all singing the Song of Abundant Life to you, so listen up, loosen up and lighten up!

CHAPTER 31

Letting Go of People Pleasing

If I am not for myself, then who will be? If I am only for myself then who am I? And if not now, when?

-Rabbi Hillel the Elder

Say No, Say Yes

If I say "no" to you,
      I say "no", not because I dislike you-
      or want to hurt your feelings.
I say "no" because I cherish my Soul
      and what you ask of me would
                 not
let me listen for what
      the world wants to whisper to me.
I say "no" to you
      not to displease you.
I say "no"
      so I can listen patiently, attentively
      for what calls to my Soul
      - and then, to be able to say "Yes!"

-Robert Cornell

Introduction

Learn to say 'no' to the good so you can say 'yes' to the best.

- John C. Maxwell

Saying no doesn't seem to belong in a book about letting go and surrender. After all, isn't saying no an expression of ego and willfulness? No, it isn't when we are people pleasers who have a hard time disappointing others and hence lose our own genuine self in the desperate desire to please others. For us people pleasers it is a difficult task to let go of our urgently felt need to give others what they want to avoid upsetting them. Then saying "no" can even be a courageous act, letting go of a great fear!

Many of us in the helping professions are people pleasers. We can easily mistake our being nice for a genuine loving spiritual attitude towards people. There are many of us people pleasers hiding in clerical collars and secular suits that don't know how to set healthy boundaries, either for our selves personally or for any institution for which we are responsible. When we abnegate our responsibility to set good boundaries, the trouble makers who complain and manipulate can wreak havoc in our churches and organizations.

Many of us who find it hard to say no are afraid of others' anger at us should we refuse their request. I can remember an exercise I did in a sales training many years ago where the facilitator was leading us in an exercise to just say the word "No"– not to anyone in particular, but just to say it aloud with conviction. As we did this, I found my level of anxiety level rising; that is how codependent I was at that time. Now I can say "no" quite easily to importuning sales people and "no" to volunteer requests that don't line up with my sense of calling. My life is way too short now to waste my precious time doing something that is not meaningful to me and that I do not have the gift or the passion for doing.

This issue of boundaries can be very confusing for some of us who consider ourselves spiritual people. We may tend to equate spirituality with saints loving everyone, sacrificing themselves endlessly and kissing lepers. But some people in the real world that we inhabit (when we are not meditating or going to Sunday or Sabbath services) can behave very badly if they are not called to account, if there is no enforcement of boundaries and codes of conduct.

So as people who want our lives to be whole, we would do well to find within ourselves a strong guardian aspect that can protect us as well as keep safe a community, an organization or a workshop that we have charge of. Our guardian aspect is not afraid of saying no, is not afraid of potentially displeasing others if they see there is something more important that needs protecting.

Another perhaps confusing thing about spirituality is that some people need to develop a more healthy sense of ego self before they try transcending this self. For if they have a fragile and unstable sense of self, spiritual work can lead them to a serious psychological breakdown in which they have a great struggle putting themselves back together again. They need to learn to care for themselves, be present for themselves and be able to defend themselves if necessary. When they can do this reliably, then they can let go of this smaller self into Spirit and trust that they can find their (healthy) ego selfhood again when they come back from Heaven to the earthly world of relationships and work.

And for many of us the spiritual life goes right along beside continued psychological work. Much of my work as a therapist focuses on helping clients integrate their spiritual and psychological selves. For many of us, psychological work will continue to be useful even when we have been on the spiritual path for many years. These should not be seen as contradictory but rather as complementary.

Self Reflection & Practice

The People Pleaser loses not only themselves in their faint heartedness, but in the end is disloyal to the Divinity within that calls them into integrity, truthfulness and courage.

For a week observe how easily and appropriately (or not) you can say no to others or set a healthy boundary with them. Take notes and journal about this. Remember to release any shame or self- judgment. You don't need that on top of feeling guilty for trying to set a healthy boundary! Also keep in mind that the pendulum in swinging the other way can sometimes lead to a surge of anger and acting out. Some of that you may have to put up with for awhile in yourself. You don't need to make a new religion out of your newly found anger but it is an important energy for your Inner Guardian to have access to!

Examine your own life and your relationships. See if there are patterns to how you have dealt with setting boundaries in the recent past. With whom do you have trouble saying no, in setting boundaries? Here are some possibilities to consider: Parents? Children? Friends? Spouse? Authority figures? Religious or other worthy organizations? People you feel obligated to? People you feel guilty about for one reason or another? People you minister to in some capacity? People who are good at guilt tripping you?

What kinds of feelings and thoughts inside you make it hard for you to say no or to set boundaries? Some examples: you feel afraid of how the other person will react if you say no or set a boundary? You want to be approved and recognized for agreeing to the request? Don't want to be embarrassed or judged in front of others for saying no? Think it isn't spiritual to say no? Think you have some kind of debt to repay to God or others?

Do you feel that you have no right to say no? If so, how could you start to give yourself permission to do better boundary setting? Possible ideas: practice saying no or setting boundaries in situations and with people you know you have difficulty doing this with. Practice what you want to say beforehand, perhaps even with a friend for support and encouragement. Inquire within yourself as to the beliefs and emotions underlying your inability to set healthy boundaries. You might want to journal on this with the part that can't set limits with others. Do this with compassion and curiosity.

IMPORTANT PRACTICE

Explore your relationship with anger; as a People Pleaser you probably repress it in some way. Often a People Pleaser will direct their anger against themselves rather than at the appropriate target. Start to develop a dialogue with your anger; it is a very important messenger to you that an important boundary has been overstepped, or that a person is pushing you for something you really don't want to agree to.

Learn to consult with your anger before it blows its (your) top off. Check in with it regularly for it will tell you many times when something is off about a situation with another person. If you are new to giving expression to anger, don't be dismayed if your first efforts blow up in your face; often you will overreact for awhile as you get the hang of it. Do not think of your anger as unspiritual; it is an important part of your guardian aspect that can protect your integrity and the safety of organizations you are responsible for!

Invitation

Mother Theresa, was once asked why the Sisters of Mercy closed the doors of their Convents in the afternoon when lines of needy people still stretched out into the street. She replied, "If we don't close the doors for prayer now we won't be able to open them in the morning."

"No" is a good and worthy word. It is the shortest of words and it gets right to the point. It protects us and the people and things we care about. Without this "No," many bad things would happen in the world. God gave it to us so we could say no to working on the Sabbath. He gave us the Ten Commandments and to obey them we have to say no to many things. How indeed could we say yes to everything and be obedient to God, let alone be respectful of ourselves and our own needs?

There is a time to say yes and a time to say no. Each is appropriate in the right time and place. The person who can never say no has neither time nor energy to say yes to what is most meaningful for them. They get lost in the urge to feed every mouth and line every palm that reaches out to them. And when they can't say no, they feel empty, drained, spent, even burnt out - and underneath that- there might be a simmering resentment. If so, it would be a good thing to listen to that resentment.

Let go of guilt, let go of fear. You don't need to please everyone all of the time, in all situations. Your job is not to save all people from themselves; even God doesn't do that! If you are afraid to say no, feel your fear and say no anyway. If you feel guilty when you say no, feel the guilt and say no anyway. And if you cannot bring yourself to say no, feel down inside yourself for the resentment that is probably hiding out there, perhaps even as depression – your resentment coming out against yourself. And know this: that anger, that resentment, that depression is trying to tell you something important!

CHAPTER 32

Letting Go of Pride & Arrogance

Pride is one of the deadliest and most insidious of poisons to be encountered on the spiritual path. When you can truly acknowledge to yourself that you are no better and no worse than any other benighted fool of the human race, you are half way there to humility. But only half way, remember!

A Humility Contest

A priest and a Bishop were arguing in the cathedral about who was the least of them. "Well" said the priest "I can never get it right at Holy Communion. I always make mistakes!" The Bishop said "I have to go to confession every week for I sin in my heart countless times each day." The deacon who cared for the cathedral had been listening in on the conversation of these revered figures and couldn't help but bemoan the state of his own soul, "Oh such a wretched man am I !" And the Bishop remarked dryly, "Well look who thinks he is the most wretched one of us."

Introduction

We human beings have a very sneaky way of trying to get around our own self awareness, to stay in control and stay at the center of the universe where we don't belong. For instance, we may put on a show of humility, or of extreme effort to seem more spiritual. Or we may study a lot of spiritual writings and look for opportunities to subtly (at least subtly to us!) drop pearls of wisdom anywhere we can to those we think in need of edification and guidance. Of course to those who see through it, this stinks but for us it makes us feel good about ourselves – even proud. Whoops! So too with "Letting Go." We may talk a good game about how we are "letting go" and becoming more spiritual, but in reality we may be just building up our own repertoire of how to stay in control and to feel proud of how spiritual we are.

There is a wonderful and humorous teaching story about Chinese Chan Master Chao Chou (Joshu in Japanese) and an ambitious, proud young monk. The tradition is that this wise old monk practiced with his teacher until he was sixty some years old, then went to see other teachers to test and deepen his wisdom until he was eighty and then taught his students until he died at 120 years of age. One day, a young monk came to him and proclaimed that he had had a great enlightenment (Letting Go of Self) experience. Master Joshu said to him, "Fine, now let it go." The monk then said to Joshu, protesting, "you don't understand! I have experienced the Great Letting Go!" To which Joshu said, "Fine then, just carry it on."

How many of us are like this proud young monk? We have a religious conversion or enlightenment experience and then we can't let it go. We try to hold onto it - which makes it fly away through our clutching fingers – and then we get bummed out about it. Or if it hangs around long enough, we go parading it around like a spiritual award for Best Enlightenment of the Year. So these letting go experiences will happen from time to time as we practice and when they do, we just enjoy them – and when they leave - we let them go.

When we have a spiritual breakthrough there is a temptation for there to be at least a temporary ego inflation as we feel an expansion of our sense of self. If we already have a high regard for ourselves, this may lead to a very insidious arrogance creeping into our spiritual lives and becoming very entrenched. Then our only hope would be to have the rug pulled out from under our feet.

For those of us who are used to feeling inferior, when we have a spiritual breakthrough, it is tempting to try to make up for lost time for how we have been held back in life by our feelings of inferiority. Then we may just try to play the same old game of overcompensating at the success game but now on the spiritual playing field. And the sense of unworthiness goes into hiding but is still there under the surface driving the whole thing.

I can well remember how I tried to make up for "lost time" when I overcame some of my inner impediments of self judgment and self rejection. I wanted to be a spiritual teacher and spread the Gospel of Liberation – but I kept getting pulled back into self judgment when I couldn't live up to my hopes and dreams. This was its own kind of delusion: again I had set up standards that I had to meet to gain my own self-acceptance. Now, more and more, I accept being just where I am. And this is an ongoing, long-term process, not perfect, but good enough.

This is so hard for young people to accept – and why should they? Their life stretches out before them, they have many things to accomplish and it is good and appropriate for them to work hard and try their best. But (hopefully) there comes a day in one's life where we don't get something we desperately want, someone we love dies, our ambition is thwarted, some early self centered dream dies within us, or some illusion that we harbored is snatched away from us by this ever changing life.

And then the real work of spirituality begins: dealing with our resentment, our fear, our resistance, our depression or our desperation to hold onto what we have. But our holding onto anything won't work in the long run. Eventually we will have to let go even of letting go, even of the role of "being spiritual." We get to choose whether we will go along gracefully with Life or whether we get dragged kicking and screaming along the whole way.

We get to choose whether to focus on serving others or on serving our own ego needs and then being frustrated that Life isn't pleasing us. And when we let go of ambition, it is not into cynicism or pessimism or fatalism, but rather into a calm acceptance of what is. From this acceptance of reality we don't struggle to get ahead, but rather we can let things play out organically with equanimity and a subtle joy. Then the process of letting things be as they are (not as we want them to be) is the Way. And the Way of letting go is the process.

Self Reflection & Practice

An argument started among the disciples as to which of them would be the greatest.

- Luke 9:46 NIV Bible

With clarity and self acceptance carefully watch your thoughts and speech regarding the following issues. You know you are having one of these issues when envy, ill will, a desire to gossip, to brag, to be better than, to be recognized, to be special shows up in your heart rather than a desire to be of service. And remember: this is a very natural human inclination translated into the spiritual realm.

So don't beat yourself up when you see it in yourself. Rejoice that you can see it and attempt to refrain from the self centered impulse! This is the most critical thing: just to see it. If you beat yourself up about being human you will just drive this stuff underground where it will fester unchecked and come out in ways very hurtful to others in your sphere of influence. Countless bible thumpers, Elders and Cardinals of the Church can attest to this from personal experience!

What do you still hold onto behind your spirituality? Remember to look carefully at your actions, not what you say you believe. Are you:

- Wanting to be seen and admired as a "spiritual" person?
- Tending to hide some of your actions from yourself and others that you are ashamed of? Secrets can be deadly. If this is the case find a counselor or Spiritual Director that you can talk to about these things.

- Wanting status as a spiritual adept that "knows?"
- Wanting recognition or success or some such thing in the spiritual arena to resolve your insecurities and doubts about yourself and your path?
- Still envious or resentful of spiritual people who are recognized and "successful?"

Do you sometimes find yourself putting others down as not being spiritual enough or being hypercritical in order to buoy up your own feelings of self worth? Do you like to gossip about other people in your spiritual community or teachers and other spiritual people in the news?

At times do you think of your status or importance before you think of serving others? Do you feel ignored, "left out" and not good enough? What other behavior and thoughts does this drive? Obsessing about getting enlightened so you can be enough? Finding a teacher to validate you? Needing people to recognize you for your achievements? Do you keep putting yourself down to confirm your own unworthiness and sinfulness as a way to ensure you are spiritual enough? Arrogance or abject groveling are two sides of the same coin.

When you feel the temptation to put others down, notice what is happening inside you. Notice the impulse. What is underneath it? The need to be seen? A sense of not being good enough? Stay with this feeling. Notice where you feel it and with compassion and non-identification, be very curious about it.

Invitation

When we have enlightenment experiences, we have gratitude for them and then let them go just like any other phenomenon, because even they are not permanent. What goes up will always come down. What comes into being will always pass away. This is the nature of any experience - even enlightenment experiences. When we cling even to enlightenment it becomes a burden weighing us down, a straight jacket hemming us in, an intoxicant to inflate us, a security blanket to hold onto. So let enlightenment and delusion alike float through the empty space of your being. Enlightened activity is not a permanent state after all but more an ongoing process of acceptance and letting go. Things come, things go; that will always be the nature of things.

Watch out for pride, it is a sneaky little devil. It can hide in your heart and pretend to be so humble, so beyond it all. And somewhere behind the outer good behavior and the kind and wise words lies a slight veil of self satisfaction in the way one's voice is so mellifluous, a momentary basking in how wise one is, a pleasure in how full of the Holy Spirit you feel when telling others what they should be doing with their lives.

And that doesn't mean you should beat yourself up; that could become just another source of pride (or shame) as well. No my friend, the work is more subtle than that. It is to catch yourself right in the moment, in the act of being prideful, to bust yourself to yourself and take joy in seeing your ordinariness. Tempted by pride just like the other guy. Nothing special about that, my dear friend! No way to build yourself up or beat yourself down by seeing that your egoic mind is just an ordinary little sneak thief like that of everyone else!

Even if you are one of those who claims to have good self esteem, if you are insisting on how great you are or your teacher is and putting others down, you have a deep vein of shame and unworthiness hidden inside. If it isn't confronted and healed, you will stay locked away in your own narcissism. If you find you are still having feelings of envy, self judgment, desire for recognition, etc., commit to healing the issue of unworthiness within your self. Most likely this is still hiding in your core identity somewhere.

Rather than holding this against yourself, practice accepting yourself just where you are, warts and all. And be radically honest with yourself. Be vigilant for any signs of your self acceptance being contingent upon meeting standards of performance. Consistently practice Self Acceptance and Self Forgiveness when you find you have fallen short of your goals and values. Let go of the desire to perform and impress others in any shape or form.

If you have poor self esteem, please let that go as well. This is not true modesty because true modesty has no opinion of itself and has no desire to build itself up or tear itself down. It is what it is and faces into the present moment with an attitude of openness, connection and a desire to serve. Learn to enjoy being of service to others in whatever way you can. This is one of the most efficacious ways to forget your concerns about yourself and be happy! Don't let low self esteem prevent you from helping others. No matter what you think the condition of your soul is, there are always others you can assist.

And then just do your very best out of love for your God, your True Self, the Path, the Truth and for those you love. Let your Love lead the Way. Let God love you just as you are, not when you will be perfectly enlightened, perfectly spiritual. Let God love you when you are feeling at your very worst. Because that is when you need love most!

CHAPTER 33

Letting Go of Being Small

Your playing small does not serve the world. There is nothing enlightened about shrinking so that other people will not feel insecure around you. We are all meant to shine, as children do. We were born to make manifest the glory of God that is within us. It is not just in some of us; it is in everyone and as we let our own light shine, we unconsciously give others permission to do the same. As we are liberated from our own fear, our presence automatically liberates others.

- Marianne Williamson

Introduction

One of our greatest sins of omission is staying small and scared and not showing up for our life. This can be such a temptation for some of us because our fears seem so believable that we are strongly inclined to keep a low profile and hunker down so we can stay safe and unhurt by any possible criticism or attack. Especially when we have been hurt or abused as children, this strategy makes perfect sense; it is how some of us survived.

And for those of us whose life has not been as difficult, still there are often challenges that dissuade us from stepping forward in our lives and we are tempted to hold back and play it safe. If we give in to playing it safe we will find that the price for this is being bored and dissatisfied with our life. The price for playing it safe is high. The price for sticking your neck out is not nearly so costly in the long run and it leads to a life that is richer and more meaningful.

The main thing that keeps us small is our fear of what we imagine might happen if we allow ourselves to show up more noticeably, to speak our truth. The fear often is that others will mock us, ignore us, criticize us or hurt us in some way. Those of us who are shy are mostly afraid in this way. We hold back because we project our own self doubt onto others. Those of us who were abused as children usually believe that to be seen or heard is automatically setting ourselves up for further abuse; this is just deeply wired into our consciousness.

For those of us who have experienced shaming, physical, emotional or sexual abuse there are ways to heal and overcome the trauma. This includes psychotherapy and trauma reducing treatments such as EMDR and the Energy Psychology Emotional Freedom Techniques. (See appendix #5) These can help relieve the intensity of fears triggered by things that remind us of prior traumatic situations. With these fear-laden memories somewhat neutralized we can move forward more easily with our lives.

For those of us with less dramatic tendencies to hide or shrink back, how do we overcome this fear of showing up for our lives? Obviously one way is to show up regardless of how much we fear the consequences. To do this there are some things that would be very helpful. One is to develop a strong desire or meaningful goal coming from the heart of love that will motivate us to face our fears and keep going on past them. With this strong motivation, and the energy of love and enthusiasm, we will be willing to face a lot of discomfort and not be overcome.

Most importantly, we need to learn to tolerate the feelings of fear in our bodies and not let the fear stop us. Meditation is an excellent means of doing this. In Zen Buddhism there is a practice called Shikan Taza, which is practicing being aware like the clear blue sky. If we let our experience flow through our consciousness without resistance, without obstruction, we begin to see our experience like the clear blue sky would see clouds.

Our feelings, thoughts and impulses, "good" and "bad", move through our consciousness and do not stay, just like clouds passing through the sky. This unobstructed awareness is a wisdom that does not identify with, does not judge, does not resist, and allows us to flow with events. When the urge to shrink and protect ourselves from potential hurt manifests, we can acknowledge it, breathe in and out freely and let it pass through our consciousness.

If the fear that keeps you small is deeply seated it can be helpful to learn to connect to your heart space where your sense of meaning and connection to others and the world resides. When you feel the urge to shrink in and become small, let your awareness move to your heart space and put your hands over your heart. This is the space of open unfettered love. Breathe into your heart; breathe in love. Gently breathe out fear and contraction and let them go. Then you can explore where the fear is in your body and deeply inquire as to its nature: is it fear of rejection, abandonment or exposure?

You may then remember the source of this fear in your earlier years and then you have an entry point to work with it, spiritually and psychologically. Bringing love and compassion to the parts of us that fear is in the end the most effective way of healing our fears. Sometimes we resent our fearful parts because we see them as having held us back from doing things we very much wanted to do with our lives. This makes healing them very difficult.

Instead, when we bring acceptance and love to them, the fear begins to melt. As we listen compassionately to our fear's stories, we begin to loosen the grip that these stories have upon our consciousness. As we work with these old fears and the urge to shrink back to protect ourselves, we begin to not believe them so much; they lose their power to hold us back. And our desire to make a difference, to do something meaningful in the world will motivate us to step out of the shadows and to share our talents and passions with the greater world around us. We begin to believe in ourselves and not let our self doubt and fears hold us back from the work that God created us for, the work that we are called to do.

Self Reflection & Practice

Loving our wounds and our fears is the Way. This is a hands on and hearts on process! And we are the ones we are waiting for to do this work for ourselves.

Make a point to become more aware (with compassion and without self judgment) of when you become afraid and your body contracts and shrinks back during the day. There will probably be a number of moments of contraction that you notice during a normal day. Notice what you do then to avoid just being with the contraction. Do you get angry? Placate others so they will not threaten you? Do you space out? Or do you avoid situations that tend to cause you to contract? Do you look for ways to distract yourself? Make a case to blame or demonize the person or situation that triggers you to contract?

IMPORTANT PRACTICE

When you feel your body contract, don't make it wrong, don't beat yourself up about it! Allow yourself to feel lovingly into the contraction and to gently be with it. You might want to put your hand over the area in your body that feels contracted to more fully bring your compassion and presence to it. Breathe into the contraction and then exhale out slowly. See what happens when you practice this way with the contraction; you may find that it softens.

Be willing to stay with the feelings and to inquire deeply into their nature. Where do they reside in your body? What size and shape are the feelings? Do they have a color, texture, weight or movement? A contraction in the heart space may be about the fear of loss of connection; a contraction in the throat is often about inability to give voice to something and a contraction in the gut is about survival. All these questions when focused through the bodily will tend to

engage you with directly perceiving the sensations, rather than thinking about, judging and resisting them.

Often, when you sink below the outer emotion of fear or anxiety and you contact what is below that, you will find other emotions surfacing: sadness, anger, a sense of unworthiness. As you engage with these feelings of contraction and fear, you probably will gain some insight as to where they come from. You may remember painful memories that parallel the current issues. You may gain a newfound awareness of or increased clarity about a core issue. With this new awareness, you can begin to move out of this old way of seeing your world. And you may very well want to do some healing work with memories, judgments and beliefs with EFT, Self Forgiveness and release of limiting beliefs. See appendices # 3,4 & 5.

Try this exercise: in a safe space, imagine that you are engaging in some activity that usually causes you to be fearful such as giving a speech, confronting a difficult person or situation, etc. Chose a situation that is personally challenging for you. It's best to start with one that is not the most challenging and work your way up to successively greater challenges. As you imagine this situation, let yourself feel that you are expanding out into the world, losing your limiting sense of the boundaries of your body and psyche. First, let yourself expand out beyond the perimeter of your body. Then let yourself expand beyond the room you are in. Continue this until you have spread out into the universe.

Before you go into a situation where you usually feel yourself contract, visualize yourself gently expanding out to a larger size. Concurrently, imagine that you feel this expansion in your body as well. Particularly imagine your heart space opening up. In your heart and in your body remember the energy of this expansion as you go into the situation that in the past has triggered you to contract. If you feel yourself balk and contract during this exercise, place your hand(s) lovingly on the area(s) of your body that feel(s) contracted. In this way you bring loving energy and awareness to the part that is fearful, most likely a young wounded part of yourself. Just bringing your loving energy and awareness to these parts of your body that feel exposed and vulnerable may be enough to release the contracted feelings you are experiencing.

You might also try giving a voice to the part of you that wants to shrink back. With compassion and a sincere desire to understand, ask it what its concerns are. You might also want to dialogue (using Focusing, free form writing or a Gestalt technique (See appendices #4&6.) with this fearful, contracted part. As you learn to listen to, accept and love this part of yourself, you will find that it cooperates more and more with your desire to move beyond your comfort zone and towards your sense of calling.

Listen to your deepest yearnings: what in your heart of hearts do you wish to do?

What is God calling you to do? Perhaps there has been a dream that has dwelled inside of you since you were young and you doubted your ability. It may be the time now to give new life to that dream and move past old fears and limiting beliefs about yourself.

Invitation

And the day came when the risk to remain tight in a bud was more painful than the risk it took to blossom.

- Anais Nin

Sometimes you may feel tight and afraid. Don't make this wrong. Let it be what it is. The wounded self is quaking and contracted. Have compassion for it but don't believe its stories of limitation. Breathe and let go. Relax down into the Godspace inside your heart. What would it be like to let yourself be as large as the heart-sky? Just breathe, inhaling deeply and gently, then exhaling and letting be the contractedness of your body and mind, just letting yourself soften past the contraction. There is nothing to be afraid of, nothing to resist. You are safe here in your spaciousness, the sky-majesty of who you really are.

Find a place somewhere within yourself where you are safe and from there, let yourself practice being without solid boundaries. Get to know how it feels, this spaciousness and freedom. This is your innate freedom and inheritance as a spiritual human being. It belongs to every man, woman, and child even if they have been hurt. We all deserve to know this spaciousness and to feel safe inside of ourselves. No one can guarantee us that we will always be safe in our outward life, but God can let us feel safe in our inner life, if we but invite Him/Her in to comfort and console us, to embrace us and reassure us.

And beyond our fears and shrinking back the Beloved calls us to be larger than our hesitations and doubts about ourselves. Love calls us to love and to serve something far greater than ourselves. We are called to be Love. He/ She calls us out into the world to heal, to nurture, to create, to celebrate the magnificence of existence. What is God calling you to do? What is lying in your heart waiting to be born? Step forward my dear; open your heart and let yourself be as unbounded as you can be!

CHAPTER 34

Letting Go of Over Identification with Mind

Not knowing is most intimate.

- Dogen Zenji

A Mind Too Full

There is a Zen story about a rather academic professor of Buddhism who comes to visit a Zen teacher. The Zen teacher invites the professor for tea and as the teacher is preparing the tea, the professor holds forth on his theories about Zen. As the professor is talking on and on, the Zen Master pours tea into the professor's cup and keeps pouring until the cup overflows. "Stop," says the professor, "can't you see that you are overfilling the cup?" " I can see," the Zen Master replies calmly, "When your cup is full there is no room for anything else to be put into it."

Introduction

In this chapter I'm inviting you to look behind your thinking mind that you often believe is "you" and running the show and realize that it is not the mastermind that you might have thought it was. Our mind, the so called rational mind that is busy planning, analyzing and evaluating everything, is not the true master – in spite of what Descartes said! Being trumps doing, including thinking, any time, for, if we don't exist, nothing else would happen! To believe that we have to prove to ourselves that we exist and to use the thinking mind as a proof of our existence seems like the kind of fundamental error that only a Western intellectual totally identified with thought could make.

Since the Enlightenment we in the West have become so enamored with rational thought that we have come to think it is the Alpha and Omega of our existence. The Western belief has been that we can understand everything and fix any problem if we can just get enough information and then figure it out rationally. And in truth, the human Intellect has been incredibly useful to us. It has been instrumental in our developing a culture that has exploded exponentially beyond our early ancestors' hunter-gatherer bands into the amazing globally interdependent technological society that we have now. The ability of the creative, thinking mind to achieve this is truly amazing. So it is very understandable that we expect that every human problem could be solved by technological advances, the use of our intellects and the scientific method. And that is probably one of the main reasons why the role of religion is fading in so much of the advanced parts of the world today.

The disproof of rationality's role as the sole motivator and master of our lives comes from many different sources: everyday experience, Mindfulness practice, psychology and neuroscience. One thing that is clear is that we have more than enough information to fix a lot of our world's problems; what we lack is sufficient collective will and the wisdom to do what needs to be done. Even in our personal lives, so often we know rationally what we should do but we don't do it. Rarely is just knowing the facts what motivates us; we need the stronger impulses of the emotions and the balance of wisdom to move us into appropriate action.

The emotions do not follow logic; they have their own way of working with perceptions, sensations, symbols and memory. Wisdom is not to be confused with knowing lots of information. For those of us who are spiritual, we recognize another deeper place of motivation, which we call Soul, Spirit, Love, or Divine inspiration. Our deep connections with the larger picture are what ultimately provide us the wisdom to create meaningful solutions to our problems. This wisdom comes from the integration of factual knowledge, life experience, and the intangible inner knowing of our deep interconnection with everything around us.

Our rational minds deal poorly with the big issues of Life and Death. For instance, our minds balk at thinking in detail about what it is like to die. It is anxiety provoking to entertain seriously the thought that we will no longer exist and there will be no trace of our existence left: in time no one will remember our name and even our best deeds will be long forgotten. Many of us, in allowing ourselves to think about this, experience a deep existential dread. Much of the time we defend ourselves from such inconvenient facts of life: in psychology we call these defense mechanisms denial, distraction, and avoidance. Indeed, we have developed extremely effective ways to avoid being present to our existential vulnerabilities. And one way to do that is to stay on the mental level.

This is ironic for we think that staying on the mental level helps us to act "rationally." But in actually it keeps us from accessing important information from our emotions and other sources of perception that will help us to make more holistic and grounded decisions. In psychotherapy it is very common for us to see clients who stay on the mental level, talking and talking about their problems, when they are actually struggling with emotions that they cannot or will not let themselves get in touch with. Sometime with my clients I use the metaphor of our awareness being stuck up in the attic of mental level functioning, while the juicy, raw stuff of emotions that we don't want to deal with are kept down in the basement of our subconscious.

When we encounter in a traumatic event, feelings and sensations that we fear could over power us, many of us go mental to maintain control. And unfortunately if we persist in staying mental, the issues will not heal. The emotions will stay down there in the basement until we are willing to open the basement door and descend down the stairs into the musty darkness of our bodies and our emotions to grapple with what is present there.

I suspect that is what PTSD and other anxiety disorders, such as panic disorder, are often about. In trauma, a person is impacted by something totally outside of their normal experience and it totally overwhelms their everyday coping skills. Then they desperately try to make sense of the episode on the mental level. They try to get themselves back under control and their usual ways of doing that are completely ineffective in such abnormal conditions. They replay the experience over and over again in their minds trying to figure out on the mental level how to cope with it.

But they can't find a way to cope with the experience because it can't be processed just on the mental level; it has to be processed on emotional and somatic levels, in the body. So they perseverate mentally on and on about the episode with no relief in sight. The way to help them regain their sanity is to gradually let them feel into the original experience until they can somatically process it in its entirety. Then it will little by little let go of them. This is what graduated exposure therapy is about: helping traumatized people gradually re-experience the traumatic situation somatically and not to "go mental" with it.

I had a very challenging episode of PTSD like symptoms myself some years ago when a set of circumstance triggered me into massive anxiety attacks. I was hyper vigilant, had trouble sleeping at night and could be triggered into severe anxiety unexpectedly by situations similar to the original triggering episodes. Since I already was a very experienced meditator, mostly what I did, as best I could, was just to keep staying with the feelings in my body, as painful as they were. And gradually the symptoms lessened and finally abated. Later, I became aware of the underlying anger that I had unconsciously repressed since childhood. This then really lessened my anxiety. But now I have to deal with being angry at times!

I can now see the gift that this experience gave me: I became intimate with my old bête noir, fear. This wasn't an intellectual or mental process at all. It was an in-the-body, in-the-present-moment dealing with the sensations of fear over and over again. It was a breathing into the fear when it arose, slowly accepting and softening my resistance to the fear and finally a gradual letting go which in no way resembled trying to figure it out in order to get rid of it. Now when fear shows up, I am much less resistant and I can much more readily relax/melt into it and let it pass through me and be gone. What a lesson – and what a price! But I am grateful for what this experience has taught me.

If our awareness is restricted mostly to the mental level, we cut ourselves off from our direct experience, being in the present moment, and in touch with our bodies. This is quite a common condition in our Western culture; we are so busy thinking about things that we miss the direct experience of what is in front of us. Apparently this is not just a condition of our current culture. Zen arose in China to bring the educated classes in that society back to the direct, vital experience of life. Already in that culture over a thousand years ago there was too much scholasticism and an inability to engage life directly, as it is, without the constant intercession of the thinking mind.

Thinking cannot engage the present moment. It can only grapple with the past and future and with abstract concepts that do not correspond to our moment-by-moment experience. Relating to the present moment through our senses is the process we call direct perception, which bypasses the rational thinking mind. If you have watched the workings of your mental process for any length of time, you realize that your thoughts are often giving a constant running commentary on your direct perception: interpreting, judging, leaping ahead of your perceptions, projecting what it thinks will happen out into the future. This may be helpful at times but often our presumptions and prejudices get in the way of our accurate perceptions of things.

If you watch yourself you will notice that your thoughts, rather than initiating action, can barely keep up with the flow of the present moment and usually lag way behind it. Try thinking your way to winning a tennis match or any other game! Our thoughts are not what usually precede and initiate our movements. Our thoughts are more like the sports commentator who is just reporting on the action that has just happened out on the field. The master of us who raises our hand, talks on the phone and drives our car is something much more mysterious and unavailable to our awareness. We can only be aware of impulses to act as they arise but not what is behind them.

If you still aren't convinced that your rational mind is not the master, consider this experiment. Researchers trying to find the source of will (volition) monitored the brain activity of subjects to investigate where the impulse to, say, move an arm came from in the brain. What they found out was that before their subjects became conscious of their impulse to move their arms, there were already electrical impulses in the brain starting to instigate the movements. So where is this will located and who is our real master?

In another experiment performed at the Heart Math Institute, even more unsettling to our usual way of understanding how our consciousness operates, subjects had their heart's neural network and their brains monitored for electrical activity. The subjects were shown a randomized series of pictures, some of which were pleasant and some of which were disturbing, such as a grisly accident scene. In the split second *before* a disturbing picture would be shown to a subject, there would be activity in the electrical impulses around the heart region. Shortly after the picture was shown to the subject, the brain then would light up in response to the picture. Whereas the heart region responded in some mysterious way to the picture *before* it was even shown to the subject, there was a slight delay between the subject being shown the picture and their brain responding to it. Spooky, yes?

Another experiment that may give us pause in proclaiming that we know who is our master was done with hypnotized subjects. The subjects after being induced into a hypnotic trance were told to do something after they came out of hypnosis when a bell was rung. When the subjects came out of the trance they were given a debriefing in another office where the bell was rung. When they responded with the induced response, they were then asked why they had done it. They answered with all kinds of reasons that had nothing to do with the actual fact that they had been induced to act that way because of hypnotic suggestion. This makes the concept of rationalization take on a whole new level of meaning!

What I hope to do by offering these examples is to encourage you to deeply question the role of the rational mind that we so much identify with as being the master behind all of our actions and the source of all the answers for our deepest questions about life. We are more often than not motivated and acting from a deeper unconscious level than the mental level. Perhaps sometime in the future neuroscience will be able to elucidate more about how our consciousness and volition work, but it is not likely that our pure rationality will be shown to be either our prime motivator or the master instigator of our actions. Our rational thinking mind is just a small part of who we actually are.

It is also important to realize that our thinking mind can significantly get in the way of direct perception. When we are fully present and not thinking we can have the most vivid experiences of living in the moment, seeing things freshly without our mind's chatter and commentary. To be lost in thought takes on a whole other meaning as we realize how preoccupied we typically are and how out of touch with the present moment. Mindfulness practice is a wonderful way for us to begin to come into the direct experience of our lives, unmediated by our thinking minds. If you aren't already practicing mindfulness, by all means begin to; it will gradually improve your experience of life.

Self Reflection & Practice

Watch your thoughts and actions for several days, especially when you are initiating any physical movement. Do you ordinarily have thoughts about doing something prior to actual moving your arm or hand? For example, watch when you respond to an itch: before you move to scratch were there thoughts to move and scratch before you had any impulse to? Or did the movement occur without your being aware of a conscious thought? Notice in general how many of your movements are initiated by impulses that are completely unconscious. Who is the master of your Life? What initiates your thought process? What motivates your actions throughout the day? Look for the master!

If you would lift your arm right now, who would be initiating it? You or the suggestion you just read on the page in front of you? If you frowned at my question just now, what made you frown? Was it me writing this a long time before you read this? Was it the letters on the page you are reading? Was it the paper (or screen) on which you read it? Or was it the light of the sun or a lamp shining on the paper or the light from the digital readout? Without even just one of these you would not have frowned. So our actions are not those of an isolated independent individual but rather the result of a complex series of interactions between "us" and the "world around us."

So tell me now, who *is* the master of your movements, even your thoughts? Don't all of the aspects of so-called external reality inextricably join together to produce your thoughts - those internal creations of your own supposedly separate mind? Work with this on the direct experiential level. Watch how you decide to actually do something. Is there a voice inside telling you to raise your hand and exactly how to do it? Are you frowning now? Have I caused you to think thoughts that you would otherwise never have thought? Who then is your master? If you look for him, you will never find him, but he is present and ready to respond when you need him. But please question the notion that this master acts separately from the rest of existence! You are inextricably interconnected to all of reality.

Invitation

Let go of thoughts of separation and self and sink below the surface of your mind, buoyed up by Being itself. Rest. Don't hurry about with your mind pushing this way and that, straining to arrive in the future or to relive the past. Pay sufficient attention to now and the future will mostly take care of itself. Let go of regrets for what could have been for there is no way to return to the past. Don't try to swim back upstream.

Your thinking mind comments and critiques, plans and frets. Some of this is useful but do not be deceived: it is not the Master. The Master you will never see; it acts behind the veil of your awareness. But you can be aware of your impulses and decide whether or not to follow them. If you are aware, you have choice. If you are not aware you are a slave to every whim and impulse that comes along.

Give up the idea of a separate self. There is no such thing. If you believe there is; try living in total isolation. You will soon find that experience to be excruciatingly empty and desolate. Your being is inseparably part of wonderful and complex currents of interrelationships. Let yourself be carried by the flow of this river of interdependency where Spirit calls you to go. Just steer yourself gently into the currents that are Love. Give up the idea that you are figuring everything out and creating your own world on your own. That is an illusion. This river of Life is moving you vastly more than you are influencing it.

When you let go of your limited sense of self, you will have more than enough energy to carry you forward into your future with this wonderful world of interbeing accompanying you on your journey. The true Master is all about you; in the sky, the bird's song, the traffic jam, and your spouse's voice. When you presume that your little ego self is the Master of your universe, you have cut yourself off from your vastness and your aliveness.

Wake up! Who is the Master? Look! Look!

Letting Go of Worldly Things

When you think you have little, you are vastly mistaken. The jewels in the night sky are yours just as much as anyone's. Who taught you to feel so poverty stricken that you need to take what isn't yours? Who told you that you were so weak and fearful that you needed to control or manipulate others?

CHAPTER 35

Letting Go of The Fear of Being with Ourselves

All the troubles of the world stem from being unable to be in a room quietly by ourselves.

- Blaise Pascal, Pensees

Be Intimate with Yourself

Seems so simple, just to be with yourself.
Yet when you try,
dissatisfaction and restlessness arise.
Old ghosts and new desires
spring forth out of the nothingness,
disturbing your peace of mind.
Stay here and get to know all of yourself:
the schemer trying to get something
to assuage his hunger- for what he knows not.
The lonely spirit crying in the night.
If you run from these ghosts,
through the whole wide world,
you may think that you have put them behind you.
But they will haunt you all your days.
Stay present with everything.
Make friends with everything.
Just don't believe their stories,
and you will have mastered your world.

- Robert Cornell

Introduction

Usually, we regard loneliness as an enemy. Heartache is not something we choose to invite in. It's restless and pregnant and hot with the desire to escape and find something or someone to keep us company.

- Pema Chodron, When Things Fall Apart

Inevitably, if we are to grow past our limited sense of ourselves, we have to spend time alone and face our own demons. When we are around other people, we always have the opportunity to distract ourselves from our fears or to project them onto others and not to take full ownership of them. As we take time apart and start watching our own thoughts and emotions, we begin to see where the real source of so much of our suffering lies. Our minds grasp onto objects of desire and push away those we dislike. The Buddha said that this was the disease of the mind that all human beings suffer from. And as we start to look within ourselves, we can't escape seeing how the ego mind which we thought was "us" and the fixer of every problem is the problem itself and not in fact subject to our so called rational will.

Meditation is the practice of just sitting still, being awake, noticing what arises in our field of awareness and not being entertained and distracted. As we sit and are present with ourselves, our issues will begin to show themselves: our restless mind and body, our fears, our obsessive clinging to things and people. Worrying about the future. Regretting the past. As we finally take our meditation seat and pay attention, we begin to see the movie we have been playing in our mind for so many years.

And guess what: we often do not like this movie. It has train wrecks in it. It contains defeats and disappointments and depressions. There are scenes of betrayal and subsequent resentments and anger towards those who hurt us. There is loneliness and the pain of abandonment. We don't find this movie enjoyable or entertaining. We want out of the movie theatre because the movie seems all too real, all too painful.

This is where so many people give up on meditation, it is sad to say. They experience this initial barrage of unmanageable feelings and thoughts and they say to themselves," This isn't working. I want to be happy and this is making me feel uncomfortable and even overwhelmed. I can't do it right." Or, "This doesn't work for me." And they move on to other things. But this first encounter with our unruly minds is often the first real insight into what is in fact the basic problem for us human beings. And the solution to the problem is also extremely counterintuitive to us at first: to learn to stay with these uncomfortable thoughts and feelings in a non reactive stance of compassionate awareness, to let them arise and fall away.

The people who "succeed" at meditation are not necessarily those who learn it easily and effortlessly. They are just strongly motivated to persist either from their own pain or a certain faith that there is something beyond their own small mind that they want to learn to open to. And they apply themselves to learning little by little how to let go of thinking, reactivity and identification with the ego's story about itself. Gradually they learn how to come back to the present moment over and over again.

So it is not that they are instant experts, they are just willing to keep practicing. And in the long run they may be better off than the person who initially finds meditation easy to practice, for they have the experience of persevering in their spiritual life even when the going is difficult. And this is an essential lesson in equanimity.

Initially, in meditation we are taught to stabilize our minds by counting breaths or being aware of our breathing or to use a word to center on and gently come back to when our mind drifts off. And we are instructed to keep doing this regardless of what feelings and thoughts come up. And finally, to watch our thoughts and feelings with awareness and compassion as they float in and out of our consciousness. Not to fix them but rather to be detached from trying to hold on to them or to push them away.

For many of us who are fixated on getting rid of OUR PROBLEM - our loneliness, our depression, or our fear - this seems like the absolute wrong direction. We want to focus on figuring out how to get rid of our problem, and instead we are told to gently let thinking about the problem go and to come back to our breath or our sacred word. How could this solve OUR PROBLEM which seems so huge and demanding? And ironically, much of OUR PROBLEM is that we deeply believe that we have a problem.

Seems kind of crazy but there you go; that is what we human beings are engaged with – problems that we have created and now believe in tenaciously. It is like Brer Rabbit who in the Tales of Uncle Remus tries to extract himself from the tar baby, but with each effort to push himself out of the tar baby with another paw, he gets himself further and further stuck to it. The more we think we have a problem and fight with it, the more solid we make it, the more stuck we get with it.

I struggled with anxiety most of my young adult life from teen age years on. I made anxiety my enemy when I had my first panic attack in my early twenties when I was flunking out of Cal Tech Graduate School. When I started meditation soon afterwards, I hoped that this practice would fix my anxiety, but it didn't. Instead, over time this practice would change my relationship with anxiety so more and more I could tolerate being with it and not looking for ways to avoid it or run away from it. And as I made friends with it, practicing being present with it, I began to see what was below it that needed healing. It was only from learning to befriend it that I then had this ability to inquire more deeply into its source and to work with this underlying fear.

Believe me, I wish that this work was not this challenging. My initial foray into meditation was like that of a warrior, wanting through sheer brunt of effort to push past fears and old sadness into the clear space of enlightenment. And occasionally I was successful in entering into this open space, but then I would crash down to earth again and again. I can remember many years ago my teacher, Charlotte Joko Beck, teaching us to just be with the contraction of fear in our body and to let it open and heal by itself. I wasn't willing to do that; the feelings in my body were just too scary for me to tolerate. I left one retreat at her center in San Diego on the verge of a full scale panic attack that went on for a couple of weeks before dissipating.

I thought to myself, " this can't be the way for me to free myself from my anxiety. This practice is only making me feel much worse." And so for some time, I quit this kind of intensive Zen meditation. That didn't mean that my anxiety issues abated; it just meant that I went back to the way I had always avoided them. I went back to being a people pleaser and a workaholic. It would only be later that I became tired of this constant efforting and anxiety, had enough trust in myself to face the pain body inside of myself and not to run from it. And with that trust and acceptance my suffering around anxiety gradually healed. No earthshaking enlightenment, just a gradual intimacy with myself, being comfortable in my own skin.

Self Reflection & Practice

The more we allow ourselves to feel the pain of our self -abandonment, the Essential qualities that we have been longing for begin to arise in us. The unfinished business of childhood begins to resolve itself in our psyches and our hearts begin to heal."

- The Enneagram Institute

IMPORTANT PRACTICE

If you haven't already done so, it would be a good time to start a meditation practice. There is no time like the present to start! Sit comfortably and become aware of your breathing. When thoughts arise, keep coming back to the sensations of breathing in, breathing out. It is just that simple. Of course, the trick is to keep connecting to the breath and not going off into reverie or worry, or planning or trying to fix THE PROBLEM. When you do, the job is to notice it and without self criticism come back to the breath. Meditation is all about noticing, simply noticing and letting go into the next moment. So just notice. And notice. And notice. Notice the breath coming in…the breath going out.

In this kind of practice, we are not interested in figuring out anything, fixing anything, analyzing anything. Just notice. Bare bones notice. No running commentary. No psychoanalysis of every little thing, just seeing and noticing. Breath after breath. If you start to think about THE PROBLEM, simply notice: Oh thinking and go back to the breath. The ego wants, insists that we obsess about how to fix OUR PROBLEM, THE PROBLEM, whatever that might be: feelings of depression, anxiety, loneliness, fear, emptiness. Meditation invites us again and again to let go of trying to fix OUR PROBLEM and to surrender back to the breath, to now. So simple. So difficult. So boring. So radical, so profound.

If you start future planning, past regretting just notice: Oh planning, oh regretting and come back to your breath.

If you start to experience difficult feelings, just notice: Oh difficult feelings, and return to the breath. No big deal.

If you start to wonder why you are doing this and what you are going to get out of it, drop doubting mind and return to the breath.

There is nowhere to get to. There is no place to go. This is it, just this moment, breath after breath. Just this moment. No Problem and no end to the Problem. Just arising and passing away. Nothing is permanent – even your problem!

Invitation

You have been restless and dissatisfied with your life for a long time. Don't you want to finally come home to your deepest self, Being itself? Aren't you tired of the same old limiting stories about yourself, the same problems that show up again and again in your life? Then practice just this moment in your body, breath after breath. There is nothing hidden here, no agenda: just a freedom that develops gradually as you gently let the drama that was your old life drop away.

Breath after breath you can let the stories and the emotional reactions go. Breath after breath you come back to this moment. Nothing fancy, it is like tasting a clear cool glass of water. It is more than time for this simplicity. You have been chasing yourself for years like a dog chases its tail. And this stillness that you can sink into expounds that there was no problem to begin with.

Whom do you chose to believe? Silent, compassionate sanity or the noisy chaos of your mind? Your ego mind tells you over and over again that you have to solve YOUR PROBLEM - and GET RID OF IT! You have run around in the world trying to find something, someone to fix YOUR PROBLEM, but all that has done for you in the past was to create more of the same problem and other problems besides. Your ego mind loves to complicate THE PROBLEM by looking outside of itself to fix THE PROBLEM.

Your ego mind doesn't want to rest with THE PROBLEM and to compassionately investigate THE PROBLEM. No, it wants to fix it fast once and for all and get rid of it! It has no curiosity – just aversion and fear. And it rushes out to reject, to fix and to control rather than to surrender into experiencing the problem from the inside out.

It is time to sit down and rest from the insanity, the busyness, the inner aversion, the incessant searching for what was in front of your very nose ever since you were born: just this breath. Just this life as it enfolds moment by moment. Just this problem that is really no big deal when you finally decide to let go and sit with it patiently and compassionately. You have been suffering with and battling against your problem for a long, long time. Is it not time now to let go and let it just be? Be with it, compassionately, patiently. Ask it to come up on your lap and to embrace it. And it will heal. Not in your time, but in God's time.

CHAPTER 36

Letting Go of The Trance of Culture

The Trance

It whispers and snarls about me:
You need this, you need that.
You are not complete or cool without it.
Others will swoon and be envious
of your good fortune If you have it.
You can be young and beautiful forever.
You can have all the things you ever wanted-
and more! Much more!
You can be powerful, rich, famous and admired,
just like in the movies.

If I listen to them, I will lose myself.
If I listen to them I will always be
looking for more and the latest
and the new and improved,
with wet bodies and perfumed breasts,
with shiny chrome and the most up-to-date features
to be found on sale today only!
So hurry up right now!
Don't be late or you will miss out
on this once in a lifetime offer!
Just sell your soul, little by little
and you can have it all. Really.

- Robert Cornell

Introduction

Mall therapy; good for you and good for your community!

-Ad seen on a local bus

Our world today is filled with a myriad of seductions and blandishments. Soviet propaganda was never this effective! The incessant blathering, whispering, ranting, urging, seduction and manipulation of Wall Street, Main Street and Madison Avenue are all around us on TV, the radio, the internet, newspapers and magazines. Businesses are constantly looking for new ways to persuade and manipulate us into buying stuff we really don't need. And they run on the same fear and greed that they preach. They hire psychologists and neuroscientists to increase their ability to convince us with just the right seductive and manipulative messages that we need all kinds of things that no one in their right mind would really fall for.

But because so many of us are not in our right minds much of the time and look for all kinds of validation outside of ourselves through possessions, social status, pleasure and power, we fall for this and buy things we don't need. We chase after status and stuff. And this keeps us in the rat race of getting, spending, ass kissing, pandering, manipulating, etc. The spiritual person has to come to grips with their relationship with this culture of media, materialism, hedonism, and hyper individualism. While opting completely out of the game and living off the grid is a viable option for some, it is not for most of us with our need to have some connection to the larger world around us. And in reality, living off the grid doesn't mean we have let go of all of our greed, insecurity and other human sources of discontent anyway.

Monastic communities provided the context for people with strong desires for spiritual development in the past but, for many reasons, this is less and less a viable option today. We need to learn how to be spiritual and to be connected to the world but not be seduced by it. The great spiritual traditions all talk about the temptations of human nature and they are as valid today as they were in olden times. Our society offers us constant temptations and we have to look them in the face, see their falsity and abstain if we are to be free.

For myself, I have tried to consciously live a life free of inordinate desires for possessions and status, but there have been times when I have been aware in myself of the desire for better things. I remember when I attended my wife's 30th High School class reunion some years ago and how so many of the couples attending had much fancier cars than we had. I could feel a sense of inferiority creeping in and I had to remind myself that I didn't need to have a Mercedes or Cadillac to be okay with myself. Nowadays I drive a little Toyota Tacoma truck that is 15 years old and I am very happy with it. It reliably gets me where I need to go and I don't care what others think about it or me. This is because I have healed much of that old core sense of inferiority that used to feed on these kinds of external differences.

It is very easy to let our culture lure you into sleep watching stupid TV shows and to waste your precious life energy with buying things you don't really need, schmoozing with people you don't really care about to get ahead, and spending your working hours frantically trying to make as much money as you can. But the price, spiritually speaking, is way too high. It's vitally important to be free, live simply and not get caught up in the rat race; otherwise we'll just become another crazed rat.

In my own life one of my temptations has been television. When I am feeling unmotivated, tired, sick, or stressed out, television can become my escape that helps me forget my current unpleasant situation. Several hours can easily go by while I watch programs and movies that are good, bad, or indifferent. Then, when I finally do become aware, I feel somewhat scuzzy, disappointed in myself for going unconscious, for wasting precious time. I feel like a person who has just eaten a large amount of unhealthy, gross junk food.

The way to freedom from the junk food of our culture is awareness – and being connected to a deep source of motivation. Not the rigid harsh indignation of the religious zealot, but rather the ongoing ability to discern: is this a good thing that I do right now? Am I staying awake or am I falling under the spell of ego needs for a false comfort and escape? We then can become aware of the false hunger pangs, the inner promptings of desire, and the sense of discomfort and not need to act upon them.

Training in compassionate mindful awareness is the best practice that I know to help us learn more and more skillfully over time to refrain from acting on the urgings of our false desires. The next best thing, when we do fall subject to these desires, is to reflect (without blame or self punishment) on how acting out of our desires has worked for us – or not. Every time we see how this has not served us, we become a little wiser, a little more able to abstain. Of course, the challenging thing here is that so many of us are highly inclined to treat ourselves harshly and, with that, little or no insight occurs. And when we have extracted the pound of flesh of guilt from ourselves, we feel justified in going back to the same fleshpots again and again to numb ourselves to how bad we feel after beating ourselves up....

Self Forgiveness can be so helpful to us when we succumb to temptation, but for many of us this seems so counter intuitive. We have often experienced from our own childhoods that the way to make sure a child (or adult) learns from their mistakes is by punishing them or shaming them. And so we have often taken on the belief that we must do this to ourselves in order to motivate behavior change. What I find to be far more effective in the long run is, without blame or self reproach, to get in touch with how unsatisfactory my attempts at comforting myself with these empty seducers actually is.

There is another thing to become aware of that usually lies beneath our desires and addictions: the way we use them to escape from unpleasant feelings of emptiness, unworthiness, sadness, anger, etc.. So when we are feeling the urge to go unconscious it is vital to ask ourselves "what am I trying to escape from right now?" This question is not to be asked so much mentally but rather to be felt in our bodies, which will usually yield the answer when we are open to listening, sensing and inquiring.

The answer to the question is often along the lines of the following list:

Low self worth and consequent envy of others.
An underlying sense of fear or anxiety.
Feelings of loneliness, boredom, emptiness.
Not feeling okay within ourselves: "I am not enough."
Painful feelings of shame and guilt.
Anger or resentment against ourselves or others.
A need to punish ourselves.
A need to numb or deaden ourselves.

Self Reflection & Practice

The first human "demon" that normally needs to be exposed is the human addiction to power, prestige, and possessions. These tend to pollute everything.

-Richard Rohr

What are you willing to relinquish to have a simpler lifestyle that allows you the time to do good deeds, be an activist for some cause, study, meditate, go on retreats, attend workshops or symposiums? Do you give up vacations or take unpaid time off from work to go on meditation retreats? Take a part time job and have to watch your pennies? Run your own business so you can decide your own schedule?

Some decisions to simplify are not easy to make, not easy to weigh the consequences of. Do you cut back on a heavy workload you have carried to keep your family at a certain level of well being you think you need to sustain? Do you do away with healthcare insurance? Life insurance? Saving for your children's college tuition? Putting your children in public schools rather than expensive private schools? Not having children? Forgoing a traditional middleclass dream of owning a house? What do you think you must have to be content with your life? Be willing to look anew at your assumptions. Journal about this. What would you be willing to give up for more time to engage in spiritual practice? Reflect and journal on this.

What are your worst addictions, unreasonable desires or compulsions that won't leave you alone? These can be for material things like eating out at expensive restaurants, buying fancy clothing, special trips, etc., or less concrete things such as prestige, recognition, status, power over others, respect, being seen as an expert, etc.

So often our compulsions or addictions are our way of trying to cover something up so we don't have to acknowledge it, feel it and deal with it. How is this true for you? Be as specific and as thorough as you can. What do your compulsions cover up? Feelings of inferiority? Loneliness? Fear? Emptiness? Lack of personal meaning in your life? What?

Practice becoming more and more aware of any feelings in your body that can trigger your binges of consumption, overwork and otherwise going unconscious. Allow yourself to feel these feelings in your body without acting out. Become curious about these feelings: where they reside in your body, their shape, texture, weight, color, texture, if they have patterns of movement, etc., This is how you begin to befriend these feelings and not let them run you unconsciously.

How might feelings of unworthiness and emptiness cause you to keep looking for outside validation through overwork, competitiveness, buying things others will admire, acquiring prestige and status? Or overeating, sexual acting out, compulsive housecleaning, etc.?

What do you say you value? What do you actually spend your time doing? Do your values and what you actually spend time doing line up? Write about this (without shame or self judgment.)

The Invitation

It lies there nudging you just below your awareness and you do not want to wake up and acknowledge and resist its push. But no matter how you try to ignore it, it moves you in ways you do not want, to do things that bring you a false sense of comfort or satisfaction. What would it be like to face your inner demons? Could it be that you will find they are based on old lies that you have been telling yourself for years? Is it possible that if you faced them, they would melt away or turn into a crying child that has been lying inside you for decades waiting for your kind attention?

What would it be like to be free of their push and shove that have kept you off center for as long as you can remember? To be free to live in the House of Love and listen no more to the sirens of guilt, shame and fear, of unworthiness, emptiness and loneliness? Learn

215

to stay my friend with the first niggling of discomfort and not to heed the false sirens of escape. When you see the ripples of their presence on the surface of your life, acknowledge them and do not be tempted to run away from yourself. For you can learn to let yourself be unmoved by them when you know their false story lines through and through and you can resist their siren songs. You know they are only hungry ghosts trying to get you to feed them a crumb or two- and finally your very soul.

You don't need all the things these voices of insecurity and unworthiness tell you that you need. You have enough. You are enough. Instead, allow yourself to be with the discomfort, the pain inside you. Love and accept your exiled parts and you will not be seduced to look outside yourself for validation. Then you are letting God into your life, you are letting your true self emerge. You will be free! Is the price for this freedom high? Yes, but worth every tear shed, every fear faced and examined, every difficult experience welcomed and plumbed for its lessons.

CHAPTER 37

Letting Go of the Need for Easy Solutions

For every complex problem there is a simple solution...
and it is wrong.

H.L. Menken

A Sufi Teaching Story

Mulla Nasrudin was searching for something in his garden. When his neighbor asked him what he was searching for, he replied that he was searching for his house keys. Wanting to help him, his neighbor joined him, asking: " Do you remember where you dropped them?" Mulla answered: "Of course I do, in my house." "Why are you looking here?" asked his neighbor, confused. Mulla Nasrudin replied, "Because there is much more light here than in my house."

Introduction

Our culture is one of impatience with difficult issues and wanting experts to solve everything quickly for us. And every day there are lots of so called spiritual experts promising that they can take away our pain easily and without any effort on our part. They offer us three steps to totally transform our lives, to scrub out our DNA, to quantum heal us and crystalize any and all of our problems away for us. The temptation is so great that I'm sure many of us have responded to some of these offerings in the past.

There is a part of us that yearns for easy solutions to life's problems that don't require much from us. So when it comes to spiritual issues it shouldn't be a surprise that we would also want simple solutions. If only we can have a great awakening, if only some guru can

217

zap us with cosmic consciousness, if only we can be born again in the blood of Jesus, if only we can find that one key to unlocking the mystery of our life, if only...fill in the blank.

But life tends to be ...complicated, with many variables affecting the outcome of any endeavor we pursue - and to require considerable long term engagement on our part. To expect it to be any different for our spiritual journeys than our life in general is to ignore the complexity of our biological evolution, our personal genetic inheritance, our family of origin issues, our cultural context, our earth's environment and how all these affect our individual spiritual journeys.

And the real work can be so challenging that when we engage with it for the first time, it seems that we are going in the exact opposite direction. Instead of going away from the problematic issues, deep spirituality asks us to go towards them, right into the thick of our pain and confusion. For us humans this just feels so against our intuitive sense of what is right. Our biology and our cultural conditioning tell us to move AWAY from our pain, not towards it.

When I started on my spiritual journey some 45 years ago as a young, intense, ambitious, anxious and impatient 24 year old, I was eager and determined to have an enlightenment experience straight away. My hope was that if only I could break through into unitive consciousness, I could fix all of the problems in my life. I started Zen meditation and after six months of diligent meditation practice, I went to my first sesshin (meditation retreat) at the Zen center where my first teacher was in charge. After the second day of the retreat I began to meditate all day and night, working on the Koan "Joshu's Mu." Tenaciously I kept this sound "Mu" in my consciousness all day like a mantra, while meditating, while we worked in Samu, and while we ate formally with Oryoki in the Zendo.

Finally on the fifth day, while the old Zen teacher Koryu Roshi, who taught my teacher, was giving Teisho (a formal Zen talk) I let out a scream and plunged into a state that I had never experienced before. I disappeared as a separate being and became the scream itself – nothing more. For an hour or so I felt so different, so much larger than my usual small self. But then my habitual ego patterns started to reassert themselves. I started to feel proud of what I had accomplished and, seeing this, I felt ashamed and tried to shout it down. Unfortunately, this approach didn't work so well; I started a war with two aspects of myself (we could say ego and superego) rather than becoming aware of them and disidentifying with them.

Today over forty years later I can look back on this experience and see how I did not know how to practice skillfully and patiently. I wanted an aggressive fast approach in which I had hoped that I could use a battering ram on my ego to make it disappear. What I could not see at that time was that it was my ego that was behind my using the battering ram, and this approach could never get rid of the ego. In fact, it would just entrench me in my self judgment and self rejection. What I also could not see was that my ego was not an enemy to be destroyed. What I needed to do instead was to heal the wounded parts of my ego so that they would not impede the workings of nonduality in my life.

After many years of therapy and many spiritual practices I know that the best path for me lies in self acceptance, self awareness and the constant - but compassionate- peeling away of layers of false beliefs about myself, the world, and others that I took in as a child and from my culture. While I have from time to time had wonderful unitive experiences where I have felt at one with others and the world, I still have work to do with my fearful small egoic consciousness, to patiently heal it and integrate it with a larger vision of the world.

It is tempting to our Western mindset to want to progress quickly and so spiritual practices that promise a shortcut to enlightenment become very tempting, especially to younger people. One of the dangers in practices that emphasize concentrative meditation and sudden enlightenment such as Rinzai Zen is that the practitioner may have some breakthrough experiences, confuse them with total enlightenment and be fooled into thinking they have transcended all delusion.

Then they are open to all kinds of mischief sneaking into their lives while they rationalize that they have attained complete enlightenment and everything they do comes out of this awakened state of mind. When a certain kind of breakthrough in consciousness is valued above all else, it can encourage both students and teachers to go over the line in their conduct and rationalize their behavior as "crazy wisdom," eccentric behavior that comes out of their so called freedom from human norms of acceptable behavior.

Unfortunately there have been quite a few examples of spiritual teachers going far outside of acceptable behavior and their students rationalizing it as their teachers practicing "crazy wisdom." In Zen this kind of bad behavior sadly happened with many established Zen teachers (including my own) in the 1980's in various Sanghas (practice communities) in the United States. Even recently (2014) the founder of the Rinzai Zen community in Los Angeles was exposed as having sexually used many of his women students for decades, even though his senior students knew about it and did nothing to stop it. There is always a danger of misconduct when individuals such as these teachers hold a lot of power in a spiritual community, have no peers to hold them accountable and there is an over emphasis on enlightenment as opposed to following Sila, precepts of conduct.

Unskillful things can also happen in a practice such as Kundalini Yoga that promises the rapid induction of higher states of consciousness. The practices of Kundalini, bringing energy up the spine, sometimes lead the spiritual aspirant into spiritual emergencies where the newly arisen spiritual energy is not well balanced or it unveils a hidden trauma.

The practitioner can then struggle with psychotic states and have much trouble coming back to a normal state of consciousness. Other times the new yogi will enter temporary states of bliss and heightened awareness, which are then confused with permanent stages of higher consciousness, possibly leading to spiritual arrogance. Such high energy practices necessitate having an experienced teacher to guide the student and to stop them from going off the rails, spiritually speaking.

No matter how much we meditate, the shadow work of uncovering our distortions of reality and our fixations is a long term project. To expect we can overcome our selfish tendencies and areas of blindness easily and quickly is likely to lead us into over confidence and outright arrogance. I was sobered to read recently about one of my spiritual teachers whom I respected and how she fared in the last few years of her life. She always valued her independence and when old age made her unavoidably dependent on others, she became rather paranoid. This was someone who had practiced with dedication and taught for a long, long time. Of course this may have been because of dementia setting in, but it does make you question how much our spiritual practices can protect us from losing our clarity with the onset of illness, old age and death. Ultimately we are in God's hands and we need to acknowledge that with humility.

I speak these words of caution to you not to dissuade you from spiritual practice, but to cause you to soberly reflect on your spiritual aspirations and your motivations to practice. It would be far better to have a more balanced practice that isn't hell bent on obtaining enlightenment immediately. Practice for the long run; practice with patience and compassion. Listen to your heart and to Love for your motivation rather than the voice of ambition. It would also be desirable to practice both Insight meditation (mindfulness practice) and deep formless meditation as complements to each other, as they bear different fruits. And it is highly recommended to have a practice dealing with your shadow to examine and heal your disowned parts. Most spiritual schools of practice unfortunately do not have such a balanced way of practicing so you should find other ways of filling in the gaps such as seeking out psychological counseling.

Self Reflection & Practice

What issues in your spiritual life do you want badly to get past? What aspects of your personality are you impatient with? Be aware that it is often your impatience and judgment of those aspects that keep you stuck! And when you let go of your impatience with and judgment of them, you begin to experience more peace of mind. So it is really important to look at this impatience and desire to quickly move past those issues that keep showing up in your life. These issues are the gateways to your spiritual journey not the obstructions!

List those things in your life that you would like to get past as quickly as possible.

Personal issues. External issues. Where in your life do you want a final solution to a problem, a problem that gets under your skin and you so want to be done with it? A problem with anxiety or depression or poor self esteem? A problem with your family? With a loved one? With a work situation? What? Be as specific as you can.

Get in touch with your feelings and thoughts about a specific personal problem. Do you feel: Impatience? Anger? Shame? Helplessness? A sense of failure? Do you have judgments about yourself or others for still having this problem? Do you have a belief that there should be a final solution? Do you fear how others are going to judge you if you don't get past this issue soon? Do you believe you should just do spiritual practices and all of your personal problems will disappear (or should) disappear? Do you feel you are a failure because you have been meditating a long time and this personal issue hasn't gone away? Look carefully at how you may be judging yourself for still having this problem. Journal on this!

Can you list all of the things and all of the people involved in this problem? Is it possible that you do not have all of the keys to the solution and you need to involve others in the solution? Would it be helpful to open up the context of the problem so you can see it in a different framework? Would it be useful for you to seek guidance from some kind of counselor who could help you to get out of the box you are stuck in? Try stepping back from the problem and address it more playfully, less intent on getting it fixed right now. Does anything else come to you?

Invitation

Go straight down the mountain road with a hundred curves.

-Zen Koan

Trying to make a great leap forward is likely to land you flat on your face! And if you insist on doing this, let it be a lesson in patience and humility. You are probably not going to transcend all of your issues in one bold leap. You most likely have too many of them. For one thing you are a human being. That already is a pretty complex problem! More than likely your issues will be resolved little by little as you live into them day by day. It's okay that your life is complicated and challenging at times. It keeps you from getting bored.

Just do what shows up in front of you. You don't have to resolve the whole thing out in one great leap forward. It's okay to take your time. You are going to get lost and confused at times. That's part of the spiritual journey! And it's par for the course in a human's lifespan. Ask wise people for advice. Seek Spirit's guidance when you get too much in your own way. Let all of your life inform your practice instead of resenting or fighting with your very human situations.

It's okay that your life isn't perfect. It never will be. You will never get it all together and have permanent peace in your outer circumstances. And it could be that your personal problems will be gifts that keep on giving throughout your whole long life. They can be grist for the mill. They can be a motivation to keep on learning and healing on this human journey you are on. It can be a source of humility when you start feeling grandiose. And make you a source of compassion for others on this journey we call life.

And anyway, what else have you go to do with your one precious human life?

CHAPTER 38

Letting Go of Spiritual Ambition

The human ego …lives out of its own self image instead of mirroring the image of God. It is that superior self-image which must die. The ego is constantly searching for any solid and superior identity. A spiritual self-image gives us status, stability, and security. There is no better way to remain unconscious than to baptize and bless the forms of religion, even prayer itself. - Adapted from Contemplation in Action, by Fr. Richard Rohr

You Are Not That Important

The only prayer that works for me
is one of love, trust and surrender.
You keep pleading with me to have
some kind of importance in the world.
Well I didn't choose you for that job.

I chose you to open your heart and to love
everyone and everything around you.
Don't you realize that I'm too busy being
with you and everyone else in this world
to have time to grant you such a request?

So relax and let go of the need
to be seen and admired,
the need to have everyone
talking about your sermons and your books,
your beautiful buildings and paintings,
your musicianship and your fame.

Just play a simple melody that any child knows.
Just walk down a street near your house
and let your heart be broken open by what you see.
I don't command, in spite of my reputation.
I just invite you through the tenderness
of your own very human heart.

-Robert Cornell

Introduction

We can see through the pretentious antics of people like Donald Trump the developer/politician (and now our President Elect) who makes a fool of himself with his boasting and his trump-eting about how great he is and how everything he does is the best. But when we look at our own lives we may see that we are tempted to self promotion as well to gain recognition.

When I started my landscape company, I was still a Buddhist monk and I used that as an interesting angle to get local newspapers to write about our new business. Of course, there was logic in this in that, being a new company, we needed to promote ourselves and get noticed in order to get work. But looking back, I also can see that I liked the attention and it answered a need in me to be, well, paid attention to – something I felt lacking as the youngest in my family.

I suspect for many of us who like to win awards, to be in the newspapers, and to be recognized in various ways for our work and accomplishments, that there is often an underlying hunger for the parental approval that we didn't get as children. For some of us the need to be recognized and honored may be insatiable, with no amount satisfying us. From a spiritual standpoint this distorts any good work that we do as we become focused on how to get recognized rather than how to do the best job and how to support the work of others who are just as important as we are.

Because we are a culture that promotes endless personal ambition, inevitably we will be tempted to transfer our ambitions into the spiritual realm. Just because we become interested in the spiritual life doesn't mean we give up all of our previous concerns about looking good, being successful and getting recognized! We take our ego concerns right into our spirituality with us. Then the question is, when the egoic mind shows up, can we see it, name it, investigate it, and heal its underlying wounds? And can we then learn to let it go, time after time? The ego doesn't generally let go of us after one struggle with it. It comes up again and again to tempt us and lead us astray. And it is our task to let go of it again and again.

We see these ego concerns taking first priority in religious circles with sad frequency. The Bishops and Archbishops of the Catholic Church failing to address clerical abuse of children and being more concerned for the property of the church and the supervising of "uppity" women religious than the healing of the abuse survivors. Evangelical TV minsters dialing for dollars. Zen priests being exposed for their sexual misconduct. The list goes on and on. And these are only some of the most egregious behaviors that end up in the newspapers. It would be foolish of us to suppose that, because we have now gotten spiritual, our egos will suddenly be chastened and domesticated and no longer of concern. If we truly value our spiritual path we will stay aware of what secretly motivates us, what impulses play out beneath our polite pious exteriors.

I can remember times when other people have been recognized for their wonderful contributions in various groups I have belonged to and I have heard within me a small, piteous voice saying, "But what about me?" I would feel embarrassed even though no one else could hear this inner lament. I have had to deal with this part of myself for years at my church and try to make sure it doesn't cause mischief. This is where one of my old family of origin issues keeps coming up. And where better than in my spiritual family, church? Then I work with the part of myself from my childhood that so wanted my father's attention; I now give it my attention and love. I no longer shame it and drive it underground, for I understand where it comes from and that the wound is still there to some extent.

Sometimes this desire for attention does come out in public and embarrasses me. Then I apologize, mend fences, and forgive myself. But this inner complaint is not so noisy as it once was, not because I have shamed it and repressed it but rather because I have found more and more satisfaction in assisting others in need of help. This has given me a much subtler (and much healthier) form of recognition that is held in the bonds of personal relationships or in the therapeutic role I have with clients.

Paradoxically, there is a deep feeling of reassurance and comfort that comes to us when we surrender our need for self importance, our need to be recognized and celebrated. We may feel a certain sadness within ourselves for the realization that fame and fortune will never be ours, thank, God. We can give up our desperate attempts to fill up the hole of unworthiness inside of us with accomplishments and can rest in simply being alive. And oddly enough this hole begins to be just a tender ache in our heart that connects us intimately with those around us.

Self Reflection & Practice

Take a fearless self inventory: where does your ego show up in your spiritual practice demanding satisfaction? Take time and reflect upon this in detail. Be willing to admit each and every dark thought and impulse for if you don't they may very well be your undoing later on! And remember that this exercise is not about beating yourself up, but rather about bringing to your awareness those aspects of yourself that need to be brought to heel and to heal. Journal on this at length.

Do you have an ambition to move ahead quickly and be recognized as advanced? Are you impatient with the slow pace of your spiritual practice? Do you focus on your own spiritual progress rather than on being of service to others? Do you have a desire for status? Recognition? Fame? Wanting to have great religious experiences so you feel validated? Be honest!

Do you catch yourself sometimes wanting to boast about your spiritual accomplishments? Do you envy others for their accomplishments or their status in your spiritual community?

Do you sometimes desire to follow a teacher blindly rather than have to question and take responsibility for your own path? Do you take pride in being their student and bad mouth other teachers and their students or brag about yours?

Do you like getting all dressed up in the outward signs of religious commitment to piety and spiritual practice, wearing cool clothes, performing religious ceremonies or esoteric practices? Is the ego part of this or is it just the delight in participating as part of your spiritual community? Look carefully.

Do you harbor an obstinacy to not listen to anyone because you don't trust them or don't want to be open to anyone teaching you anything? Would letting someone else teach you something feel like they were being superior to you and consequently would feel degrading to you? Do you always want to do things your own way? Do you believe that you know the Way better than others?

Do you have a desire to gossip about and/or make fun of clergy, others in authority, or members of your own spiritual community? Do you envy or resent others who seem better recognized or more successful than yourself in their spiritual accomplishments? Are you are tempted to speak badly of them?

Look inside yourself for childhood wounds and deficits you are trying to compensate for with spiritual ambition. Instead, use that desire for external rewards to motivate you to heal your own wounds, to re-parent yourself, and to let God heal you. Use your own personal pain to empathize with others and to support them on their healing journey.

Take a specific childhood issue you are still working with. Begin to love and accept that part of you. Spend time each day loving and comforting that part of you and bringing it to God/Divinity to heal its wounds. As you heal, be of assistance to others with the same issue.

Invitation

Your life is not about you; your life is about Life. Whenever you hold back and desire a thing for yourself, you have diminished yourself. Open your heart and let go of the need for recognition and status. Let your concerns encompass others; as you help them to heal, you will also heal and you will not need so much bolstering of your ego with success and superficial spiritual consolations.

Let go of the need for quick results. It is only the ego that needs this. The True Self is content with what is in front of it each moment, "good" or "bad." It is patient with and caring about others. It is not looking for goodies for itself. Remember this when you are impatient and feeling overlooked and that life isn't being fair to you.

God sees into your heart. Let Him/Her heal with His/Her love the deficits and hurts you have suffered. Whenever you feel the urge to look outside of yourself for validation, come back within yourself to God, the Fountain of Love. When your heart is full of the connection to Him/Her and to others, you already have all that you need!

When you are connected to the abundance of God's Love you will never experience yourself as lacking anything. Remember that any longing for something outside of your self -for recognition, success, status- is a sure sign to return to God, to Love. Then you will be given what you need and have plenty to share with others.

CHAPTER 39

Letting Go of Busyness

The rush and pressure of modern life are a form, perhaps the most common form, of its innate violence. To allow oneself to be carried away by a multitude of conflicting concerns, to surrender to too many demands...is to succumb to violence.

-Thomas Merton

Listen

Stop. Listen.
Your Soul is calling to you.
But you are busy with the too many things,
some bright and beautiful,
others heavy and dark.
But go below this.
Go deeper:
your Soul is calling to you.
You are larger than you think
and your Soul knows.
It knew before
you were even born.
It knows that the world waits for you-
for the one precious thing
you were born to do.
Listen to the silence
that is below the too many things.
It too knows what

you were meant to be.
Let go of fear, let go of shoulds.
Your Soul is calling to you,
inviting you into the great world
that is waiting for YOU.

- Robert Cornell

Introduction

Half an hour's meditation each day is essential except when you are busy. Then a full hour is needed. – Saint Francis de Sales

One of the contradictions in modern day life is all of the time saving inventions we have at our disposal and yet so many of us don't have the time to be still and listen to birds or to look at a sunset. Many of us work long hours and don't get home early enough to spend quality time with our family at night. Some people work hard to get things they really don't need. And some, of course, have to work to scrabble out a meager livelihood for themselves and their family.

Other more wealthy parents wear themselves out driving their children here and there to too many things: martial arts, ballet, language school, play dates with other children etc., etc. I look back at my childhood and remember the long unstructured times I had playing out in the woods by myself – some of my best memories - and I wonder: what would have become of me had my time been structured like a modern child's time is today. Would I have become even more of a workaholic?

How do we pull ourselves out of this vortex of intense, constant busyness? Because our whole culture is caught up in this speed and pressure, it is often hard for us to see that we are not living at a healthy pace of life. As in addictions work, the first thing to acknowledge is that we have a serious problem, that our life is out of balance, if not that we are totally out of control. Many of us complain about our frenetic pace, our feelings of being overwhelmed but we do little more than complain to our friends and co-workers.

And for some of us committed workaholics, our complaining almost has the quality of bragging. As they say in the Anonymous Programs, you have to be "sick and tired of being sick and tired." And of course, there are more and more people today that struggle just to make ends meet. But many of us who are fortunate and relatively economically secure still find ourselves overloaded with too many projects at work, too many volunteer commitments and too many activities for our children.

For some of us we have to literally bottom out. One of my clients became severely ill for many months with an autoimmune illness before she could see what she was doing to herself. That long recovery proved to be a boon to her, for it forced her to be idle and that gave her time to take inventory on how her life was out of control with her over focus on work and how she was cut off from her heart. Gradually, she pulled back on her professional and volunteer commitments and found a new lease on life. She had come to see that the drive underneath her relentless schedule had been to prove to the world that she was competent and now she did not want to fight that battle any longer. She was competent enough. She determined to be okay with a lighter work load and to spend more time with her family.

While many are underemployed in these times, there are a lot of us who are overemployed, who drive ourselves past what is healthy and in the long run lose out on our family life, our health, our spiritual life and any peace of mind. As Jesus said so poignantly "what is it worth to gain the whole world but to lose your own soul?" What is it worth to own another property, to win another award, to land another contract and to be stressed out, to feel the loss of ourselves in the process?

This demon of busyness lies deep within many of us. It is fed by fears that we aren't good enough, that we don't have enough money, that others are getting ahead of us and that we can never have enough of the security that money buys. Like all compulsive processes, it is driven by fear and like all things fear based it can show up as what our culture likes to generically call "stress." Therapists have all kinds of stress busting strategies, but all too often they give their clients band aides to reduce their stress with breathing techniques or mindfulness exercises but don't lead them into a deeper examination of the things underlying their busyness and over commitment that are the real cause of their stress.

If we want to have spirituality in our lives, we have to be willing to slow down and get out of the rat race at least for a regular time of quiet and reflection. There is just no other way. Nowadays you will see many self help articles that tacitly accept the rat race of your life and try to show you how you can "fit" your spirituality into that frenetic life style. It then becomes just one more thing to do on your checklist and to feel bad about when you can't "get it done." What these articles don't tell you is that spirituality requires a different frame of mind. It is not about fitting 3 minutes of "power meditation" into your already hectic schedule. It is not about trying to learn how to keep as many balls in the air as you can but rather about asking the fundamental question of what is beneath trying to juggle so many balls in the first place.

Young adults have an especially challenging situation these days in our culture of instant virtual connectivity. While our personal digital devices have given us untold benefits in terms of time management, access to information and global access to everything and everyone, they also have a dark side. There is a growing culture of addiction to these personal devices. Everywhere you go you see people on their smart phones, texting, emailing, checking their Face Book page, their whatever and surfing online. And this is not even touching on the prevalence of male addiction to internet pornography. Now we no longer have any space in our lives to reflect and just be present for we have something in our very hands to run to anytime we have "time to kill." Time that could give us more space we leave behind for more stimulation, more news, more "likes", more texts, etc., etc.

I was talking to my 30 something dental technician this week about this issue. She comes from rural Montana and she used to take about two hours a day to be quiet and write and reflect on her day. Now the minute she wakes up in the morning she reaches for her smart phone to look for texts, emails and to go on Face Book. She knows this is not the best use of her time but also seems unable to release the hold these things have on her. She has lost the space she once had to inquire into what is meaningful and what would nourish her soul.

When we do give ourselves some space and time to be aware, to take stock of our lives, we begin to see how our minds are racing into the future, check lists in hand, and what beneath our awareness is driving it all: fear and desire. We begin to see the thoughts and feelings that drive our overwork: fearing the possibility of being a failure, fearing not being good enough, fearing losing our job or falling behind others, fearing not making enough money, desiring to please, to impress, to earn strokes, to avoid angering or disappointing others, comparing ourselves to others, feeling over responsible, etc., etc., etc. And we see our desires for more things for our children, more money, more security, more power to overcome the simmering fears that lie below our usual awareness. We also realize we are afraid we will miss a great opportunity with our business or we need to build a nest egg for our retirement or provide for our children's education.

Sadly, this insecure mindset will never give us peace of mind. And this insecurity is rife in our country today with so many changes afoot and the middle class feeling under great pressure and uncertainty. When we give ourselves space to notice, we also become aware of an underlying sense of internal pressure. When we are incessantly busy, we develop a habitual internal momentum that keeps pushing us forward from one task to another. It becomes a feat of courage to get out of the rat race if only for a moment, for then we can get in touch with this underlying anxiety and pressure. And we don't like it; it feels edgy and uncomfortable, so we look for distraction to take our minds off this uneasiness.

A number of years ago, when I would start to feel overwhelmed by the demands of my landscape business, I would go up to the small mountain town of Wrightwood not far from where I live in Pasadena and stay by myself at a lovely B&B there for the weekend. I would come up to the mountains with so much carried on my back that for the first day there mostly I would just lie around listening to Brahms chamber music and sometimes crying. I was being my overly responsible self and trying to please demanding clients would send me over the edge, trying so hard to address all of their many concerns. I would get caught up in the trance of having to please them no matter what and fearing that I would fail. It would take me a few days to return to sanity so I could come down from the mountains and resume my life. Without the silence of those pines and the granite boulders, which made no demands upon me, I could have lost myself.

At some point we may finally be willing to get off of this endless treadmill, to take a leap of faith. And we allow ourselves to take a breath - and to be aware that we are breathing. Very simple and so easy to miss when we are running on empty. As we slow down and take things off our schedule, we can then see the anxiety playing out in our mind that drives the whole thing forward.

We need to be with our anxiety, let it be and not run from it back into the swirling vortex of busyness. And then we have the choice to question the unfounded fears and let them go, to no longer be driven by these anxious thoughts about success and failure, pride and shame. Like all addictions, our compulsion to busyness takes time to heal. We will have our moments of falling off the wagon and we will suffer the consequences through stress related illnesses, burn out, or damaged relationships.

Then we will let go again and perhaps this time surrender even more, learning to keep coming back to the present moment and the simple tasks at hand. As we let go of busyness and learn to be with our experience in the present moment, our life takes on a decidedly better quality. We can enjoy the simple pleasures of our lives and not need a lot of how-to manuals and magazine articles to tell us how to do everything perfectly in our over busy lives. We keep our lives real simple and we don't take on more than we can manage. We learn to trust our own intuition because we now can tune into our senses and gut feelings. We learn to live more in our bodies and on body time.

There is the wonderful story concerning Julia Butterfly Hill who found her calling in environmental activism and lived for over two years in a redwood tree called Luna in order to save it from being cut down by the Pacific Lumber Company. Before that happened, she had a life changing event where she was involved in a horrendous car accident involving a drunk driver.

Here are her own words (courtesy of Wikipedia), "As I recovered, I realized that my whole life had been out of balance...I had graduated high school at 16, and had been working nonstop since then, first as a waitress, then as a restaurant manager. I had been obsessed by my career, success, and material things. The crash woke me up to the importance of the moment, and doing whatever I could to make a positive impact on the future. The steering wheel in my head, both figuratively and literally, steered me in a new direction in my life."

Self Reflection & Practice

Have patience with all things, But, first of all with yourself.

-Saint Francis de Sales

IMPORTANT PRACTICE

Give yourself a whole day alone to reflect upon your life and the quality of its rhythm and pace. Go away someplace out of your usual territory, away from your usual concerns and tasks. Take no electronic media, books or entertainment with you and take a notebook or journal to write in. In this quiet open space, consider the question of how happy you are with the current pace of your life. Let your body be the main part of this inquiry. Some of us drive our bodies like machines. Let your body speak to you as you feel into the level of energy present, the emotional tenor present, any aches and pains. Listen to that pain in your neck and shoulders, that knot in your gut. What would they like to say? Do you feel fatigued or rested? Content or sad? Peaceful or anxious? Calm or irritable?

If you are not happy with the pace in your life, what would you be willing to give up to reduce the speed, stress and demand you feel in it? What voices in you tell you that you cannot let anything go? Are these healthy voices, or are they the voices of fear, guilt or insecurity, the need to be admired, recognized or to please others? One way to tell this is to look inside and consider letting some commitment or responsibility or desire go that is feeling burdensome and not conducive to a healthy life balance. What is the emotional tenor of any voice that tries to convince you otherwise? If it is fearful or motivated by fame or ambition it is not healthy. If it is a voice of calm, caring and interest, or one of sober reflection, then it is healthy.

There are difficult issues to consider when you have children. Are your children getting enough quality time with you? How much time do you let electronic media entertain them instead of your engaged presence? Can you let go of trying to meet every need you think your children have? Are you overinvolved with their homework? Do you think they must have all of the latest electronic gadgets and cool clothes and stuff? Are you sometimes driven by a fear that they will fail, not get into the best schools or be unpopular? If any of that is driving your over involvement with them, start to pull back and look carefully at your beliefs and behaviors about parenthood. Read a good book such as *Love and Logic for Raising Responsible Teenagers* by Jim Fay and Foster Kline.

Are you someone who is over responsible except when it comes to taking care of yourself? Do you find it difficult to say no to any request at work or from a friend? Does your family always take priority over your spiritual needs?

We need to look at all of the pressures we put on ourselves to get ahead. Attending social events we don't really want to be at for business reasons. Not being able to turn down a committee post for similar reasons. What are we setting up as our ultimate values? Where our time is spent, there our values lie.

There's inevitably a price for getting out of the rat race, and we have to look seriously at the price we pay to keep being a part of our culture's increasingly material focus. What do you want your legacy to be? To get your child into Harvard Law School so that they could be a corporate lawyer or a CEO? You owned the best car ever? You grew your business so you had lots of people working for you? You made sure you could retire comfortably? What do you want your legacy to be? Write about it!

Think deeply about what your actual needs are without the whisper of anxiety breathing in your ear. Write about it. Question if a need is based on fear or on faith.

Invitation

Is that all there is, is that all there is? If that's all there is my friends, then let's keep dancing.

-Peggy Lee

Time goes by and your heart cries out "when do we get there? When can we ever stop?" And if you ignore it long enough your heart may go silent and dead. Then you will wonder: what happened to my love of life? Where did it vanish- and will it ever return? This is the living death where materialism and technology have replaced the connections of your heart to people and things that have meaning for you. Is this virtual Zombie life what you want?

Let go of those inner voices that say to you: more, more, not enough! Take a chance and get out of the rat race. Take another path that is slower and quieter, where you can hear yourself think and breathe. You don't need the second house. You don't need your children to go to Harvard. You don't need that fancy new car. You don't need the designer clothes. You don't need the latest Man Toys. You don't need precious jewelry. You don't need all that stuff the culture says you need.

Everything you buy, you pay for with your life energy and time and you have to take care of it and keep it secure, besides. Live simply with less stuff. With this you create more space in your life to live! Move more slowly, with deliberation. Then you will be able to breathe and notice little things that make you smile. Come back to this moment where a bird happily sings to you in the morning and a garden welcomes you home at night. Take a nap in the afternoon and work later in the night when the phones are silent. Spend time with your family, friends and your pets. Have time to putter and garden a bit. Find time to meditate. Keep asking yourself what you really want in life. Let yourself live deeper into your Life.

CHAPTER 40

Letting Go of Noise & Distraction

Are You Listening?

The invitation is there.
Always.
Whether you realize it or not.
The wind in the pines
constantly expounds the Dharma.
Whether you hear it or not.
The rocks speak of suchness.
Whether you stop-
to sense it or not.

- Robert Cornell

Introduction

The age in which we live, this non-stop distraction, is making it more impossible for the young generation to ever have the curiosity or discipline... because you need to be alone to find out anything.

- Vivienne Westwood

We know it: anyone that is at all sensitive is aware of it. We are deluged with noise and distraction in our everyday environment. With the technology available today, there are few places where we are not connected to, if not immersed in, all kinds of media. There has never been a society so immersed in such a seductive stream of ongoing entertainment, advertising, political talk, 24/7 news, pornography, and all of the electronic media younger people now occupy themselves with. One report I saw recently said that the average teenager texts or receives a text eighty times a day. Perhaps this leads to a feeling of being more connected to others, but I seriously wonder if it also leads to so much distraction that they can't get in touch with themselves.

For many of us there comes a time when the distractions and noise are too much. We crave silence. We want to hear nothing but the quiet tick of an old fashioned clock, the purr of a cat on our lap or the gentle sound of rain outside. This is a portal into our inner sacred realm. Buddhism talks about how the trees and rocks constantly expound the Dharma (spiritual teachings) of suchness. And we instinctively know this; nature and its sounds and sights lead us to a quiet space within where we hear and see with directness and simplicity what lies around us. No future to plan out and worry about, no past to regret. No present to miss by our living in our heads in concepts and words.

And in this we can find great peace of mind. We are not being manipulated to buy the latest thing; no demand is being made upon us, our worries drop away from us. There is just this invitation into Being: just listening, just seeing. The smell of pine trees, the rustle of leaves, the call of a bird or squirrels squabbling in the trees, the feel of a breeze on your face. The mind goes quiet and you just hear the gravel crunching underfoot. All is at rest inside of you so that you disappear and are just "this."

But silence can also be a portal into whatever fears and other negative emotions and thoughts we have been running away from. That is often why we distract ourselves so much in the first place. Can we stay present in the face of our fears of being quiet, "non productive," "irresponsible," vulnerable long enough to recognize these feelings and thoughts and to befriend them and let them go? Something like an addict having the jitters going off drugs, we often will find it difficult at first to let down and be still when we have an opportunity to encounter this deep silence.

This silence allows us to become familiar with ourselves deep down inside. In this lack of distraction we can see what we experience each moment and learn to befriend it. That is the purpose of meditation retreats: to give us ample time to settle down inside and to know ourselves in the deepest way possible: to know ourselves beyond the idle chatter of our monkey mind, beyond our limiting fears and sticky desires, to have an intimacy with the world as ourselves.

Even though I have been meditating for some 45 years now, I personally still need a lot of time in silence: a regular time or two of meditation every day and then a quiet day a couple of times a month where I turn off my cell phone, shut down my computer and all of its connections to email, Facebook, Linked In, turn off the TV and let myself be with myself and my experience as it unfolds through joy, anxiety, sorrow, alertness, sleepiness and a myriad other experiences. This is how I keep in touch with myself and with the world as it is unfolding right NOW.

Self Reflection & Practice

As we hone the ability to let go of distraction, to begin again without rancor or judgment, we are deepening forgiveness and compassion for ourselves. And in life, we find we might make a mistake, and more easily begin again, or stray from our chosen course and begin again."

Sharon Salzberg

How much time do you give yourself during your regular work week to be with yourself without distraction and busyness? What would you be willing to do that would allow you to slow down and be present? Turn off the TV at home? Not text or be on the Internet so much?

Notice when you are seduced into mindlessness by noise from media: TV, the Internet, etc., etc. Catch your self from going asleep and numbed out and turn it off. Even if you are in a public place, ask for it to be turned off when you can.

Practice taking quiet times every day when you are not so busy. Perhaps it would be on the drive home from work. Try turning off the news, the talk radio and just be with yourself as you drive home. You may find that you are calmer and more available to your family when you arrive home.

What keeps you from being still? Notice carefully what in you perpetuates restlessness and the fear of stopping. Watch your mind and what it says about the fear of disappointing others, failing at something, not meeting a deadline, not getting something done you feel responsible for, etc., etc. Often it is the fear of these things that keeps us running on our treadmill. And if we let these fears continue to drive us we never find the time to still our mind and become free of these fears.

Be open to where your invitation to stillness is coming from in your day. Allow yourself to follow it. It might be a sunset, a child's laughter, a piece of music. Let the world sing to you: just listen, look, be open to perceptions that carry you into the simple beauty of this precious present moment.

Try stopping just once a day, every day, for fifteen minutes and check in with yourself. In this non-doing, what does your heart say? What does your mind tell you? What does the world whisper to you in the silence?

Try being present when you are waiting in line at the market, the bank or anywhere else where there is a line up. At first you may notice your annoyance at having to wait in line but eventually you may find that you actually appreciate the "excuse" to slow down and check in with yourself.

The Invitation

The water in a vessel is sparkling; the water in the sea is dark. The small truth has words which are clear; the great truth has great silence.

- Rabindranath Tagore

You can let all of the electronic gadgets that you have tell you what your life should be, constantly texting, tweeting, Face Booking. You can sit at a table with friends and be texting others and never see what is in front of you. You can keep taking pictures of your life and sending them to your friends to share and miss your real life that is playing out right in front of your nose. Wake up! Your life is not meant to be virtual. Your body needs contact with earth and real people. Put away your infernal eternal machines for a weekend and live a real unvirtual, unmediated life for once. See what it is like to be in your body and not living in your mind.

Silence is something your soul needs like the oxygen you breathe. Don't be afraid of it, for silence is the deepest language of God's speaking to you. Enter into the quiet and let your busy mind go, as you sink deeper and deeper into the stillness of now. Go find a place that will welcome you and make no demands upon you. Maybe it's in a quiet room in your home that is neat and clean. Perhaps it would be by the ocean where the wind playing on the waves would speak to you of deep quiet things. Perhaps it is in the mountains where the trees whisper of something you know not what and the rocks speak of countless eons of being.

Sit down and rest my friend, rest on the bosom of your mother earth who has born you all of these years. This is your true home. In this quiet place, when you notice the voice of guilt, fear of failure, over responsibility, future planning buzzing in your ear, just let it go, for it is nothing but unnecessary noise. Let yourself be with yourself and the world that supports you unconditionally. During your days, learn to move unhurriedly, and to listen beyond your worrying, planning mind to the sounds of the world, to look at the sky and birds and trees.

The world does not worry; it just is. Let this isness and its silence sink into your very bones. This is who you really are; so when distraction and worry show up know that they are just like clouds in the sky, fleeting in nature. The blue sky is permanent; the clouds are just passing through. Cultivate this awareness of the present moment; this is the foundation of your soul. This is the bedrock of your consciousness. This is the corner stone of your temple.

Challenging Practices

Some practices are relatively easy and then there are some that are incredibly difficult. As we mature, we can gradually take on more and more such difficult practices. But some of us Life just throws into the deep end of the pool, whether we are prepared to swim or not. Those of us that are so unfortunate - or so lucky - to be roughly handled in this way often experience a major shift in their lives. We do not will these things to come along but we can let ourselves soften under the onslaught and not fight against the blows of fate we experience. If we try in any way to manage our dark journey, we are more likely to let our egoic minds in to call the shots and try to regain control.

CHAPTER 41

Loosening the Grip of Addiction & Compulsion

Addictions or compulsions are misguided attempts to avoid our natural suffering and grasp desperately onto pleasure. When we are willing to face our discomfort and fears we are starting on the road to sobriety and freedom.

Same Thing Again and Again

You keep doing it.
It worked once -or at least you think it did.
Your dad hugged you when you showed him
how high you could jump.
Your mother kissed your booboo
so it wouldn't hurt anymore.

You're still trying to get it-
but it doesn't come anymore.
You still jump, hoping for someone's hug
You still get hurt, always hoping
that someone will care for you.
But no one comes and hugs you,
no one applies a Band Aide
to your hurting soul.

You are left feeling alone and uncared for
and the pain wells up inside of you,
looking for some love, somewhere.
And then - you abandon yourself, again,
with the false promise that you'll be back
once the skies are clear and bright.
You know what this is called:
Insanity.

                            -Robert Cornell

Introduction

Today I had to sit with a mother and father who decided to call the police on their 30 year old son who had been stealing from them for the last six months. He had been acting out his gambling addiction insanity, stealing from them to get money to gamble. His motivation – or so he said- was so he could make up his past debts to them. Sometimes he would win a little of the money back but it was never enough and then he would continue to gamble and lose it all – and more - again and again. Even with all these losses, he still maintained the crazy irrational hope that he could win back all the money he had taken and get out from underneath his shame and resentment.

I had seen him in therapy and he had some insight into the possible causes of his gambling addiction, but not the willingness to let go of his pride (and his shame) and to surrender to the fact that he could not control his addictive behavior by himself. And he was not willing yet to surrender to the finality of the fact that he could never make up the money he had stolen. That would have meant he would have had to give up his desperate attempts to get the money back and instead accept final humiliating defeat and to ask for forgiveness from his parents and himself. He admitted to me that, even though he had friends he could call when the urge to gamble came, he would not call them. And so the time finally came when his parents gave up, had enough, and reported him to the police.

What does it take for us to finally realize that what we are trying to do from our egoic mind's twisted perspective is never going to work? The saying "insanity is doing the same thing again and again expecting a different result" is so incredibly true. Yet, even faced with the fact that, again and again what we are doing isn't working, we often just keep doing more and more of the same thing. "Okay I failed this time but if I just do it harder and more often, then it will work," we say to ourselves. "If I just love him more he won't beat/leave/betray me. If I just make this much more money I'll feel good about myself."

We can't get out of the mindset that has got us stuck in this losing game. We must be able to change the whole way we are looking at the situation.

The way we have to do that is to surrender. Let go of the way we see ourselves, let go of our pride, let go of our anger, our self righteousness, our resentment and our sense of victimhood. We have to admit we are powerless over our situation because we can't see our way out of it by our own means. With these kinds of core issues, nothing will work but a big letting go – a surrender of something very near and dear to us. Something that is so familiar to us and so much a part of our identity that we are loathe to let go of it, even though it causes us so much pain and grief.

In my own life I spent some twenty difficult years as a Zen student tenaciously trying to practice with great intensity. In my meditation practice I would try so hard to be present – and it was this very trying that was the barrier although I didn't know it at the time. The breakthrough finally came for me when I was willing to contact the deep sense of unworthiness that drove this frantic efforting and begin to heal it, first with the acceptance I received from a counselor, and then finally with my accepting and loving myself and my brokeness.

It was only when I was finally sick and tired of all the endless efforting and could let go into just not trying to get anywhere, that my heart and mind opened and a new vista appeared. From this new vantage point, all of the insanity of my efforting seems just that -sheer insanity- driven by my distorted way of seeing myself. My pain had to become so great that it finally brought me to my knees and I had to give up my precious image of myself as one who perseveres, no matter what. This is the way so many of us live our lives. We live out of a false life script and try to make our life work by certain rules and strategies that usually come out of our wounded childhoods.

This doesn't work, but we just keep trying over and over again to make it work. This is the insanity that underlies all addictions and compulsions. And finally, if we are lucky, we hit a brick wall that we cannot get past; we bottom out in great pain. And then we are finally broken open to seeing how we have created our own suffering by living a false life shaped by our old way of seeing the world around us. And then we are gradually willing to let go.

Self Reflection & Practice

As you look at your life, where do you keep trying the same thing over and over again, hoping to get a different result and all you meet is frustration? If God is loving, why do you think he/she doesn't give you what you keep trying to get with your useless repetitive behavior? Journal on this.

Look at this in some detail for it may open up a way for you out of this suffering. Do you keep trying to please someone who seldom is thankful or kind to you? Do you keep working frantically out of some sense of a fear of not surviving or a fear of failure? Do you act compulsively out of a fear of displeasing others or a sense of guilt? Where are you specifically addicted to people, things and places? What rules and strategies do you use again and again with indifferent results? Do you keep trying to get love and attention from someone who cannot give it to you?

What are you addicted to that never satisfies you and leaves you feeling empty again and again? What is that big empty hole in you that you keep trying to fill up, to satisfy with more and more stuff that ends up leaving you feeling endlessly disappointed?

Try being with this hole inside yourself, rather than resisting it, running from it, or defending yourself against it. Let yourself feel it in your body and breathe. It will not kill you. Let it be however it is - without your constant fearful mental commentary convincing you of how terrible and catastrophic it is. Staying compassionately with this empty hole inside of you is the most healing thing you could do for yourself – and probably the scariest thing you will ever do! But it is the way to your ultimate liberation.

Try giving up one of your addictive or compulsive behaviors for a week and see what comes up for you. Journal every day on what feelings surface and what old stories show up in your head. Use a friend as an accountability partner to check in with because you will be tempted to fall back on your old dysfunctional addictive, compulsive behavior. And if this doesn't work, surrender to the fact that you are addicted and need professional help.

Invitation

If this program doesn't work for you, you can always have your suffering back.
- Anonymous program saying

Surrender looks hard but it is so much easier than trying over and over again and failing again, and again, and again. Maybe it is time for you to let go of all of that compulsive trying to get it right. You'll never get right what you were never intended to do in the first place. Maybe you have been trying to climb the ladder of success all of these years and you are finally realizing that your ladder is up against the wrong wall. Maybe you have been avoiding the fact that your marriage isn't working the way you hoped it would and you have to confront this fact and do something about it. Maybe you have been collecting degrees for decades and you still feel inadequate. And maybe you keep trying to make the pain go away and it's finally time to face it.

Relax. Stop. Stop trying to make something happen or to keep what you fear from happening. Just allow yourself to stop, if even for a minute, and relax. You can always take up the effort to control things again, if you want your suffering back. But give yourself the gift of some time to relax, to rest, to stop trying so hard. Get away from the craziness and give yourself some time to reflect on what is going on in your life. Perhaps you will sleep a lot, maybe you will even cry when you let down the burdens you have been carrying for such a very long time.

Allow. Look again at your situation and allow yourself to possibly see it differently. Are you trying to hold up the sky all by yourself? Are you trying to swim upriver? Are you trying to push a rope uphill? Does the responsibility you carry belong to someone else? Do you actually not have any control over the situation? Are you trying to please someone who is almost impossible to please and you think it is your job to please them? If any of this is true, why are you trying so hard?

Maybe you are not the person that you thought you were ten or twenty years ago. That's okay. You can be different now. Most people change with all those additional years of experience and maturing. It's okay to admit that you have failed at something. It's part of life. Everybody does it. If you need to grieve your losses, do so. If you need to, take some time off, if you can. Don't rush back on the scene and act out the same old drama just like you have so many times before. Create some space around you that isn't caught up in your old, old patterns of thinking and doing.

Surrender. Let go of blaming others. Let go of self-hatred and self-rejection. Let go of guilt tripping – yourself or others. Let go of your desperate effort to control things. Let go of perfectionism and being a control freak. Let go of excessive worrying. Let go of workaholism. Let go of FEAR. Open yourself to the possibility of Grace. And when you find that you can do this – not perfectly – but enough, you may find a new ease, a new sureness in yourself. You are enough.

CHAPTER 42

Allowing Ourselves to Suffer

The more you try to avoid suffering, the more you suffer, because smaller and more insignificant things begin to torture you, in proportion to your fear of being hurt. The one who does most to avoid suffering is, in the end, the one who suffers most.
— Thomas Merton, "The Seven Story Mountain"

Crucifixion

You don't have to climb up on a cross
(mostly the affectations of self proclaimed
martyrs preening for attention).
Just fully enter your life and that
will give you pain and sorrow enough.
When pain comes to you, as it surely will,
Don't run from it. Don't numb out.
When there is a gaping hole within you
don't run for the nearest comfort.
Sit down in the ashes and be present
with what you never wanted to embrace.
This is how you let God in.
This is how you find your Resurrection.

- Robert Cornell

Introduction

The most beautiful people we have known are those who have known defeat, known suffering, known struggle, known loss, and have found their way out of the depths. These persons have an appreciation, a sensitivity, and an understanding of life that fills them with compassion, gentleness, and a deep loving concern. Beautiful people do not just happen.

- Elisabeth Kübler-Ross

Spirituality is not about purposely avoiding pleasure and punishing yourself through self inflicted suffering. Usually such masochistic behavior is motivated by a kind of self hatred and denial of life. But that is not to say that the purpose of spirituality is to eliminate all suffering. Suffering will always be a part of our lives, for we will lose friends and loved ones, we will experience aging and the loss of our health – if we live long enough. And because of the nature of Life, our conditioning and our basic human nature, there will be everyday situations and environments that we will experience as unpleasant or even painful.

Mature spirituality invites us into a new relationship with our inevitable suffering. Rather than resist and resent this suffering we face it with courage and acceptance. We don't make martyrs of ourselves, and we do not struggle with this suffering. The interesting thing about working with acceptance and not resisting is that our suffering becomes less painful. When we don't tense up our bodies against the feelings of suffering and we don't spin out catastrophic stories that we tell ourselves about our suffering, it often becomes less intense and more workable.

There are many, many kinds of suffering: from physical illness to public speaking to being involved in situations and with people that we don't like. The more we continue to avoid and resist these kinds of life experiences, the more we make ourselves smaller and smaller, more and more rigid. We fail to grow and overcome the petty peeves and personal dislikes that cut us off from the larger world around us. We can very clearly see this with older people who have allowed themselves to be the victims of their own small pettiness and bad moods.

In my own life I can see how many times I reacted negatively and unskillfully to my pain and fear and because of that I did not accomplish important things in my life. This was particularly true in my becoming a monk and training for the Buddhist priesthood. In my practice as a monk, I would fight to overcome my fears and suffering or I would avoid issues that brought up my fears and suffering. This fighting with and avoiding my fears kept me stuck for a long time. It was only later in life that I began to have a healthier relationship with my suffering and learned to work much more skillfully and constructively with it.

Our only wise choice as human beings is to face all of our life: its suffering as well as its pleasures and not to retreat into a numbed out or reactive shell we build around ourselves to avoid the inevitable. The more we avoid being open to all of our experience, to our vulnerability, the more we are alienated from ourselves and from God, Simple as that. The walls that we build up to protect ourselves are the very barriers that cut us of from Life and God.

The first Noble Truth that the Buddha expounded was that Life is Suffering. To our Western pleasure seeking minds this seems so negative. But for those of us who have struggled unsuccessfully to avoid suffering all of our lives, it may seem like a great relief. It acknowledges the truth that we have resisted for so very long a time: that there is no way to completely avoid suffering in this human life. Accepting that suffering is an inevitable part of life, the only thing we can do is to learn to face into our suffering, not to run away from it, to accept its presence, not to resist it. Oddly enough, this becomes the gateway through which we can find our liberation.

As most of us should know from experience by now, it is not pleasure that we need to learn how to engage with, humans are mostly hard wired to soak up as much of that as they can! No, it is suffering that we need to learn to open to when it shows up. And it is with suffering that we need to learn how to inquire into its very nature and not to fear it and fight it. And in this deep engagement with our suffering many benefits accrue.

If you look at the great leaders of mankind, the one thing that stands out is that they all were well acquainted with suffering: their own and the suffering of others whom they embraced and supported. Jesus of Nazareth, the Buddha, Abraham Lincoln, Gandhi, Nelson Mandela all experienced great suffering that arose from their leadership. We can fairly accurately say that the more suffering they were able to face, the greater their character. But let's be clear that this is not a masochistic suffering brought on by self hatred. And it is not a melodramatic playing out of martyrdom. It is a suffering for the love and sake of others, one's fellow men, one's country – and oneself.

If we are to be authentic and generous human beings, what the Jewish people called a "mensch," we have to accept our allotment of suffering and even take some additional suffering on for the sake of others. And this is not to say that this suffering has to look heroic: mostly that is the act of narcissism trying to look noble. There are so many ordinary people who carry on with the little challenges and pains of their daily lives without complaint. And there are many of us who care for others in ways that remain hidden to others. These people are the unheralded salt of the earth that keeps the human race alive.

Self Reflection & Practice

Character cannot be developed in ease and quiet. Only through experience of trial and suffering can the soul be strengthened, ambition inspired, and success achieved.

– Helen Keller

Remember to engage these questions from a place of self acceptance and fearless honesty!

Spend time reflecting upon your relationship to your personal suffering: How do you work with your own suffering? Do you try to push through it? Just try to ignore it? Resist and resent it? Deny it? Avoid it as much as you can? Numb it out with overwork or addictive processes? Do you sometimes sink into it and have a "pity party" and act out of it? Journal about all of this. It is one of the most important things you can learn to deal with more skillfully and consciously in your life!

Think about your experiences with rather intense physical pain and emotional suffering: how you have dealt with them? Do you tense up against the experience of pain or can you breathe, let go, and soften into it? Have you had experiences with pain or suffering lessening as you moved into a more accepting place with it? Reflect upon this.

What do you tell yourself when you are suffering? Can you accept your suffering as part of life and that others have suffered just as you now are suffering? Do you sometimes freak out when you think that the pain will never end? Or can you just accept the suffering and trust that it will end at some point? Do you blame yourself or others for your suffering? Do you think that you are being punished for something? How do these thoughts help or hinder you in dealing constructively with your personal suffering?

How are you when it comes to being with others who are suffering? This is a very important clue as to how you are with yourself when you are in your own pain, so examine this carefully. Do you quickly try to cheer them up? Can you just be with them in their pain and not try to avoid it or fix it in some way? Do you avoid spending time with friends who are suffering? Do you get judgmental and impatient with people who are suffering?

IMPORTANT PRACTICE

The next time you have some physical or emotional pain, practice being with it in an accepting, non-reactive, non-judgmental place. Put your hands over the places that are experiencing suffering or pain. This is a very tangible way for you to increase your sense of presence with yourself. It is as if you were saying to yourself: I am with you right here in this painful experience. See how this might soothe the edges of the pain.

Remember to breathe into the pain and not tighten your body or breath as you are with your pain. Observe neutrally and gently the quality of the pain: is it sharp or dull? Heavy or light? Hot or cold? What color is it? What texture does it have? Where does it sit in the body? Does it move or stay in the same place? Practice perceiving the qualities of your pain directly in the body without your mind coming up with its usual labels and judgments. See if your relationship to your pain shifts in anyway as you relate to it in this different way.

Invitation

This was the first time I heard somebody put it like that: There is space around my unhappiness. That space, of course, comes when there is inner acceptance of whatever you are experiencing in the present moment.

- Eckhart Tolle

Pain can be your enemy. Or pain can be your companion or even your teacher and savior, inviting you to go deeper into yourself. In any case, you will inevitably experience suffering in your life and the only important question is how you work with it.

The first step is acceptance. Let go of resistance and judgment of self and others. Say to pain, "Hello, I feel you, pain. I feel you in my body. I accept you being here in my life." The next step is to breathe and soften your body around the pain. Consciously release any tightening you feel in your body that is trying to block and resist your experiencing the pain. The breath is a good way to release such tightening. Always remember that every breath out is another opportunity to relax, to let go of any tightening or resistance. As you breathe out, imagine breathing the pain and any resistance to it gently out of your body. Let be. Let go.

The third step is to investigate with genuine curiosity the experience of the pain. Touch the pain with the lightness of a feather on its surface. Be gentle with yourself as you explore the pain. Where do you feel it in your body? What color does it have? What texture? Does it have a weight, a density? Can you see any movement or change in the pain as you neutrally observe it over time?

At all times in your investigation, watch your mind for any stories it will tell you about your pain. It can concoct all kinds of horror stories about how the pain will never end, that you will die of some horrible disease, how much you want it to go away and what steps you might take, etc., etc. Watch this commentary carefully so as not to be carried away by it and be discerning as to whether or not some of what your mind says is helpful. Be aware of that which is not useful and let it go!

Acknowledge that others have had and still others are experiencing pain just like your own. You are not alone in this. To have a human body means that some will have pain like yours. In your suffering, let yourself be in solidarity with all those who have suffered this pain. They are human beings just like you and have vulnerable bodies like you do. At some point in your experience of suffering, perhaps you can realize something you have gained from the experience.

Perhaps you have become more compassionate with others who suffer. Or maybe you see the frailty of your own life and know that you have to focus on what gifts you have yet to bring into the world. If that is the case, thank your suffering for these blessings. If and when your pain abates, be sure to acknowledge your gratitude for the return of health and appreciate the miracle of having a healthy body and mind.

CHAPTER 43

Allowing Ourselves to be Broken Open

Suffering is not meaningless. If we allow it, it can open us up to the infinite, unbearable compassion for all that lives, including ourselves.

The Wall Breaker

All of you undisturbed cities,
haven't you ever longed for the enemy ?
If only He had besieged you
ten long earthshaking years,
until you were desolate and in mourning,
until starving you suffered under his hand.
He lies like the countryside outside of your walls
and he knows how to outlast those whom he visits.
Look out over the edges of your roofs:
there he encamps and doesn't grow tired
and does not diminish or become weaker.
And he sends no one into the city
to threaten, to make promises or to persuade.
He is the great Wall Breaker
who works in silence.

--Rainer Maria Rilke, translation by R. Cornell

Introduction

This is a scary poem. Rilke is sometimes like that in his poetry. Probably the poem is scary to us because it tells us that there is some force in the universe that doesn't like the walls we erect to protect our false identities and our personal comfort and that this force will eventually visit us and break down our walls. The poem talks about cities –actually us– that are comfortable and complacent behind their walls. And then Rilke says rather strangely to us, his audience, "Don't you long for the enemy that would lay siege to you?" That doesn't sound like anything we would consciously want!

And yet, there is a longing deep within us to have the walls between us and the world broken down so that we are no longer confined behind them and we can- yes- taste freedom. But from Rilke's words we can tell that the cost for this freedom is going to be high. We will have to endure hardship and suffer as the Wall Breaker silently has His way with us. This sounds quite a lot like the chapter in the Bible on Job with his sufferings and his struggling with his situation and arguing with God over his lot. And when Job stops fighting with God and accepts his painful situation, he gets his life back.

So wait a minute: interestingly, the Wall Breaker doesn't threaten, doesn't make demands, doesn't cajole. He sits outside of the walls and does His work in silence. What kind of an enemy force is this? Perhaps His threat to us is more in our minds than in actuality. The reality for most of us is that we resist and put walls up against much of our experience - which we judge to be unpleasant or threatening. Perhaps if we allowed our resistance (our walls) to our experience to fall down we would be freer.

There is a wonderful and painful scene in a classic movie, *The Pawn Broker*, where the old man at the center of the movie starts to come back to life. After the Holocaust in which his wife and children were taken away from him and exterminated by the Nazis, he came to the United States and became a pawnbroker who was gruff, remote and unfeeling. But events in his present life begin impinging on his walls and he starts to have flashbacks of his family – and his deep grief at losing them. In the defining moment in the movie, he connects with this grief that he has deeply repressed, by bringing his hand down on a spike that he uses for holding his bills, running it through the palm of his hand. And in feeling this great physical pain, he comes back to life and faces the deep pain buried within him from so long ago.

This is so incredibly human. When terrible things happen to us or our loved ones or our community we have two basic choices: we can allow ourselves to be broken open by the event or we can shut down and build a thicker shell. We can open our hearts and feel the pain and the connection with those around us or we can harden and close off. This is not to discount the prevalence of PTSD and real trauma in horrendous situations.

But often traumatic situations in our lives blow us out of the water, turn our lives upside down and, oddly enough, have the potential to help us to grow beyond the confines of our narrow self identity.

We humans are by nature cautious and we tend to stick to tried and true ways much of the time. This is especially true of the way we see the world and how we relate to it. In fact, therapists and psychologists rate the severity of a person's mental condition by how tightly they hold onto their stories about themselves and how others have treated them and how the person behaves in rather repetitive and rigid ways. Even for those of us who are less fixed and rigid, it is critical for our spiritual growth as to how we respond to what impacts us from the outside.

When I was a Zen monk studying and practicing in Los Angeles, I was the perpetual good little boy who tried zealously to become enlightened and worked so hard to get my teacher's approval. But I was stuck, stuck, stuck. My solution then to being stuck was to try harder and harder to concentrate and be completely present in my meditation and the rest of my life. But this was just the workaholic solution I had taken my whole life, now just played out in the spiritual arena. Finally my teacher admitted to the community that he was an alcoholic and went into the Betty Ford Rehab Clinic for two months. During that time, all my teacher's secret sexual relationships with his women students came out. I was absolutely outraged about his sexual improprieties.

I felt blindsided, betrayed at a fundamental level by the teacher in whom I had put all of my hopes for recognition and spiritual progress. But as the good little boy chewed on his anger, it gradually dawned on him that he needed to question for himself whether his relationship with his teacher and his own way of practicing were really serving him. And the answer that ultimately I came to a year later was: No.

And I walked away from almost 15 years of study with this man and the possibility of getting his approval as a Zen teacher. I walked into a new life as a laymen, still practicing Zen, but also having a career as a landscape designer and contractor and family man. The training I got from this change of direction was enormous and I have no regrets that my life took this turn. And I could have been stuck for a much longer time if my teacher had not betrayed me and stirred the good little boy into some really gut wrenching self examination.

As I look back at my life, most of the big forward steps have been initiated by crises of one type or another: flunking out of the theoretical physics graduate program at Cal Tech, the betrayal by my Zen teacher, a shortage of work in my landscape business that pushed me to decide to study to become a therapist, a bout with prostate cancer that gave me another chance to choose where I was going to graduate school in psychology. For that I am forever thankful to my cancer (especially since I am still alive)!

Self Reflection & Practice

Reflect on traumatic or difficult events in your life. What effects have they had upon you? Do you see yourself as having grown from these events or do you see yourself as being merely a survivor of them? How has your dealing with them, positively or negatively, affected your life?

As an experiment, try revisiting a traumatic memory and be willing to be compassionately and courageously present with yourself as you remember it. Does your willingness to be open and present to the memory change the way that you now relate to it and to yourself in any way? Journal on this.

Do you still find yourself avoiding certain memories because they remind you of a traumatic event in your past? Try facing into such a situation in your life now and see if you can work through the fear and resistance. If you can do this, note how you change from this experience.

If the trauma you have experienced in your life is really deep and complex, it would be an excellent step forward to get therapy for it. Eye Movement and Desensitizing and Reprocessing (EMDR) or Energy Psychology Emotional Freedom Technique (EFT) could be of assistance to your healing from trauma. Realize that most childhood trauma is complex trauma and that this takes some time and effort to work through and heal. In addition, all of the processes explained in this book about befriending, engaging, and re-parenting our vulnerability and our wounds are good basic methods of healing and moving forward.

Invitation

Things come apart, we feel undone. But then we pick ourselves up and determine to go on. If we inquire deeply into our experience, we will heal and release old patterns of compulsion and repression. The bone that has been broken becomes stronger. The old fears are healed and released. We find that we have an inner strength that we had no idea we had. Now we know what we are able to overcome, and we can move ahead with more self assurance, more dignity. And yes, we may limp, as Isaac did after his encounter with the dark Angel, but that is a small price to pay for our liberation and a new name

We know in our bodies as never before that there is both a vulnerable and an indestructible part of us that lies beyond -and in- all of the heartache and tragedy. We have come through and we are not the same. We have been through the purging furnace and we are purified even if there are burns on our bodies. You may not have chosen this, but you know now that in some way you have been blessed, even though you cursed your lot while you struggled through. At some point you were willing to let go down into the pain and you came out the other side. And something fell off your back: an old fear, a holding back that you no longer need.

Now you stand in front of the path forward and know this: whatever lies ahead is workable. Whatever pain and suffering there are in store for you can in fact purify you and enlarge the compass of your wisdom and compassion. Pain is not to be feared and you can expand the compass of your concern and engagement. Now you can move ahead with confidence and equanimity.

CHAPTER 44

Accepting Death in Our Lives

As you enter the later chapters of your life, you become aware of your death accompanying you. This is not a morbid thing as it makes you really appreciate what you have and realize what is really important.

From Tertiam Quid - by Kathleen Stroup

> For even so
> like this moment,
> we go,
> we go.
> Glorious.
> Brief.
> We go.

Introduction

I have had the good fortune to be close to many people during the time of their dying. This gets to be a regular occurrence in your life if you live long enough and you are willing to be present with the passing of those you care about. As I have lived longer and faced more of my own fears, I have found that being with loved ones and friends who are dying has grown easier and easier for me to experience, and it has brought the gifts of caring and intimacy and a confirmation of what is important in life. The thought of my own death does not cast a pall over me as it did many years ago. It is inevitable; it is a necessary and unavoidable part of living, not to be dreaded and not to be obsessed about.

I remember the first death I experienced up close. I was a monk at the Zen Center and a young member of our community whose Dharma name was Ryokan was dying of Leukemia. He was a good ten years younger than myself and I found it very difficult to see his frail body lying on the couch shivering under blankets, the white pallor of his face, and knowing that he was going to die soon. His father and mother were grateful that we visited their son, but I felt relieved when we left. It was personally so painful for me to be present with the suffering and the death surrounding this young man.

The second memorable death I was present with was that of Rosemarie Head. When I first met her in the early 1980s she was the president of the Los Angeles chapter of the California Landscape Contractor's Association. She welcomed me into the association and made me feel very much connected to her and others in the group. Rosemarie had a way of doing that; she probably had a hundred friends who thought they were the most special one in her life. The first intimation that she was ill happened when she was attending a landscape contractor's professional convention in Puerto Vallarta and she complained about a pain in her back.

Rosemarie and I had teamed up to build a Water Conservation Demonstration Garden as a memorial garden for her late husband Henry Soto at the L. A. County Arboretum. Halfway through the project, she became deathly ill from late stage pancreatic cancer. She was a brave woman and as she dealt with her illness she made provisions for her children and for selling off her nursery business. The last time I saw her she was in a coma and very near to death with her breath coming laboriously. When the dedication of the Henry Soto Water Conservation Garden was performed several months later, I was overcome with sadness that she was not there to be part of the ceremony.

I was not present when my father died, but I visited him for his 99th birthday celebration several months before his passing when he was in the nursing wing at the retirement home where he and my mother lived in Kingsport Tennessee. Six months prior, he had fallen out of bed and had broken his hip. Now he was confined to bed, in a lot of pain and had to use a urine bottle when he peed. I remember helping him with the bottle and cleaning him up afterwards. He said to me in his low key self deprecating manner that "his weenie had shrunk." I smiled at him and we both looked with deep love at one another. This was the last time that I saw my father and I still remember that long look of love that we shared with each other.

My father and I had shared good times and bad times with each other. As a teenager and young man I had been very hurt that he had not shown much of an interest in my studies and scientific research. This left me with a lot of buried anger that showed up by my not attending my own graduation ceremony at Indiana University and telling him to leave once he and my mother had driven me out to the California Institute of Technology to start graduate school. But my father, in spite of this, kept quietly loving me and never hurt me back. (I only learned of my father's hurt from my mother some years after he had passed away.) Eventually when I had children and matured I came to understand and appreciate my father for his quiet understated love and acceptance of me. When he passed away we were complete with each other.

Many years later, many deaths later, a dear friend of mine, Kathleen Stroup, was diagnosed with Stage IV colorectal cancer. Kathleen had nursed her dying husband until his death and had then taken care of her dear sister Deidre when she was dying. Now she faced her own death. Katherine and I both had been in the same year of the University of Santa Monica Spiritual Psychology program and we had become close friends. She was very generously helping me to put on some spiritual small group programs at All Saints Episcopal Church and during the time we were working on our second program, she found out that she had colorectal cancer that was so advanced that it was inoperable. She continued to help me with that program until she became too weak to attend the meetings.

Kathleen did not lament her misfortune; she dealt with it directly, without self pity, she acknowledged it and continued to live in acceptance and peace to the end. She made a wonderful trip to Ireland with her niece before she could no longer travel, and when she returned, we stayed in regular touch. On one of my last meetings with her, we "ate" poetry together. She loved poetry as much as I did and we read aloud to each other some of our favorite poems. Our time together was precious, intimate, sad, but beautiful in a way that I could never have guessed time spent with a living, dying person could be. At her memorial her niece prepared a beautiful video of Kathleen singing and reading some of her poetry; it was as if she were alive again and adjuring us to enjoy our lives to the fullest in the love which is Spirit.

Tonight in writing this and looking through some of Kathleen's poetry for one to use for this chapter I was touched by the sadness of never seeing her again in my life – the warm hearted lady who never complained and who was so generous with her caring and her time. This is one of the inevitable hazards of loving someone; we will miss them until we ourselves pass away. I suppose that I will be accepting of my death when it comes. It might be of prostate cancer, which I have had for 20 some years or it might be from some other cause. I would hope that it is not soon because I still feel that God has some things for me to do – but as the Rabbi said, "You never know."

Self Reflection & Practice

Reflect upon the deaths of family members and friends that have been close to you. Where are you at in your coming to terms with these deaths? How present could you be with them in their passing? What is difficult for you in being with the dying? Do you have regrets, feelings of guilt or a sense of incompletion over some of these deaths? If so, journal on this.

If you have regrets and feelings of guilt, this would be an excellent opportunity to give voice to them and to heal and let go of them. You might find the exercises on Self Forgiveness to be helpful in this. If there is something incomplete, try using an empty chair process to talk this through with the deceased. Imagine in your mind's eye the deceased in the empty chair and talk to them. If you feel so moved, you might take the role of the deceased and reply to yourself, creating a dialogue as you talk back and forth. If you do this, remember to switch chairs between roles to keep the energy pattern of person in the dialogue.

Where are you at with the possibility of your own death? Do you feel your life is complete enough that you could let go now? If not, what is it you had better start doing, now?

As an exercise, you might write your own eulogy. When you do this write about only your good traits, your loves and your passions. Write about what you have learned in this journey you have been on and what has been most meaningful to you. Write also about your wounds, your healings, your hopes, and perhaps what you had hoped to accomplish but did not. You might then get in touch with what is most important to you now in your life in a much more visceral way! What does the fact of dying, yours and others, mean to you about Life and the world being a safe place – or not?

Invitation

Stars have died so that we might live. Their ashes are in our flesh and our bones. Without their deaths we could not live. Without death there could be no life, one thing dying so that another might in turn be born out of its flesh and ashes and live. You will die, I will die, we all will die someday. Of this we can be certain, but not the time nor the conditions under which it will happen. It is okay, it is normal, this is how life/death works in this world of impermanence and change.

Life will go on as it has for eons, species will die, new ones will take their places in the order of things, and the human race will make it...or not...into the far future. This is not entirely up to you and me. We do our best and we are along for the ride with every other living being on this little fragile earth island we call home. Our job while we are here is to love and to serve our fellow beings of all kinds, to help care for our little planet, and to celebrate our living in this fleeting precious moment. And when it is time go, to turn it over to our sons and daughters to carry on with their children. And on and on and on...

CHAPTER 45

Engaging the Horrific

There is a really deep well inside me. And in it dwells God. Sometimes I am there, too. But more often stones and grit block the well, and God is buried beneath. Then he must be dug out again.

Etty Hillesum

Introduction

With some terrible events the mind grinds to a halt and is silent before them. There is no way to find a good ending to them, to paint a silver lining around them. We can only stand still in the face of such horror and suffering and honor it with our silence and earnest intent to do whatever it may take to prevent such a thing from happening again in our lifetime.

This is a difficult chapter that I didn't want to write. When it started to come forward in me, I felt quite a bit of fear that I had to be willing to stay present with. And then there is my reticence to being pretentious or hypocritical writing about something that I haven't personally experienced and undergone – at least not yet. But for honesty's sake I had to write it because it is part of our reality and there is no way to sugar coat it.

There are terrible things that have happened for billions of years to our planet. It was born in violence and it will probably go out of existence with the violent explosion of our sun. In between the beginning and the ending have been many other cataclysms. The moon was wrenched out of the earth some 4 billion years ago. There have been at least two great die offs of life on this planet: in the Permian Period and at the end of the Cretaceous Period, when the dinosaurs were killed off by a large meteorite smashing into the earth in the Yucatan peninsula of Mexico. We could comfort ourselves by the probable fact that but for this meteorite impact it might still be dinosaurs running around on the planet instead of us mammals. But that is rather the easy way out.

Life as we know it on this planet could still be wiped out by another meteorite crash-or perhaps even more likely now by our own human carelessness and folly. More recently, we have seen the great menace that we humans are to ourselves with our use of technology to destroy other human beings as well as other life on the planet. Perhaps the most disturbing episode in recent human history was the Holocaust, the systematic annihilation of some six million Jewish people and other "undesirables" by the Nazis. For some in Europe this caused the death of their religious beliefs to the point that some said that God had died.

How do we to maintain a spiritual perspective that acknowledges these realities and neither falls into pessimism and nihilism or into some naïve rose-colored-glasses Pollyanna spirituality that denies these terrible truths? The answer for me does not lie in any abstract theological analysis or argument but in my very personal willingness to experience whatever shows up in my own life: death of loved ones or my own dealing with chronic illness, acts of nature (God, if you will). And to simply be present with the reality of horrendous tragedies that I cannot put a positive spiritual spin on. One amazing example of how a human being can deal with absolute darkness is the life and death of Etty Hillesum, a young Dutch Jewish woman who lived and died in the Holocaust. She had done much inner work and when the Nazis showed up in her native Holland she did not hide but went out to help her people in their pain and suffering. She could have escaped but instead she chose to stay with them even knowing that it would mean her own death. All of this is related in the beautiful account of her life during the holocaust, *An Interrupted Life*. When she was transferred with other Jews by rail to her eventual extermination she threw a note off the train that was sent on to friends who saved it so that it could be part of her story. She said in the note, "We go off singing."

Etty didn't have on rose colored glasses, but she did see her reality from a very different perspective than the people around her. She could transcend her own perilous situation and keep her mind and heart open even under these most wretched of conditions. At one point in her musings in her diary, she speaks of seeing a young German soldier and being able to have compassion for him even though he was serving as part of the instrument of her people's destruction. It is like Jesus's last words, "Father forgive them for they know not what they do."

We humans have seen horrendous things in our history: plagues, the collapse of civilizations, terrible wars. And we are most likely going into another terrible trial as Global Warming comes upon us in future years. This together with over population, too many young men unemployed in Africa and the Middle East and a virulent fundamentalist version of Islam, makes for a very uneasy time in the world. There are no simple solutions and it will challenge us in ways that we in the United States have not been challenged since the Great Depression and World War II.

Do we still have it in us, in the age of Trumpism, to persevere and to do what is necessary, not only for our own wellbeing and that of our families, but for the whole planet? These crises that will require us to go beyond the limited concerns of our own families, our communities and our country and to be willing to make sacrifices for the sake of our whole earth and human family. Can we meet this challenge? It will take a spiritual growth that transcends ideology, religious and political narrowness of mind and an ability to open our hearts to the other as never before. Get ready for this journey brothers and sisters for it is coming upon us already!

Self Reflection & Practice

Spirituality is ideally engaged with the world around it. Spirituality without engagement is tepid, weak hearted and does not challenge us to grow. If you haven't already done so, start researching and becoming more informed about the difficult and challenging issues surrounding us today. Poverty, economic inequality and injustice, money in politics. Environmental degradation, Climate change, overpopulation, religious extremism, political and racial strife in impoverished areas of the world. Extremism and racism in our own country. These are part and parcel of our spiritual journey upon this earth of ours. These are hard and dark truths and are part of what we have to face as caring spiritual human beings. Our spiritual journey is not to distance ourselves from these issues but rather to feel them more acutely and to engage with them.

Where is your calling to heal the world? Political polarization, and the influence of hugely wealthy vested interests? Massive over population in areas of the world that are least able to meet the needs of more human mouths to feed? Religious fanaticism and turbulent masses of young men in poor areas of the world? Lack of education for women in Africa and the Middle East? Growing right wing movements in the developed world? Droughts, heat waves and their impact upon vulnerable human beings and animal and plant life? Loss of rain forests, and the potential mass extinction of life forms like no other extinction since the Cretaceous Period? The poor and troubled in our own country?

Know that inaction is a much a choice as action is. How do you avoid feeling hopeless and overwhelmed? Where do you feel called to face the difficulties of the future? Political action? Service in your hometown? Making changes to your life style? Environmental action? Consciousness raising? Think about what you care deeply for. And start with small steps to do what you can do. Join with others for this work requires many hands and hearts. Caring community is the only way to make a difference.

Invitation

For I was hungry and you gave me something to eat, I was thirsty and you gave me something to drink, I was a stranger and you invited me in.

- Matthew 25:35 NIV Bible

The world is calling to you by your full legal name. No one else can fill your shoes, brothers and sisters. There is no one that can do your job, no one that has the gifts you have and is in the place where you live. There is a stream that waits for you to clean the trash out of it. There is a redwood needing your protection from the chainsaws that would fell it. There is a song in your heart to be sung to call others into awareness. There is a research project on isopods, algae, and fish that needs your expertise. Everywhere in the world there is a need waiting for you to do the beautiful and necessary things you were born to do.

Listening to the voices of the world, Kannon Bodhisattva, with her many hands compassionately gives to each what is needed. We are her hands and we are the things that she gives to those in need. Your heart is the heart of Kannon Bodhisattva, listening deeply to the sounds of the world around her, heeding the cries of those in pain. Your heart is the heart of Jesus ministering to the poor. Your hands are the hands of Mother Teresa caring for the sick and dying. May your ears become more sensitive to the sounds of suffering around you, reaching out past your own zone of comfort. May your heart grow stronger in its love and desire to be of service.

Being of Service: the Ultimate Practice

When we love, we cannot help but want to be of service. To love and to hold back from our desire to help others would be tantamount to shutting down our love. So love and serve, serve and love. Each fulfills and deepens the other. As you love another, you find more ways to be of service to them. As you serve, you find more reasons to love. With the eyes of love, you see clearly that you are giving yourself a great gift when you serve others.

CHAPTER 46

Falling in Love with Everything

The only spiritual work there is, is to fall in love with everything again and again and to say "thank you, I love you."

I'm Not Myself Today

I am not myself today.
I saw you coming up the street, like a thousand times before.
Only this time you were my long lost brother, my long lost sister.
Stupidly I asked," Where have you been all my life?"
And you stood there, not knowing what to say.

Oh, can I hold you closer to me than I am to myself?
How did I ever miss you?
I saw you these many years
but I just could not see.
You were white/black/brown/yellow/red.
You were old, you were ugly. You were sad and tired.
Not of my class. Not Republican, Not Democrat.
You dressed poorly. You had bad breath.

But somehow something today opened up inside of me
and I saw you in your beauty as for the first time.
If only I can hold onto this treasure and never forget it, ever.
You were so beautiful that I could not help
but fall in love with you over and over again.

- Robert Cornell

Introduction

Buddhists have a practice for opening their hearts where you meditate in detail on the idea that, because of reincarnation, everyone else in the whole world was once your mother who gave birth to you, raised you, and loved you. While I'm not a believer in reincarnation, it seems clear that we human beings could use a practice for being able to open our eyes and see that everything around us is the Beloved. Perhaps we could come up with a practice that is just as profound and just as rich as this one so that we could break through our ego's optical delusion of individuality and isolation.

There is a beautiful, funny, sad, gentle movie called *Everything Is Illuminated* where the main character is a young American of Jewish Ukrainian descent. He is a bit obsessive compulsive and shy. He works as an accountant who is not very well connected to either himself or to the world around him. Somehow he feels called to go to the Ukraine to find the woman who saved his grandfather from the Nazis. He goes on a series of funny, offbeat and touching adventures in the Ukraine and he is quietly transformed. When he returns to the US, as he goes through the airport terminal, everyone he meets turns towards him and looks at him with love. And we realize: the reason they are looking at him this way is because that is the way he is seeing them as if for the first time in his life.

Perhaps we could contemplate how difficult life is for other people and animals and plants and even rocks and dirt, even though we usually can't see it. We can imagine fairly easily the life of an old woman who walks along the sidewalk, bent over and know she has had a hard life. And we will be walking in her shoes soon enough. Harder to imagine, but hopefully still possible, is seeing the lives of people who are not so savory in our eyes: the ones who seem to act unconsciously and inconsiderately, who are dirty and uncouth. There are probably reasons for their ill behavior and perhaps you can in your mind's creativity fill in the blank for them. The more we get to know people in detail, the more difficult it is to judge them. Often for people who behave badly, they have been abused in all kinds of ways in their past.

Animals don't have it so easy either. If we think in any detail of the farm animals that we raise and butcher, we will cringe at our being an accomplice to the massive suffering that they go through to provide us with our meat. Even stones have a hard life. Most rocks that we see in our walking around came from quite some distance from where we encounter them and they got quite beat up getting to where they reside now. Life is hard for all beings and all things. It would be good for us to think tenderly of everything that we encounter.

Perhaps we could make it a practice to greet everyone and everything that we encounter in our daily lives as if they were our brother or sister, because in a real way they are! They have all come out of the same billions of years old star stuff as we have. Maybe you could say mentally to yourself: hello Sister Cat, Dog, Squirrel, Bird, hello my dear ones. Good to see you today, Grandmother/father. How are you my son/daughter/sister/brother? And then your world could become re-enchanted, and it would be illumined from the inside of your heart, my dear.

Once many years ago, I was leading a Sunday Interfaith worship service with a bunch of Boy Scouts I had been mentoring for the Environmental Merit Badge over the weekend. As part of the service, I asked the boys to go around the campsite and find something to put on our makeshift altar to celebrate and appreciate as part of our environment. One of the boys, undoubtedly a wise guy, put on the altar a squashed aluminum beer can that someone had dropped on the ground.

I thought of what our former Rector at All Saints Church, George Regas, would have said and I shared it with the scouts. "Lord I know that your heart is broken by how we don't take good care of this world that you have given us. Please open our hearts and our minds so that we might be more caring. Amen." I don't know how the boys felt but I truly felt the sadness inside of me well up over how careless we are about the well being of this little planet we live on.

In my therapy practice, there are magic moments when I fall in love with the beauty of a client who has been open and vulnerable. This is what makes being a therapist one of the best jobs in the world: I get to fall in love over an over again with so many people young and old on so many different journeys. This blessing has come to me only because I have kept practicing letting go of fear and judgment, learning to simply be present. As I let go of fear and judgment, it is natural that I can see people's inner beauty; this is each person's natural inheritance and it is often my job to help them to see their own beauty.

Self Reflection & Practice

We have talked before about giving up judgment of self and others. That is one of the main barriers to loving others. So it is very important to practice this again and again until your eyes can open to others beauty – and to your own beauty. For when you fall in love with others, you fall in love with your own Being, which is inextricably joined with their Being. Every day become more and more aware of your judgments and let them go as soon as you can.

Spend some time reflecting on and appreciating everyone that you normally come across in your life: bosses, co-workers, spouses, children: everyone. Reflect on the good qualities of everyone, even the ones you have some reservations about. You can surely find something good in every single one of the people around you! If you can't, then reflect upon how their childhood must have been difficult to make them as difficult as they are!

In your daily meditation, bring one person to mind and think lovingly about them. With your hand on your heart, send them loving thoughts. With the information you know about them, think on how life has been difficult for them. If there is resistance to this, acknowledge it and let it go and come back to sending them love. Also, don't forget to send yourself love too! You are no less deserving.

Think of all of the people that you are dependent upon for your well being: janitors, gardeners, trash collectors, farmers, cooks, mail people, doctors. Teachers, police, pilots, service people of all kinds. Even lawyers and bankers and politicians! Think on all that these people do for you. Each day pick one particular person who serves you to think kindly of. Send them love and appreciation for what they do for the quality of your life.

Think on your favorite places in nature, museums and parks. Remember animals that you love and that love you. Send all of these good things love and appreciation. Send love and appreciation to all of these things that you carry in your heart and the whole universe, our galaxy, our planet. These all feed you and sustain you now and have nurtured you in so many ways in the past. Even distant suns that exploded, died and provided the elements that now reside in your body: the calcium, iron, magnesium, sodium, potassium, phosphorus, nitrogen, oxygen- and bromine and iodine too!

Invitation

Everything in the world is a part of us. Everything in the world depends upon us and we upon it. There is no line that can be drawn that says, "No this is not a part of us. We can exist independently without this." If we were to start to remove things from the world, at first we might not notice, as long as they were far, far away. But before long, the things removed would impact those we are in relation to and we too would be affected.

Without the plants, we could not breath or eat. Without animals we would have no meat. Without bees, many of the crops we depend upon would not flourish. Without birds, our crops would be overcome by harmful insects. Without worms, our soils would become hardened and depleted. Without microbes in our bodies, we could not survive as they outnumber our own cells and help us to draw nutrients from our food. We earn our bread by serving others and they in turn earn theirs by serving us. We depend intimately on each other and it is good for us to remember how interdependent we are with one another.

It is a right and a good thing to give thanks to you God, our Alpha and our Omega, our beginning and our end. It is a right and good thing to give thanks to all of you myriad things and beings through which our live is sustained. Amen.

CHAPTER 47

Being Obedient to the Call

The third time he said to him, "Simon son of John, do you love me?" Peter was hurt because Jesus asked him the third time, "Do you love me?" He said, "Lord, you know all things; you know that I love you." Jesus said, "Feed my sheep.

- John 21:11 NIV Bible

Introduction

Probably the greatest way for us to learn to let go of our excessive concerns about ourselves is to be of service to others. When out of compassion and caring we can give up our convenience and our personal agenda to serve others, we grow in wisdom and compassion. For me, Jesus is the great role model of service. When he asks his disciple Peter if he loves Him and Peter says yes, Jesus instructs him to care for His flock. If Peter really loves Jesus it is tantamount to caring for His little band of followers.

As we all know too well, there is no end to the problems and the people in pain and need in our very imperfect world. It is tempting to close off our hearts and focus on our own needs and those of our close families, because our own needs are demanding, the needs of others seems so great and our ability to effect any change seems so minimal. Probably there is also a fear that, if we would let ourselves really feel what we could feel, we would not be able to look away and we then would be going down a path that could ask a lot from us. Perhaps, our fears tell us, too much for us to handle.

Our minds will rationalize our fears and tell us that realistically there is nothing that can be done, but our hearts, if we heed them, stubbornly tell us that something must be done. It is good that our hearts are so unreasonable, otherwise the wonderful things that great men and women have done for the world would never have been undertaken in the first place. It is a good thing for us personally to listen to our unreasonable loving hearts;

if we just listen to the cramped narrowness of our so called rational mind that likes to weigh the chances of success and gauge our potential personal risk, we will be unlikely to take on the difficult and unmanageable tasks at hand in the world around us.

It is important that the inner voice we hear is not the nagging voice of Guilt. We can often feel guilty that we should be doing something that we are holding back on. It is okay to feel this kind of guilt, but it will never take us very far, for Guilt is in fact the child of Fear and Shame. These negative emotions don't have the power that Love and Compassion do to stay the course and face whatever difficulties lie ahead when we follow the call of our hearts. So don't listen much to Guilt. It might seem like the stirrings of conscience, but usually it is an echo from the harsh voice of our Inner Critic.

Love is the true guide. It never lets us down. We may have to practice some level of discernment as to what is appropriate to give our life energies to, but Love is the initiator, the transformer, the true motivator and it will far outlast any pangs of guilt or flashes of anger we may feel about the plight of the poor or our wounded Mother Earth. And Love is wonderfully unreasonable; She will nudge us, invite us to open ourselves to a larger world than Fear in all of its guises ever will.

One thing that we don't put into the equation of pluses and minuses of our rational thinking mind is the energy and enthusiasm that we get from helping others. When we are of service to others, our world expands and we are lifted out of our narrow concerns. I remember a clear cold winter's day in Indiana when I was in my early teens and I was doing some chores for pay, clearing people's driveways of snow. There was one old woman who could use some help but she didn't have any money to pay me. "That's alright." I said and I proceeded to shovel the snow off her driveway. I felt really good afterward and whistled all the way home, with the air biting my cheeks rosy and freezing the drips on my nose. I felt truly alive! There is something that feels intrinsically good about being of assistance to others.

I was talking to my daughter last week and she was telling me how much she liked being of help to others. She has her own struggles to be financially secure, but she really likes giving advice to and supporting younger creative artistic people via Twitter, blogging and other web related communications. She was thinking it was odd in some way that she wanted to do that in light of her own financial challenges, but for me it is a natural part of growing up. And if we are not expanding our locus of concern as we near middle age, it is not a good sign for our future contentment. If we are not involved with helping others, our lives will dry up and we will not be living a full human life.

One of the temptations that is most common in our lives is what are called the sins of omission. These are not the "hot" sins of sexual misconduct, murder, etc. They are the failings of the faint of heart who are fearful of stepping forward to share themselves and their resources with others in need. Many of us are guilty of these sins much of the time. We look away from the homeless and we do not donate enough time or money to worthy programs as we heed the promptings of our fears about tight finances and lack of time and energy for our own family's needs. It is so easy to let our fears and worries override our concerns for other people and the world around us. So every way in which we can overcome the voices of fear in ourselves leaves us more open and available to be concerned with the needs of others. This is why spiritual practice is so important.

Self Reflection & Practice

The first question which the priest and the Levite asked was: "If I stop to help this man, what will happen to me?" But... the good Samaritan reversed the question: "If I do not stop to help this man, what will happen to him?"

-Martin Luther King, Jr.

Where have you felt called to service in the past? How have you responded or not? How did you feel when you did or didn't respond to the invitation to be of service? What does this tell you about the power of being of service?

Do you sometimes feel guilty that you don't do enough? How could you let go of this guilt and let your heart come out more in response instead? Practice for a week being present in your heart as you go about your day. When you see sorrowful things on TV, in the newspaper or as you go around your town, put your hand on your heart in response. Let your heart respond first rather than your head. At night, at the end of your day, journal from your heart, listening for its invitation to you instead of nagging guilt

What issues keep pulling at your heart strings now? Give yourself some time to get in touch with your heart's concerns. Write about them and describe what makes you heart hurt or swell up. Discern what you can personally do and what is beyond your ability to effect change upon. Focus upon what lies in your locus of control. Join with others to do the things you cannot do alone. Invite others into your work. Don't be concerned with who gets the credit when good work is done. It's God's work anyway!

Chose one thing you can do to help make a difference in the world. It does not have to be a huge thing; it needs to be something that resonates in your heart. Give yourself time to do some research on a least one issue and keep your heart open to what it is feeling as you do this. Read with your head AND your heart. Perhaps journal on your reactions to what you are reading. Commit to doing something to be of service.

Where do you hold back in serving others? What concerns cause you to hold back? Write them out. Put them on paper and then let your heart address them. Usually these are the voice of fear. Pray to God/ True Self / the Beloved to lead you into your calling and reassure you about your fears. Listen every day for some inner promptings.

Invitation

In your world, listen to the murmurings of your heart, for it speaks the great truths of your life. Don't be afraid to feel what you feel. Let your heart be touched, to be sad, angry, even broken for the things you see going on around you. Let your mind serve your heart and not the voice of self interest and fear. Let your heart sing its unique song that it wants to share with the world. Turn off the TV and the angry talk radio with their non stop blaring and blathering and bluster about distant disasters and blame and outrage.

Let your mind and heart settle and stop being numbed by the overwhelming weight of it all. And then go down a city street near you and look open heartedly and carefully at the street and its people. Don't be afraid to let your heart feel what it feels. For whom, for what does it care? The poor? The mentally ill? The injustice of the rich taking advantage of the poor? The devastation of our environment, plants and animals? Let your heart speak of its cares and concerns for others. Watch out that your grief and sadness do not turn to despair. Be in community. Stay in touch, week in week out, to what your heart says to you and to what it pleads with you to do.

Start with something. It doesn't have to be big. Start with something you really care about. Something close by, almost right under your nose, that is hard to avoid. Don't worry that it seems too little a task. If you let it, it will take you towards much larger and more challenging places to be of service. Be sure that you keep being led by love and delight, for the work can get heavy at times. Judgment of yourself or others will not keep you engaged when the going gets tough. Love is the way.

CHAPTER 48

Serving in Our Personal Relationships

"We're all seeking that special person who is right for us. But if you've been through enough relationships, you begin to suspect there's no right person, just different flavors of wrong. Why is this? Because you yourself are wrong in some way, and you seek out partners who are wrong in some complementary way. But it takes a lot of living to grow fully into your own wrongness. And it isn't until you finally run up against your deepest demons, your unsolvable problems—the ones that make you truly who you are—that we're ready to find a lifelong mate. Only then do you finally know what you're looking for. You're looking for the wrong person. But not just any wrong person: it's got to be the right wrong person—someone you lovingly gaze upon and think, "This is the problem I want to have." -Andrew Boyd, Daily Afflictions

The Journey of a Marriage

Now I see you as you are, my dear
not as I wanted you to be, but as you are.
I have lived with you far longer
than I lived in my parent's house
and you know me more deeply than anyone.
We have raised children and
worked together to build a life.
We have seen our parents off to their end
and one of us will most likely see
the other's eyes close for the last time.
You are my love and my companion
on this journey, my dearest.

Introduction

There is an old Buddhist story about heaven and hell. In hell, people are seated at a table with a sumptuous meal spread out before them, but they have to eat with very long spoons. And as they try to feed themselves, they can't get the food to their mouths because of the length of the spoons. So they desperately try over and over to get food into their mouths but fail and their anguish grows as they starve.

In heaven, the people sit at the same wonderful banquet and have the same long spoons but they give their attention to feeding the other person across the table from them so every one gets their fill. There is much satisfaction and joy around this table as each person looks for morsels that will be particularly pleasing to their partner across from them.

Our close relationships with others can feel very much like heaven or hell; probably nothing is more rewarding or challenging in our lives than our personal relationships with other people. They don't think like us, have the same values or the same viewpoints. And besides that, they can often make demands upon us that can feel like impositions at times. And yet almost all of us feel a strong need to be connected to the other people in our lives. For the spiritual person the ideal is that, at some point, we feel called to give back to those around us and to be of service to them. We let go of our needs and start feeding the person across the table and lo and behold, we find ourselves being fed as well.

What our service to others will look like is as different as each one of us, but there are some commonalities. We are called by Love to be kind to those around us. This means that we learn to be careful with our speech and say only what is true as far as we can tell and we speak out of a desire to be caring and helpful. That doesn't mean that we don't speak up about things that others might find difficult to take in; it is important that we can say difficult truths to one another as well as kind words of encouragement and support.

Our relationships are full of opportunities and challenges for loving others, being of service, truth telling and discernment. And for growing into our own full adulthood. When is our love blind and when is it true and deep? When are we serving others and when are we enabling them? When are we telling our truth and when are we acting out and making unfair accusations? When are we drawing healthy boundaries and when are we being selfish? When does our anger serve to clarify and when is it unruly and destructive? There are probably no better places to grow spiritually than in our relationships with our families, friends, coworkers, bosses – and enemies.

Today we don't need to retreat into a monastery; our spiritual training occurs right in the midst of our daily relationships if we stay awake to the opportunities that lie all around us. There is no better place for our old family issues to surface than in our intimate and everyday relationships. Our boss at work can trigger our mother/father/authority issues. Our spouse will be our biggest opportunity to have many of our deepest, rawest relationship issues triggered so we can become aware of them, take responsibility for them and work to heal them. And as we heal our old hurts and wounds, we are able to be more present and more loving in our relationships. Our focus becomes more about being of use to our families, friends and business relationships, rather than what they can do for us.

As a therapist, the overwhelming majority of the work I do is helping people with their relationships with others: spouses, life partners, co-workers, children and parents, bosses and subordinates. This is primarily where our inner work lies: to heal ourselves so that we can be clear about our relationships with all of these people who can really push our buttons at times. Lately I have been working with a woman in counseling that has the same issues at home as she does at work: she takes on more responsibility than is healthy and appropriate for her and feels alone, unsupported and resentful. As we explore and unpack the origin and nature of this pattern in her consciousness, it is making a very real positive impact on how she relates to herself, her husband, her children and her boss and associates at work – and how she sees her relationship with God.

Currently, I am finding myself considerably challenged by setting boundaries with a client who pushes my buttons. There is a pattern of him pushing me to get more from me than is healthy for either me or for him. If I give him more time than our usual hour and I don't bring to his attention the ways that he tries to manipulate the situation, he will not learn how to get along with others whom he angers with his actions. Because of my own personal issues, it brings up a great deal of anxiety for me to calmly but persistently remind him of the boundaries of our therapeutic relationship. So our work together is not only his work but also my work; I have to keep working on my issues so I can be clear, non reactive and help him with his relationship issues.

Self Reflection & Practice

"A new command I give you: Love one another. As I have loved you, so you must love one another.

-- John13:34 NIV Bible

Where do most of your relational issues show up? At home with your significant other? With your children? Siblings? Parents? At work with your boss or subordinates? Journal on this in some detail. Go over recent sore points that have stirred you up: can you see any patterns to your difficulties with others?

What are some of your relational issues with children, parents, bosses, peers, subordinates?

>Trust / intimacy with your significant other?
>Over responsibility at home or at work?
>Being a resentful martyr to others at work or your family?
>Fears of inadequacy or unworthiness?
>Of being unlovable?
>Fears of being abandoned or rejected?
>Fears of being betrayed?
>Not feeling respected or supported by peers or family?
>Fears of judgment or punishment by authority figures?
>What else?

Journal on this, remembering to exercise Forgiveness of Self and others as you do this! When you clear up your old issues you become freer and more capable of doing the right thing at work and at home. How have you seen this playing out in your life as you work on your own issues? Appreciate what growth you have achieved thus far and think on where your future steps might take you.

IMPORTANT PRACTICE

Chose one relationship in your life that you would like to improve. Set an intention to use this work as a way to heal and grow spiritually and psychologically. Take some time to sort out what are the specific issues that you have with this person. Do your own personal work to deal with any resentments, judgments or fears that you have regarding this person. How have they hurt you in the past? What do you fear they will do to you in the future? How do they remind you of issues that you had in your family growing up? How might you now be of service to them?

Invitation

If each spouse says to the other, "I will treat my selfishness as the main problem in our marriage," you have the prospect of great things.

- Timothy Keller

Can you see the opportunity in each and every interaction "good" or "bad" that happens at work and at home? If you have clear intent and stay awake, you will be learning every day of your life and there will be little room for a sense of victimhood to arise. Then every day of your life you are in training in the School of Love and Wisdom. Even your so-called enemies, should you have any, will be your teachers. If you have clear intent, you will learn more and more how to be of service wherever you are. Your mundane life becomes your monastic training center.

If you heal your issues, your life will open up and you will become a wise, compassionate and helping presence to those around you. They will find solace, guidance, and caring in your presence. So you don't need to look for grand things to accomplish in life; just show up each day and watch your mind and open your heart. This will be sufficient to make the world around you better. And if you are called to accomplish some great work, be aware that your relationships with the people you encounter in that work are just as important as the work itself! You do not accomplish anything of lasting value if you trod over the heads of your subordinates. So stay humble and focus on being of service.

CHAPTER 49

Serving in Our Community & Country

Nothing that is worth doing can be achieved in our lifetime; therefore, we must be saved by hope. Nothing which is true or beautiful or good makes complete sense in any immediate context of history; therefore, we must be saved by faith. Nothing we do, however virtuous, could be accomplished alone; therefore, we must be saved by love. No virtuous act is quite as virtuous from the standpoint of our friend or foe as it is from our own standpoint; therefore, we must be saved by the final form of love, which is forgiveness.

"The Irony of American History" - Reinhold Niebuhr

Introduction

Today there is so much dissension in our political discourse regarding what we should do for the betterment of our countries and our communities. We are witnessing a degree of political polarization that sometimes makes finding common ground to be able to move forward feel like a hopeless task. The rise of Donald Trump in the US and the rise of other polarizing populist figures in Europe such as Marine Le Penn have unfortunately made this polarization even more acute. The basis of this polarization always lies in fear and resentment, where the aggrieved groups perceive that they have been treated unfairly and now mobilize to defend themselves and their rights, inevitably at the expense of the welfare of those demonized as the Other.

And yet, some people seem to be able to bridge this gulf and do good work that is supported by conservatives and progressives alike. Father Gregg Boyle here in Los Angeles is someone whose work is praised on the left and on the right. There is something about a person who is working from their heart that seems to touch people of all beliefs and ideologies. Father "G" as he is known by his "homies" is a man who has worked tirelessly to help black and brown people leave their empty ghetto lives of drugs, gangs, and violence. He is one of these special people who works from his heart without rancor or class or racial hatred.

While there are many issues such as Global Warming that raise ire on both sides and that need urgently to be addressed, how can we do this in a way that does not unnecessarily raise the hackles and paranoia of the other side? Can we find a way to our own hearts and those of others whom we are in disagreement with, so that the language of right and wrong can be laid aside and we can speak of what lies on our hearts as well as our minds?

In a recent documentary, *Years of Living Dangerously*, a climate scientist from the University of Texas in Lubbock reaches out to her fellow evangelicals and speaks to them in their churches about the impending climate crisis and how, as stewards of the earth, Christians are called to take care of the earth that their God has bequeathed to them. And in spite of their suspicion of science and secularism, they begin to be open to what science is telling us about our impending future.

Can we reach out across boundaries of ideology and politics and listen to the other and their concerns? Marshall Rosenberg in his work in Non Violent Communication has found a deep path towards reconciliation and mutual respect. Perhaps if we could let go of the red meat of political vituperation and slogans, we could begin to acknowledge the fears, the needs, and the hopes that lie in the hearts and minds of coal miners in West Virginia worried about feeding their families and environmentalists fighting coal ash pollution in the streams of that same state.

The heart is the right place to bridge this gap, not the fear based mind with its tendency to be judgmental and reactive. When we allow ourselves to come together and listen from our hearts, to be vulnerable and deeply honest, then we can begin to struggle together to find solutions that will allow us all to work and to live free of pollution and environmental degradation. We all breathe the same air, we all need work to support ourselves and our families. We are all in this together.

More and more I come to the deep realization that regardless of what our own particular beliefs and politics are concerning global warming and over population, we are all in the same boat. If we pass a point of no return and face escalating temperatures, we will all be on this same overheating overpopulating earth ark. All of us: liberals, conservatives, animals, plants; all in the same boat. And rather than becoming angry about this, it sobers me. I don't feel so angry at conservatives for denying the implications of climate science and wanting to hold onto their jobs and their economic focus. They have their own fears and concerns as do I.

And I have to look at what I am personally willing to do. Invest in solar power to be installed on my house? Cut back on plane trips and the use of my truck? Ride my bicycle to work sometimes? Try to drive as efficiently as I can when I do go out? Cut back on watering my garden? Contribute to environmental and population control efforts? Separate and recycle our household trash as carefully as I can? And of course, I need to vote on what we as a community and country will do about these urgent issues and support financially those political leaders who support my values.

My guess is we will face an extreme global crisis within the next decade or so caused by Global Warming, overpopulation, and water and food shortages. This will wake many people up out of denial and, hopefully, their focus on their own concerns. It is going to be hard, very hard, but it will take such a crisis to get our attention. That's our nature as human beings: we don't do well with long-term issues that slowly creep up on us. The issues have to hit us upside of the head before we are wiling to make the difficult changes that will save us as a civilization. And when this happens, it will not serve us to lord it over those who were in denial of the threat. We will need to work with them to see how we can help keep businesses and the economy afloat in times of great environmental change and challenge.

Mostly, we can listen to our hearts and do what we are called to do. Our actions speak far more profoundly than our words. And I suspect that's why people like Father Greg Boyle here in Los Angeles earn the respect and admiration of people of all political stripes. He is practicing loving and serving hurting people. It's hard to take exception to that. When we sacrifice our own comfort for others, it's hard for others to be judgmental about that. When we take a position on some issue, let's start with our own need to let go of something near and dear to ourselves. It's not that the wealthy should not be asked to pay more in taxes, but let's not keep ourselves out of the equation of who is going to pay for environmental healing and economic justice.

SELF REFLECTION & PRACTICE

Intellectual understanding blocks empathy. Empathy lies in our ability to be present without opinion.

Marshall Rosenberg, Non Violent Communication

Everyone is entitled to their own opinions, but they are not entitled to their own facts.

Daniel Patrick Moynihan

Think on the things that you most care about in our society that have become political footballs and a means of hating and demonizing the opposition. Birth control and abortion.

Home and Charter schooling vs. public school funding. Textbook wars in our schools over evolution and sex education. Campaign contributions and the legal status of corporations. Global warming and how to reduce carbon emissions. Gun violence in our schools and nation. Drug addiction and enforcement policy. The prison/ industrial complex and the vast over-incarceration of minority citizens. Militarization and spending our treasure and young people's blood on far off wars. Economic inequality.

Think on one of these issues that you are deeply concerned about and that you can feel angry and judgmental towards those opposing your position. As a Non Violent Communication exercise, allow yourself to have some compassion and understanding of what your opposition feels and what their needs are. Not what you judge as wrong and stupid about their ideas and actions, but what their actual needs and concerns might be. What basic values and needs might they have that you, in part, might share with them? How could you feel into their world in a way that you might be able to bridge the gap between you and them?

One of the most difficult conversations to have is with people whose world view is very different than our own. And often these people are our own family. Make some time to meet with people who have very different views on one of your key issues and have a respectful dialogue with them. When you find yourself getting heated and argumentative, breathe and return to your heart. Always intend to speak from your heart about your cares and concerns. And be equally willing to hear from them about their needs and concerns. What concrete things could you find agreement with them on to support in your own community where political sloganeering has less relevance?

Where can you personally make a difference? Put your time and energy into those things you believe in. Don't just contribute money to good causes. See to it that you are giving of your own energies to help make things better in this hurting world.

IMPORTANT PRACTICE

Now that Donald Trump is our President, there is a need to be more engaged in the political life of this country as never before. Spiritual people sometimes have a tendency to pull back from political engagement and to see the whole process as sordid and unenlightened. We can no longer afford that kind of attitude!

Whether you did or did not vote for Trump, my belief is that the man, because of his personality structure presents a danger to our country that we have never seen before. As David Frum, a conservative commentator who is an editor of the Atlantic Magazine said recently, it is critical that we defend our institutions

such as the free press, the constitutional checks and balances of Congress and the Judiciary.

What I invite you to continue to do throughout the Trump Presidency is to check his words against his actions. For those of us who voted against Trump, we must be careful not to jump to paranoid conclusions while at the same time being vigilant. For those who voted for him, I urge you to keep watching his behavior and asking yourself if these are the actions of a thoughtful and compassionate leader. If not, then oppose whatever actions of his that you feel are not based upon the welfare of this country and its diverse people.

Invitation

Out beyond our ideas of right-doing and wrong-doing, there is a field. I'll meet you there. When the soul lies down in that grass, the world is too full to talk about. Ideas, language, even the phrase 'each other' doesn't make sense any more. - Rumi

So much right, so much wrong. We argue about the causes of the weather even as it destroys crops and puts poor men and women out of work. We bomb far off places and kill women and children so our own children will - perhaps – be safer. We can be sure that these poor people are dead under our missiles but not so sure if we are any safer. Surely these things break God's heart. We can do things to put it right. We can vote and we can protest and we can remind others that those children we kill have parents with broken hearts too.

We see so much of our world descending into rage and chaos. How do we keep our own hearts and minds from descending into anger, fear and despair? Always be working for a better world, in your little corner of it. There are many things beyond our control. Be sure to focus your energies on things that are within your area of influence. Lead with your heart and think with your head.

What could you do today that you have been afraid to do in service to others? Before you volunteer other people's money and time, dedicate your own treasure and energy to what you believe in. Put your money where your heart is. Put your engagement where your values lie. Our actions always speak more loudly and profoundly than our words and political slogans.

CHAPTER 50

*Serving in Our Religious &
Spiritual Communities*

The religion of the future will be a cosmic religion. It should transcend a personal God and avoid dogmas and theology. Covering both the natural and the spiritual, it should be based on a religious sense arising from the experience of all things, natural and spiritual, as a meaningful unity.

– Albert Einstein

Introduction

For those of us who are of the older generations, one primary concern should be bequeathing to our children and their children viable and relevant religious/spiritual communities that support spiritual growth and inculcate the basic human values of selflessness, kindness, and integrity. There is good and necessary spiritual work to be done in our religious communities, yet increasingly we see younger people leaving mainstream religion and looking elsewhere for ways to frame their lives. How are we to find new ways to be meaningful to the Gen Xers and Millennials who more and more find our religious traditions outmoded and irrelevant?

Much of our current religious traditions are stale leftovers of dogma, rituals and beliefs that were useful and relevant to a prescientific period but do not meet the needs of our current technological society. But unlike the secularists and atheists who say that religion is irrelevant, it seems to me that religion is always relevant to the human condition- as long as we remain humans with hearts that need healing and unruly minds and bodies that need development and discipline.

Until we are able to overcome the worst aspects of our human nature there is unlikely to be a time soon where religion or spirituality is irrelevant. What are irrelevant and destructive are the toxic religions that continue to appeal to our tribal identity and fear. And in spite of modernity, there is still much of this fear based tribal religion. This shows how deeply seated egoic consciousness is in mankind. It is so easy for it to highjack religion in the service of ignorance and fear.

Modern brain research is showing us in considerable detail what we need to address in our religions of the future: how to control our worst impulses and foster our best feelings of love and compassion. The practices of mindfulness, loving kindness, and letting go of the negative impulses are as relevant today as ever and science is backing up this age-old need for discipline and wisdom. How this wisdom is to be expressed in new religious rituals, language and world views remains to be seen. And we can be a part of this work! It is not just a job for the professional clergy class, it is something we all need to engage with.

For myself, I have less and less interest in doctrine of any kind. While I attend an Episcopal church regularly, many of the old doctrines and rituals are not very meaningful to me. I could care less about the concept of the Trinity, the Virgin Birth and even the Resurrection. And while I may not care so much as other parishioners about Communion I do care about my *community*. I regularly practice loving presence, but I seldom invoke Jesus in prayer and I pray very little in any traditional manner.

I meditate every day and empty myself but seldom pray or have a conversation with God in the way more traditional Christians do. I am half Buddhist and highly value mindfulness practices but I also practice a kind of loving devotion to Love itself. Admittedly, this may seem strange to many, but it is how my religion has evolved on my spiritual journey. As Thomas Moore said in a recent book, I seem to have created a *Religion of One's Own*.

This may seem dangerous to some but for me it is because I take my religious life very seriously that I cannot accept other's concepts and doctrines as foundational truths. As the Buddha said profoundly, "Do not believe something because I have said it...but rather accept it because you have tested it in your own experience and found it to be true." For me, religion is about your life experience. You will be led to some truths through other's teaching and example but eventually if you just live another man's faith you are selling your life very, very short.

When I lead meditation groups at my church, I am not concerned about what beliefs and doctrines the members of the group have (indeed, we have one very spiritual atheist)! What I am concerned about is exploring human consciousness with them in meditation and examining our life experience to see what we can learn from it. I quote the Bible and the Buddha. Wisdom is wisdom, wherever it comes from. Love is love wherever you find it. How we can open our hearts, heal our wounds and be of service to others are the real issues. What we believe about various doctrines or beliefs, whether it be the Resurrection or Reincarnation, frankly I have no real interest in.

This is an experientially based religion with little doctrine and centered on the day-to-day, moment-by-moment learning to be fully present to Life as it shows up. It is about the continual effort to let go of one's default programming and to open one's heart and mind to the world and the people around us. It is about liberation and about healing. It is about Love and about Service. It is about forgiveness and about creativity. In a way, a religion of this kind is a very simple one, because it has little if any dogma or doctrine. But in another way it is a demanding path to follow. You build it with your own mind and your own heart and your own hands every day of your life. And you co-create it with others and with the Beloved.

As human beings we are wired to be in community. This goes especially for when we engage with spirituality because spirituality is about connection with our fellow human beings and the world around us. If you are trying to practice spirituality by yourself without connection to others you are really missing the boat. We learn real spirituality in community. Why? Because we not only get support and connection with our fellow disciples, we also can get royally pissed of by these same people and that is a great part of the learning and healing we have to do! This becomes the sand that gets stuck in our shell and helps us to create the pearl of wisdom, if we but inquire into what is below our upset. So don't be surprised if you have problems with some of the people in your religious community.

The question is not how to keep this from happening but rather what to do skillfully with the situation once it does. This is one of the beauties of community; you get your face rubbed in your stuff. This is not the problem with community; it is the very essence of its importance in spiritual practice! I once had a woman in a small group I was leading at church comment that she was so glad that the group would last only 6 weeks because she didn't like a couple of the people in the group. Little did she know what she was missing with her judgmental attitude! Because of that, I no longer do short groups; I want participants to rub shoulders (and egos) with each other and to learn from the experience.

If you have given up on church or synagogue or temple, then look at creating your own spiritual community with others. This might be a long term book study group, a meditation group or a worship group – or even better, some combination of all of these. We all need support at times when things are difficult in our lives and we can also learn a great deal from each other. In addition, there is a kind of symbiotic energy that arises when many come together to worship, study and practice. In a healthy spiritual community there will be many who can help you and many who can use your help. We learn how to let go of our judgments and willfulness and to be present with and to serve others.

Self Reflection & Practice

Tradition is the living faith of the dead, traditionalism is the dead faith of the living. And, I suppose I should add, it is traditionalism that gives tradition such a bad name.

-Jaroslav Pelikan

Community is necessary for one's spiritual practice. The essential thing that we are learning in spirituality is how everything is intimately connected. So how are we going to realize this without being engaged in community? Humans are intensely social animals. To deny this and try to practice spirituality on one's own is rather like trying to swim in a sand dune in the desert.

Where do you feel you are called to practice and serve in spiritual community? Do you feel that you have the kind of religious or spiritual community that you need? If not, what might you be willing to do to have such a community? Move? Help to create one in your hometown?

This does not have to be a large group or formal church, mosque or synagogue. It could be an intentional small group that focuses on certain spiritual teachings and seeks to put them into practice in everyday life. What is important is that the group meet regularly (at least twice a month.) Does this give you any ideas for how you might find or co-create a spiritual community?

It is always a good idea to set aside regular times to go on a spiritual retreat, say a couple of times a year. Do you already engage in such practice? If not, what might you find near you to provide this need? How might you help to create such an opportunity in your own community if it's not available already? Retreats can be in one's own home with fellow committed practitioners.

If you are not already serving in your spiritual community, what is getting in the way of this? Of course you may have heavy family obligations such as a newborn or a sick family member to care for. But if you are too busy making money or raising your children or some reason like that, seriously consider what your spiritual community means to you. If you are not making some kind of contribution (besides money) to your spiritual community, you are not going to get much out of it. And of course, there will be times when you have to step back because of other commitments, but if you always hold back, you are cheating yourself.

Invitation

Do you have a dream for a true home away from home: a place where you can be more real than anywhere else? If that is not happening now in your spiritual home and you find you always go there in your Sunday best, then my friend you need to look somewhere else! Look for a place where deep honesty and the courage to be true to yourself are practiced. If you have to, help to create this with others. It doesn't have to be in a big building and it doesn't have to happen on the Sabbath. The Sabbath may be important but remember that the other six days are equally so for spiritual practice! Small circles of people who are willing to be real with each other are better for spiritual growth than places that have big shows with charismatic leaders who inspire but don't lead you courageously into looking at your dark places.

Listen for what you need and listen to what your family needs, if you have one. Don't be afraid of rolling up your sleeves and pitching in to help create intentional community. The spiritual home of tomorrow may not look like it does today. You don't need big spires and large congregations to get close to God and yourself. Some of this real work of spirituality now happens mostly in the basements of churches where broken people get honest with one another. They are called the Anonymous Programs. This is true church. If you're not finding that vulnerability and deep honesty somewhere in your spiritual home, you are missing the essence of the work! If you are reading scripture but not reading between the lines of your own life, you are missing something. Have the courage and conviction to admit this and keep looking!

FINAL THOUGHTS

Letting go is such a hard -and rewarding- spiritual practice. And there is time to even let go of letting go. If we just obsess all the time about letting go we could become rather ascetic grumpy difficult old prunes. Not very juicy, not very pretty to look at, nor very sumptuous. So it is important for us to take delight in our world, to let it nourish us, comfort us, and heal us. We can't do all of the work of Spirit by ourselves; we need the love and support of our loved ones, the assistance and guidance of that which is greater than ourselves and the expansive and powerful support of this beautiful earth we dwell upon. All this supports and feeds us; we cannot do it all by ourselves; this is not a boot strap kind of operation.

So please take delight in your life. It is a good life. Sure it will have its challenges, but whose doesn't? Let yourself enjoy the good things in your life. Rich desserts from time to time. Good wine. Great food. Coffee! Beautiful surroundings. Movies, Music. Love making. Jokes and laughter. Downright silliness. Teasing and arguing with your partner; they deserve it you know! Family that loves you and you love them.

A gentle heart can take this all in and savor it without trying to hold onto it. Indeed, the more we can let go of our rigid demands for life to be on our terms it seems the more we can enjoy it just as it is: baking hot days and beautiful sunsets, traffic jams and quiet evenings at home, difficult arguments with your spouse and love making with them, having to pay more taxes and getting a lovely birthday gift. All as it is and all okay.

And desire is good. We desire good things for our life and when we get enough and feel loved enough, another desire naturally arises within us: the wish to be of service. Our intrinsically loving heart nudges us along towards caring for and helping others and that circle of love expands out further and further. At some point in our lives the issue becomes, how can I serve, what will be my legacy to this beautiful world that has given me so much? And this desire will carry us forward, further out into the world.

There is a wonderful man in my church named Don Thomas who has had considerable challenges himself. He recently lost his dear wife to dementia, he himself has many physical challenges and yet he goes to Malawi several times a year to serve there as a physician. And his daughter wrote this beautiful poem to celebrate her father. Here it is, by Gillian Kessler's permission:

Father II

In this picture
there is yellow green earth.
Dark black skin.
An old white man walking with a small black child.
Big boulders border the periphery.
The old man wears a baseball cap,
presumably to keep the sun at bay,
the little dark boy is in a sports jersey,
a bright orange number "3"
across his middle.
The boy looks off, a dark heaviness in his eyes.
The man looks at the boy.
There is movement in this picture.
The kind of movement that comes from open spaces.
Connection of only this. Only this moment.

I think of you and the movement I know.
You were gone at dawn, gone to save lives, run the show.
Words like crisis and trauma and emergency part of the
daily vernacular of our family though, I really didn't know,
at all, what was going on.
You left and then came home.
Slipped in somewhat quietly.
Gently sorted through mail.
Made yourself a dark drink,
ice softly floating.

We didn't make a lot of time for family reflection.
Didn't recount the day's events over a lively dinner table.
Didn't have loud, boisterous debates over homework or chores.
We all did our thing. We observed the things of others.
We moved like outsiders
in a shared space. Daily dialogue was routine.

So perhaps that's why this photo of you is so arresting.
You sharing this quiet moment in the green yellow grass
with this small black boy.
You living humbly, saving for months,
then packing your bag of tricks
and venturing across continents, across lifetimes and worlds
to carve out such simplicity.
This simple dialogue between two humans.
It doesn't matter right now if the drugs you've found will
help save this boy's mama. It doesn't matter if he is sick.
The only moment you both have is now.

There are no eight children to pay for, worry about, disappoint.
There are no wives, no colleagues, no competition.
There aren't massive bills and college funds and larger homes.

There is this quiet walk,
the gray boulders,
the soft hum of the wind.
There are the questions that you ask.
The way that you listen.

After your stroll, you will both return to the village.
Everyone will greet you with their wide, white smiles and you will
clasp their dark, dry hands.
You will hold their babies.
Play their games.
Hear their songs.
You will surrender to simplicity
in a place ravaged
by disease, by shame and be
the father that you never had
the chance to be.

- Gillian Kessler

Peace be with you, my friends.

Developing our Connection to Our Higher Power

As we deepen our awareness of our inner connection to ourselves and our Higher Power through spiritual practice, as we internalize a set of values and principles to guide our lives through our reading of spiritual and religious texts and participate in a worshipping/practicing community, we grow a wisdom part of ourselves that can guide us when we are susceptible to the influence of our limited egoic consciousness. This wisdom part that we develop within ourselves can function like a wise and loving father or mother when we feel we are off center and reactive to the events around us.

We can develop this connection to the wise part of ourselves through regular meditation, praying and opening to Spirit's loving guidance. Ideally, when we realize we are being reactive, we remove ourselves from our all-too-busy life, go to a quiet space, re-center ourselves in Silence and Prayer and reconnect to this Source of Love and Wisdom that comforts, heals and guides us. When we are reestablished in a relatively good place, we ask Spirit to speak to us, then stay in silence waiting on Spirit to answer. Note that Spirit may or may not give us thoughts; what we may instead receive is a Felt Sense or intuition in the body that leads to some forward movement on our part. More about this in Appendix Four.

When we are upset there is another very useful means to facilitate this listening for Spirit by putting one hand over our heart and the other over our belly to move us out of our head and deep into our interiority. As we feel into our bodies in this manner, we are connected to a source inside of us that is calming, loving and healing. It is as if by putting our hands directly on our bodies, we are saying to ourselves: "I am here for you. I care, love and support you." There is a profound comfort that we may feel from this simple exercise that can take us out of our upset and allow us to be present with and listen to Spirit and our Wise Self.

Then, when we feel calmer and we can open more readily to the presence of Spirit, we can begin a dialogue with Spirit that could look something like what follows below. This dialogue could be written out or could be a heart centered internal dialogue between our wise part and the part of us that is feeling upset.

Us: Spirit, I need guidance from you.

Spirit: What do you want to talk to me about my Dear?

Us: I am troubled by_____ and need your support and help healing this issue I am facing in my life.

Spirit: You have my full support and attention, my Dear.

Then you can continue this dialogue until something resolves. You will feel an energetic shift within you when you get some clarity, peace, encouragement and guidance from your Higher Power. It is this shift that tells you that you have had a significant movement in regard to the issue at hand. This is a very useful practice to help you keep centered as you go about your daily life, checking back with Spirit on a regular basis.

APPENDIX TWO

Developing Basic Trust

The presence of basic trust indicates that you have the innate sense that life is fundamentally benevolent, and that benevolence exists independent of you and your actions. You will have this sense to the extent that your grounding in the universe has not been disturbed.... The disturbance of basic trust is a significant factor in ego development because the perspective of ego is diametrically opposed to the sense of basic trust.

- A. H. Almaas, Facets of Unity

Those of us who have had consistent parenting probably have this basic sense of trust already, which when present, is taken almost for granted. But for those of us who don't, we must gradually build this basic trust by first and foremost being consistent and trustworthy to ourselves. As we practice staying non-reactively with our own experience, "good" or "bad," we begin to build this basic trust in ourselves. Then we know that we will not abandon ourselves, even when we are experiencing difficult feelings or sensations. We practice being non-reactively present to our experience first of all by letting go of negative judgments about our experience and negative scenarios that our minds may project from our current experience.

For instance, if we feel a challenging emotional pain in our heart space, we place our hand over our heart to be present with ourselves. If we experience resistance to being with this pain, we can soften the resistance by using our outbreath, to let ourselves relax into the experience. By lengthening the outbreath and thereby slowing it down, we deepen the relaxation response, reducing our anxiety. Finally, we can gently affirm in our minds that every experience and every situation we meet in our lives is workable. Even this pain is workable and we are willing to be with ourselves.

We also build basic trust by being consistently kind and nurturing to ourselves, even with our fearful and hurting parts, just as a good parent would be with their hurting child.

Our tendency as humans is to not want to experience such fear and pain so we typically move away from the parts of us that experience these "negative emotions." We may do this by distracting ourselves or numbing out with alcohol or other drugs or compulsive activities such as over eating, sexual acting out, workaholism, etc. Or a controlling self abusive part of us may surface to try to whip us into shape. This moving away or against is self abandonment and abuse and it sets up a lack of trust in ourselves. So when we notice our tendency to want to space out, to avoid, to numb out, to act out, or act against, we determine to stay present with our experience as it is in the moment. In this way we begin to rebuild trust in ourselves.

For those of us lacking in basic trust, doing Self Loving exercises on a regular basis is an excellent practice. To do this, put one hand on your heart, one on your gut, and send yourself loving thoughts and energy towards that part of you that is distrustful and afraid. You might want to whisper such things to yourself as, "You are safe. You are okay. I care about you. I'm here for you." You can send loving energy to yourself or let it come from God or another religious or spiritual figure that is important to you. I had one client who was deeply connected to Mother Mary, the Mother of All Sorrows, and bringing Mother Mary to mind helped her to be calm when she was feeling scared and uncertain.

Sounds and music can also be of great comfort when you are feeling off center and upset. Pictures of nature and other spiritual subjects, icons and mandalas can also be used to develop further a sense of wellbeing and safety. Chose carefully music and images that are helpful to you in inducing a feeling of inner peace. Good friends, warm religious and spiritual communities also are great places to encourage us and support us and they also help us to develop more of a sense of trust in the world and in people.

Practicing Self Forgiveness and Self Compassion

Many of us who experienced abuse or a lack of nurturing in childhood tend to perpetuate this harshness or coldness in relating to ourselves in our adult lives. Because we had no model for being kind to ourselves, we tend to treat ourselves as we were treated by our care givers. Others of us who did not receive sufficient mirroring and encouragement from our parents may engage in perfectionism and base our self esteem on our performance and people pleasing. All these childhood situations set us up for developing severe Inner Critics and Perfectionistic Pushers that monitor our performance and barrage us with a steady internal commentary on how we are failing to meet our own impossibly high standards. And the fact is, that no matter how hard we try and how well we succeed, that success gains us only a temporary amnesty from our Critics and Pushers.

This self criticism is very important to heal if we are to heal our relationship with ourselves. One way to begin to develop a healthier, more loving and nurturing relationship with ourselves is through the practice of Self Forgiveness and Self Compassion. First we learn to become aware of the Inner Critic and its habitual dialogue, which has gone unnoticed and unchallenged in our consciousness for a long time. So we are going to have to practice noticing this inner abusive stream of criticism as soon as possible so we can interrupt its momentum. With the momentum broken, we can then move into Self Compassion.

With Self Compassion we direct loving thoughts and wishes our way. Since this is not our usual want, we need to practice this on a daily basis. We learn to have empathy for our shortcomings as being only human. We take ourselves off the hook of constant comparison to others and to rigid standards of conduct. We come to understand how many of our weaknesses are not of our own making. We start to treat ourselves as a loving parent would their child. We avoid harsh self condemnation and only give ourselves useful feedback when we make a mistake. We learn to take responsibility only for what we have some control over and not for what others blame us for.

In Self Forgiveness, we begin to practice taking back in our consciousness the judgments we have been holding against ourselves for years. As we have had this habit of judging ourselves for years, we should be patient with ourselves when we begin to try to let go of these judgments. Usually, it will take many times of forgiving ourselves before forgiveness really sinks in and the self judgment lifts from our backs and shoulders.

To help the Self Forgiveness to really sink in, hold your hand over your heart as you repeat, "I forgive myself for judging myself as being _____." Fill in the blank with whatever judgment you are making against yourself. For instance, "I forgive myself for judging myself as being stupid and incapable of learning." And you can keep wording the Self Forgiveness in slightly different ways to try to be exhaustive of whatever judgments you are holding against yourself. In the above example, it might be, "I forgive myself for judging myself as being slow in math work. I forgive myself for judging myself as being terrible at taking instruction. I forgive myself for judging myself as being incapable of improving my math abilities. I forgive myself for judging myself as being stupid."

As you continue to practice this Self Forgiveness, you will feel a certain lightening of mood, an energetic shift in the body when you are getting to the bottom of your pile of judgments against yourself. This is the sign that it is working as this shift is not something that just occurs on the mental level. If it just stayed on the mental level, it would be of little benefit to you.

Self Judgment always has an energetic presence in the body that has a very heavy, hurting feeing tone associated with it. This work is not complete if there is any residual of this heaviness still remaining in your body. So after the practice of Self Forgiveness around a certain issue, it is always a good thing to see if there is any of this residual negative energy present as you bring the issue to mind again, in the case above this would mean looking at how you might improve your math abilities. If there is no charge left, you can easily think this through without that heaviness reappearing.

Focusing and Listening to Our Body's Wisdom

One very useful way of increasing our intuitive non-rational mode of accessing and processing information is by tuning in to our bodies. There are extensive and rich neural networks around our heart and gut areas and these networks are in profound and complex interactions with our brains in the playing out of our consciousness. Interestingly, there is more feedback going to our brain from the heart neural network than from our brain to the heart's network. We often talk about a "gut" hunch or something "weighing on our heart." These are common sense ways that we acknowledge that there is something important that we gain through our bodily awareness. The brain processes these body-based inputs with its own to come up with important information about our relationships with others, our environment, etc.

Focusing was a specific set of skills developed by Eugene Gendlin to help psychotherapy patients get in touch with their body/mind connection when they are stuck on the mental level or dissociating in some way from their emotions. Focusing is more then proprioception or contacting the internal sensations of the body; it is these sensory inputs plus emotions and their interactions with the intelligence of our thinking, processing brain that produce what Gendlin called a "Felt Sense." It is this Felt Sense that helps therapy clients to effectively process their feelings and get in touch with important non-rational ways of processing information and connecting to one's inner motivation.

In this appendix I want to introduce you to the basic steps for this process of Focusing and if you are interested, you can read further in the literature. There is a free E-book available through Amazon called *Focusing – Learning from the Masters* by Lucinda Gray. Ann Weiser Cornell's book, *Focusing in Clinical Practice*, gives a very detailed and nuanced description of how to do this practice, both for yourself and for clients. Focusing is a critical skill to employ in the kind of subtle, highly experiential processing that we are doing in the exercises in this book. We must be able to drop below our habitual ego-filtered, mentally prejudiced ways of relating to our inner experience if we are to heal and grow beyond our fixated dysfunctional patterns.

In Focusing, we first take time to notice what is present in our body: perhaps a tightness in some musculature in our body, a fluttering sensation in our belly, etc. We let ourselves contact these sensations directly without the usual overlay of analysis and commentary as to what we THINK is going on inside of us or how we like or don't like the experience. This is the same attitude we have in mindfulness practice: a willingness to directly contact the feeling/sensation with suspended judgment/analysis. We hover at a certain distance that keeps us from feeling overwhelmed by the experience and but not so far away from it that we are disengaged from it.

Letting our thinking mind go, we feel into it, explore it and let ourselves process this somewhat nebulous, still undefined sense within us. We will not get a highly linear, intellectual description of what is going on inside of us from this process. Rather, our description to others or ourselves will be full of feeling words, analogies, metaphors, images and other non-linear means of description. It will sometimes be vague and clumsy as we struggle for words as we contact our experience. For example, "When I think of that situation, I feel this slightly hot contracted band across my chest. I feel somehow constrained, held back. I almost have the feeling...the sense of being on a leash."

As we let ourselves wrestle with the unknowing and vagueness of this process, some newfound awareness may spring forth- a realization that we have never had before. For example, a client describes to me how she has a deep pain near the base of her neck, she stays with it, explores and describes it further to me and comes to the realization of how long this shame-pain has lodged there in her neck and how she has carried that for her family from a very young age. She can then process much of the anger against her mother and father that she has held inside herself, unacknowledged for years.

Clearly, this is not a rational/deductive process but rather a tentative, intuitive, non-linear process of inner exploration that leads to new insights and the ability to make shifts in attitudes and changes in behavior that can be profound and lasting. It is not just new information that is gained but more importantly a new way of processing emotions that have heretofore been blocked and are now freed up, allowing us to move forward in our life. In Focusing, you are birthing something new and at first unformed in yourself. Patience and the willingness to stay in not knowing for awhile is needed in this rich gestational process!

To practice Focusing bring to mind a situation where you have felt stuck in habitual emotional reactivity and behavioral rigidity, and where you are feeling anxious, angry, frustrated, confused, powerless to change and perhaps even despairing. Let yourself remember details of the situation that bring up these uncomfortable feelings, allowing yourself to feel whatever you feel. Do not rush to find a solution as you would most likely find your usual old solution again which has not been working for you. Let yourself rest in not knowing what to feel or to do.

Step back slightly from your habitual stories about the situation and your habitual emotional reactions to it and judgments about it and see if anything else might arise that could surprise you. Perhaps a forbidden emotion you ordinarily do not allow yourself to have. Perhaps an entirely different way to look at and relate to the situation. Perhaps a hitherto unacknowledged impulse or feeling that in the past you would have quickly suppressed. Perhaps an image that leads to an insight or a newfound emotion. Listen for things you would not ordinarily pay attention to that could be clues for a new way forward out of your present impasse …

When something new arises be sure not to dismiss it out of hand even if it seems downright strange or unfamiliar. In fact, the more unrecognizable the intuitive message is the more likely it will have something in it that will lead you out of your present impasse. Learn to pay attention to and play with something if at first it doesn't make sense. Remember, if it doesn't make sense in your old world view, think about how helpful this old frame of reference has been for you in the past!

Einstein said, "we cannot solve a problem on the same level of consciousness that created it." Similarly, when we are stuck in a rut in our life and cannot seem to get out of it, we are trying to solve a problem with the same consciousness that created it in the first place. Focusing allows us to step back from our usual way of perceiving and processing the situation in our rut and find new ways to relate to this rut and to move out of it.

Tapping into Healing

I won't go into detail here over the theory and practice of Tapping or EFT as Gary Craig's very informative and generously provided material on his website www.emofree.com contains most of what you will ever want to know about this technique for free. What I want to discuss instead is what to realistically expect from this procedure and to both expand the limits of its usefulness as seen by some practitioners and to warn about using it as the latest panacea for all that ails the psyche.

Tapping works best on simple traumas or phobias. In some cases these can be relieved in one treatment session. More complex trauma can require many separate treatments over quite some time. Because of the cost of such an extended course of treatment, it would be advisable for a person to learn the techniques themselves and to treat much of their own symptoms. One proviso about this self treatment however, is that one should not do it on very traumatic events which could cause one to flood with unmanageable feelings. These traumatic memories are best left to getting assistance from mental health professionals.

Something that I have noticed that isn't remarked upon by others using this technique is how it can help surface feelings that are buried or split off. A person who tends to repress emotions or stay on the mental level may be helped to access these emotions with the EFT protocol. I have done the tapping protocol with several such clients who have quickly accessed emotions that they otherwise would have repressed or split off from. If you find yourself or a client stuck in numbness or a particular emotional reaction to an event and you suspect there is something else going on that you just can't access, try tapping on the emotion (or numbness) that is present and you may find yourself breaking through into an emotion that lies below the presenting one.

For example, you (or your client) feel stuck in anger towards someone. Use the set up statement 'Even though I feel angry when I think of (the situation) I completely accept and love myself." And as you tap on the points, describing the feelings that are present - in this case anger - you may find yourself (or your client) sinking into another emotion such as sadness. Typically, the stuck emotion is serving as a protective emotion and the emotion that you sink into is a more vulnerable emotion that has been avoided. This can be a very useful way to uncover vulnerable parts so that they can be worked with more consciously and directly.

Working Compassionately with Our Subpersonalities

We think of ourselves as a unified whole, except sometimes we don't act that way! It isn't uncommon for our actions to take us by surprise and for us to say things like, "I don't know what came over me. That is so unlike me to do that. That just wasn't me that did that." In such a case, most likely some unconscious, unacknowledged part of us has surfaced, much to our chagrin. There are many useful psychological practices for working with these unconscious and unintegrated aspects of ourselves. One type of process is what we call "parts work." There are Voice Dialogue techniques developed by Hal and Sidra Stone and the extensive work of Robert Schwartz, in his Internal Family Systems, which is very thorough and logically developed. I particularly recommend the book, *Self Therapy* by Jay Earley as an excellent introduction to IFS work.

Psychologically, our consciousness is more like a committee than an individual. Given certain circumstances, we behave in one way and given other circumstances we behave in another. An easy way to think about this is to recall how we relate to children, how we relate to our boss or employees, how we relate to our spouse, etc., etc. We probably bring out very different aspects of ourselves in these clearly different situations, and quite appropriately so. However, when we have parts of ourselves that have been repressed or split off, they are hard for us to access or become aware of. As an example, if we were instructed in our childhood not to get angry, we may have a hard time getting in touch with our anger when it is appropriate.

In other cases we overemphasize some aspects of ourselves and this is often a way that we learned to protect ourselves or to try to make up for what we perceived to be our deficits. For example, if our competency was not validated by our parents, we may feel incompetent and have the need to over compensate as an adult, to be perfectionistic or super successful in what we set out to do in life. Or, if our parents were very critical of us, we may internalize a very strong Inner Critic to try to protect ourselves from the criticism of others. So parts work helps us to connect and work with the parts of ourselves that have either been repressed or inappropriately emphasized. With the case of repression, we try to connect with the part of us that might feel the forbidden emotion. We could dialogue with it through free form writing (or inner dialogue) where we give ourselves permission to just write freely about how we might feel if we were not forbidden to do so. Or we might invite ourselves to feel the forbidden emotion through role play or inner exploration.

With an over expressed part such as an Inner Critic we might dialogue with it and see if we can renegotiate a new, more constructive role in our lives or we may decide just to hold the line with it and not let it beat us up when it starts in on us. Even more to the point, we may find a wounded part of ourselves that this overexpressed critical part is trying to protect. If for instance, we are trying to protect a shamed part of ourselves, we may have a Perfectionist or Pusher Part that tries to make us perfect or very successful to avoid the shame of failing. When dealing with a protector part, it pays to try to lovingly contact the vulnerable part that it is trying to protect. When this vulnerable part is loved and nurtured, it has no need for the protecting part's overzealous guardianship.

According to the Internal Family System, as related by Jay Early, there are Protectors (Managers and Firefighters) and wounded parts that may be of various ages (Inner Children, Inner Teenagers, etc.) that have been turned into Exiles. Exiles are parts of ourselves that we have repressed or disowned to avoid the pain that they carry. Managers are the unconscious programming that we use to try to keep the pain of the Exiles from surfacing. In cases where an Exile threatens to surface with its intense psychic pain, the Firefighters will intervene to distract and numb us out through various addictive or compulsive processes.

Using the Internal Family System framework, we can look at a repeating pattern in our life and see what is happening below the surface of our awareness. First, we may become aware of a compulsive pattern such as people pleasing. We can dialogue with this protective part (Manager) to find out what its function is, i.e., what it is trying to protect us from. In the case of people pleasing, most likely it is protecting us from feeling rejected or threatened. When we ask the protective part to stand aside and it allows us, we can relate to the Exiled part that lies behind it, in this case most likely the Inner Child that carries the fear of rejection or punishment.

Then we can begin a loving dialogue with this vulnerable part that has been exiled. We develop a loving connection with it that allows us to understand its world and to help it to heal. We can also use the Mindfulness and Self Compassion practices described in the following Appendix in our relating to the Exile and its fears and pains.

Mindfulness and Self Compassion in Working with Thought and Emotions

Love the Lord your God with all your heart and with all your soul and with all your mind and with all your strength.

- Mark12:30 NIV Bible

Meditation and contemplation in their manifold forms are some of the most common practices in worldwide spiritual traditions. Why is this? Perhaps because so many different wisdom traditions found these practices excel in transforming ordinary human consciousness for the better from self centered reactivity to unconditional love and compassion. We are going to discuss two types of meditation practice here: the practice of loving kindness and what has come to be called "mindfulness" in our current culture

There are many books on mindfulness practice so I don't intend to go on about how this is practiced. What I wish to do here is to include a few pointers about mindfulness practice that may not always be brought out. First of all, the Chinese word that we translate as "mind" actually has a more holistic meaning. The two ideograms that make up "shin" mean heart/mind so it would be better to translate the practice as heart/mindfulness. We Westerners have a rather head-centered culture and if we frame this practice as mind based, we are likely to emphasize one aspect of the practice to the detriment of the other. It would be better if we thought of this kind of practice as a body/mind practice – a way of joining and harmonizing body and mind.

If we are head centered, the danger is that we can take this kind of practice as a way to further cut ourselves off from both our emotions and our bodily sensations. By practicing mindfulness where we see ourselves detached and looking out from our minds, we may be subtly disassociating from bodily sensations and emotions. It would be better to hold our awareness centered in our body and especially in the heart region to emphasize the development of compassion for both ourselves and others. In this kind of meditation, we can use the breath as something to center on and come back to as well as use it to soften any resistance to our experience that we may encounter within ourselves. With this practice there is no emphasis on concentration but rather to gently connect our heart/body/mind to our experience as it unfolds in thoughts, sensations, emotions, etc. in the present moment.

The practice of Loving Kindness is one of the most healing and transformative meditation practices I know of. Love is the greatest and most profound emotion that a human being can have. It heals all wounds, it allows us to expand and transcend our limited self centered world view and it moves us to extend ourselves in the service of other people, the planet and all life. To do Loving Kindness, sit in a comfortable and upright position. Put your hands over your heart space and bring your attention there. Then imagine a bright clear golden light shining from a source in front of you. This is the energetic manifestation of love. Imagine you are breathing this golden light into your heart center, which is like a chalice. Keep breathing this golden light/ love energy into your heart-chalice until it is full and then breathe it back out, returning it to Spirit. Also, you can send it out with the outbreath to anyone on the planet; those you love, those you have difficulty with, those in need and distress.

There are many variations you can do with this meditation; the commonality is that they are heart centered. Perhaps you can move to your heart space just by becoming aware of it or by placing your hand over your heart space. Perhaps you want to recite some affirmation as with a traditional Buddhist version: "May I be at peace. May all beings be at peace. May we all attain release from suffering and ignorance." In whatever manner you do this Loving Kindness meditation, repeat it until you feel your heart space warm up and enkindle with loving energy. Sometimes you will experience your heart aflame like a furnace of love. And always extend your loving to those around you. Be sure to share it and it will become more and more expansive over time.

When you are upset, you can use Loving Kindness Meditation to good effect. Sit somewhere quiet and bring your awareness into your heart space. You may experience a tightness there; if so, breathe gently into your heart space and release the tension out with the outbreath. Put both hands over your heart and send loving kindness to yourself. You may use an affirmation as mentioned above or just send loving energy towards your heart. If you are holding the upset somewhere else in your body, you may want to put one hand there, keep one hand on your heart space and continue to direct loving kindness to both your heart and the other place holding the upset. Talking to yourself like a kind and wise parent would as you do this can also be extremely useful. A good book describing this practice is Tara Bennett Goleman's book, *Mind Whispering*.

Starting & Facilitating a Study / Practice Small Group.

A group can be a wonderful and effective way to engage the material in this book. This book is meaty with challenging exercises and perhaps sometimes the meaning of some part of the text will escape you. With a group of people, each will bring different experience and knowledge to the group, which will complement that of others. Additionally, being in a small group provides support for engaging in study and exercises that at times can be demanding. The first thing to try is finding out if there are existing groups in your area that might be appropriate for this kind of work.

can use search engines like Google and Yahoo and use search terms such as Spiritual Book Club, Spiritual Growth, etc., including your hometown. Also you can use MeetUp. com to search for a group or to set up your own group; this is easy and inexpensive. And of course, you may use the old fashioned word of mouth networking with friends or at your church / temple / mosque / Dharma Center.

To start a Study / Practice Group, think about where you can meet and what you want to practice with others before you put out an invitation. To make it easier on yourself, you may want to get a few people to agree to share the group responsibilities before you put out an invitation. Eventually, as the group matures, probably more people can facilitate and support the meeting. You also can decide if you are going to have a break during the meeting, serve anything to drink or eat, etc.

At the first meeting, you want to establish some guidelines. Your first duty to your group as leader / facilitator is to make the group feel safe for every participant. I would recommend the following for developing this sense of safety in the group:

Confidentiality. It is important that people can have confidence that anything they say in the group will not be talked about outside of the group.

No cross talking or advice giving, especially in any check in. At least initially, this is important. Later you may find that some interchange is beneficial but at first I strongly urge you not to allow crosstalk. Some people can hardly listen to others before they are analyzing and advising the person sharing or telling the group how they had a similar situation. Also, when people cross talk and interrupt someone sharing, they are likely to cut off those who are less talkative and open and discourage them from further sharing. There is nothing else so effective at shutting down openness in a group as this, so don't let anyone get away with cross talk and advice giving! You can be tactful and still hold firmly to this rule.

Form a circle in your meetings, or as near as you can to one. This helps keep the group connected, it is easier for everyone to see and hear each other, and it encourages equal participation. A check in period at the beginning of the meeting is always a good idea in a spiritual practice group. This gives everyone the opportunity to share something significant that happened since the last meeting. Encourage the sharing to be related to the subject at hand and not meander purposelessly.

Talk about politics and religion should probably be disallowed in the group. Talk of politics and religion are good ways to get people to talk from their heads and scuttle any movement towards true intimacy and vulnerability!

Try to let everyone have equal time but don't force anyone reluctant to share to do so. In time, with safety, most people will open up. You might want to use a timepiece in your check ins to let everyone have the same amount of time. It helps to have a regular way to start and continue check ins where someone volunteers to go first and then you go clockwise (or counterclockwise) around the circle.

Keep the group conversation on task; don't let it be sidetracked into other areas of conversation. Have clear guidelines as to the purpose of the group and hold to it! If you are not using a book as a central organizing focus, agree beforehand as to the topics to be discussed in the group. The leader needs the subtle skill of intervening if the group starts to get off topic or someone in the group begins to wander and be tangential. Often a good clarifying question can bring the sharing back to topic. For example, "You started talking about _____ and then you began to talk about _____. How do you see these two things as being related?"

It is good to have a consistent structure to meetings: consistent starting and stopping times and a regular agenda such as, a beginning centering / meditation period, check in time, discussion of book material, assignments of reading and exercises for the next meeting, etc. In groups where there is a skilled facilitator, you could have dyads where some of the material is engaged with in a more experiential way.

Beginning and closing rituals are helpful to give the meeting a consistent sense of opening and closure. Rituals and structure give participants a sense of safety that they know what to expect from one meeting to the next, so if something is challenging for them, they have the structure as a support. One good way to finish the meetings is to stand in a circle and have someone offer a prayer that summarizes and completes the sense of the meeting. Also, members of the group can be invited to say a prayer into the circle for anyone that they are concerned about just at the end.

Printed in the United States
By Bookmasters